D0363751

The Making of the Scottish Landscape

The Making of the Scottish Landscape

R. N. Millman

B. T. Batsford Ltd
London and Sydney

First published 1975

© R.N. Millman 1975

Printed and bound by Redwood Burn Ltd, Trowbridge and Esher
for the publishers B.T. Batsford Ltd, 4 Fitzhardinge Street, London W1
and 23 Cross Street Brookvale NSW 2100 Australia

ISBN 0 7134 2838 4

Contents

The Plates

The Maps

Without recourse to the notion of 'landscape'
the geographer runs the risk of writing either
too purely analytically or too much descriptively
and, with either fault, of destroying the
essential character of the subject.

J. M. Houston, Introduction to *The
Western Mediterranean World*, Longman, 1963

Preface

This book traces the evolution of the mosaic, or palimpsest, of physiographic and cultural elements which comprise the modern countryside and townscapes of Scotland. Since the past is the key to the present, a chronological analysis of the moulding of the Scottish landscape, as evidenced by land-forms, cultural relict features and documents, helps us to explain the appearance of the modern rural and urban fabric in terms of its origins.

To date, nothing similar to W.G. Hoskins's *The Making of the English Landscape* series (Hodder and Stoughton) has been attempted for Scotland — probably because of the great lack of early documentary sources and, to a degree, arch-aeological evidence, compared with England. There is no equivalent to the Domesday Book in Scotland: the first comprehensive maps and written records of the character of the Scottish landscape come, respectively, with William Roy's military survey (1747-55), the estate surveys from the mid-eighteenth century and in the First Statistical Accounts. In contrast, during the last two hundred years, in the age of agrarian improvement and the rise of modern industry, communications and centres of population, there has been copious documentation and field evidence.

Scotland has had a very different economic, social and political history from England and this is much evidenced in her landscapes. James Caird, in the *Scottish Geographical Magazine* of 1964, described the Scottish countryside as 'a landscape of revolution rather than one of slow evolution' — substantially a deliberate creation, mainly of the eighteenth and nineteenth centuries. Moreover, despite increasing trends towards stereotypes, regional differences in Scottish landscapes remain very marked as do their English counterparts — assisted by comprehensive modern conservation and planning policies. Even the casual tourist cannot fail to notice the change in rural and urban house styles and materials from England, together with the different layout and use of fields, the composition of field boundaries, woods, gardens, farm buildings, and the distinctive moorland areas of the Highlands, Islands and Southern Uplands. However, regional differences in landscape, dialect and local customs in Scotland do not correspond so closely with historic counties as they do in England, because of the different ways in which Scottish society evolved in the past. On the contrary, although distinctions are becoming increasingly blurred today, the historic two-fold division between Highlands and Islands and Lowlands, focused on rival clan and family loyalties and involving lairds, chieftains, merchants, church affiliations and the lives of peasant farmers, was of greater relevance in the making of the modern cultural landscape. One legacy of this, at the local level and quite ignored by the reformed local government boundaries, are the residual names of some of the medieval fiefdoms, like Atholl or Bredalbane, Buchan, Strathbogie, Strathmore, Cowal, Cunninghame, Fife, Galloway and Kintyre, which may be considered the nearest Scottish equivalent to the French *pays*.

This book attempts to consider the making of Scottish landscape in an integrated and original way, stressing the essential continuity of that landscape and of the sequence of changes within it. Wherever possible, reference is made to the changes as observed by various topographers, notably over the last two centuries, with the aid of contemporary maps and other illustrations. Of necessity, the greatest emphasis in the book is placed on the period after the Act of Union and the 1715 and 1745 rebellions, followed by the collapse of the clan system, the Improving period, the clearances and the disappearance of run-rig cultivation, and then by the rise of modern industry, urbanism and communications. This period saw the steady reorientation of Scottish financial, commercial and administrative functions and social life towards the economic, social and governing influences spreading from England. However, whilst this period is the best documented, the treatment of earlier centuries presents a bigger challenge, since much local detail is then the subject of conjecture.

The last chapter takes the story through to a point about twenty-five years after the first comprehensive planning of landscape development was initiated in Scotland. It is written at a time when revisions in planning and local government procedures and recommendations from the Select Committee for Scottish affairs seem likely to influence very considerably further landscape changes during the last quarter of the twentieth century. Some of the changes that have occurred in recent years have generated much controversy — some of this based, it seems, on a lack of appreciation amongst certain interests of the essentially changing character of landscape, for something which is the product of time and events can never be a static image, like a postcard or a photograph on a calendar.

Within the constraints of research time, access to source materials and above all space, this book can only attempt a broad, impressionistic account of the making of the Scottish landscape, often involving considerable generalization. Because of this, conscientious Scottish readers and scholars may well detect certain errors or oversimplifications of detail that could be eliminated in a much more comprehensive and meticulous study. This book cannot attempt such an approach: rather, it is intended, in part, to provoke others, particularly Scots, with the leisure, interest and resources, to write county or perhaps regional studies for Scotland in the same spirit as that of the county writers for W. G. Hoskins's *The Making of the English Landscape* series. This hope is that of an Englishman who has come to know and delight in the character and variety of the Scottish landscape as a fascinating field of study. If this book helps a wider readership towards a better understanding of the making, and essential character, of the Scottish landscape and to a greater appreciation of its capacity for change, it will have achieved its purpose.

1   The flat, windswept landscape of Orkney, with the county town of Kirkwall in foreground — a burgh founded in medieval times. The huddle of houses and narrow *wynds*, together with the twelfth-century cathedral define the old town; beyond this, characteristic Victorian and modern Scottish house styles are evident. In the background, the pattern of large square fields and smallholdings dates from agricultural Improvement in the nineteenth century. The landscape of north-eastern Caithness is in many ways similar.

John Dewar Studios: Kirkwall, Orkney No. 3695/5

2   The east coast of Sutherland: Helmsdale, with Strath Kildonan and the bleak, mat-grass, bracken and heather-covered moors behind. Helmsdale, with its distinctive grid layout, two kirks and nine-teenth-century style Scottish cottages and houses abutting right on the streets, was a creation of the Duke of Sutherland to provide alternative employment in fishing for crofters evicted during the infamous clearances in Straths Kildonan and Naver in the early 1820s. Telford's road of 1809 crosses the Helmsdale river via the twin-arched bridge.

John Dewar Studios: Helmsdale, Sutherland No. 3693/D3

3   The landscape of the far west: Borve, Island of Barra, Outer Heb-
      rides, Inverness-shire. The shell-sand beaches have behind them tracts
      of machair, sometimes cultivated, otherwise crofters' common graz-
      ings, where the acid, peaty soil is tempered and better drained
      through mixing with the basic, wind-blown sand. The ancient
      gneiss, stripped bare by glaciation, forms headlands and hills
      inland, rising above peat bogs and hundreds of lochans. The
      mixture of isolated crofts and crofting townships with adjoining
      plots is, in its present form, largely the result of nineteenth- and
      early twentieth-century reorganization.

      *Cambridge University Collection: Borve, Barra, Inverness-shire,
      looking NNE from O.S.grid reference 32/653005. Number APX
      83.*

4   The West Highlands of Scotland. The ancient glaciated volcanics of
      Glencoe (left) give rise to a rougher, more serrated range
      compared with the ice-smoothed slopes of the Mamore Forest
      (metamorphics, right). Glencoe and, even more evidently, Loch
      Leven are deeply ice-scoured valleys etched out along ancient lines
      of structural weakness. Loch Leven, shallow at the mouth and
      almost blocked by a post-glacial fan, is a typical sea loch — a
      miniature fjord. Scrubby remnants of the once very extensive pine,
      birch and oakwoods are scattered along its northern shore,
      Forestry Commission plantations in the distance. Foreground: the
      British Aluminium works and village (1904), linked to Fort William
      and the South by the A82 (built during the Great Depression).

      *John Dewar Studios: Kinlochleven, Argyll/Inverness-shire border
      4223/5.*

Note on the use of geographical names in the text

Throughout the text, the author has tried to maintain consistency through using initial capitals for compass points and other descriptive adjectives only when these form part of widely recognized names of regions or localities within Scotland, as distinct from their general usage. Thus one reads North-West Highlands, Inner Hebrides and Outer Hebrides, in the form in which they often are given in atlases, but south-east, or south-west Scotland, the latter also being known as the Borders and Galloway respectively. Descriptions like south-east Scotland and the Borders are not entirely synonymous, but their geographical content has developed with use by a variety of writers, not simply geographers. The Southern Uplands are generally written with capitals as are the Central Valley or Central Lowlands. Indeed, the Lowlands (south of the Highland fault-line boundary scarp), the Highlands and the Islands are names which have well-recognized culturo-historic as well as geographical connotations in Scotland, as distinct from the west coast or eastern lowlands of Scotland. Likewise, the North-East, or North-East Scotland, comprising Aberdeenshire, Banffshire, Morayshire, Kincardineshire and sometimes Nairnshire, is distinct from north-eastern Scotland which can also include the lowlands around the Moray Firth and even lowland Caithness. A comparison may be found here in the distinctive use of East Anglia compared with eastern England. The Western Isles (Inner and Outer Hebrides) and Northern Isles (Orkney and Shetland) are widely accepted with capitals; indeed, some writers have even adopted the use of the West, Central or Eastern Highlands and the West Coast when referring specifically to these areas, in the same way as they would use North-West Highlands, Lowlands and North-East. This practice, however, is not used in this book. Finally, the South, to a Highlander, has a fairly specific connotation in referring to the Lowlands and England.

Hence, while every effort is made to ensure consistency in the text, some debatable styles of geographical names may be found, depending largely, perhaps, on the view of the reader.

Note on sources, dates and referencing systems used in this book

Besides references to material in the Scottish Record Office, the National Library for Scotland, the British Museum and other libraries, the author has gathered information and examples from widely scattered sources often revealed through his own field researches through which he has obtained a considerable acquaintance with the Scottish landscape. In particular, two types of problem arose in preparing this book: namely, instances where detailed documentation is often lacking or, at best, fragmentary; and facts, observations and examples quoted in a number of authoritative books and papers for which it is difficult to track down the original sources. Besides which, in this book, space regrettably does not allow full reference to all the sources which are available to the reader wishing to pursue points of detail for further study. To overcome this, and to reduce tedious textual references to a minimum, a list of principal sources, combined with suggestions for further reading, is given for each chapter in an edited bibliographical section at the end of the book.

The author will be able to acknowledge errors and omissions that are brought to his attention by readers in any subsequent edition.

Spelling of place-names has been standardised largely in accordance with Johnston's *Gazetteer of Scotland,* revised by R.W. Munro, third edition, Johnston and Bacon 1973.

The author is indebted to Dr David Turnock for the use of Figures 6-10, to Miss A.J. Winser who compiled the index and proof-read the text, Mrs G. Booth who typed the manuscript and Mr Ken Wass who drew the maps for publication.

1 The form of the ground

No study of the Scottish landscape would be complete without an introductory account of the origin and distribution of its landforms. These are the ligaments upon which the cultural palimpsest has been developed, chiefly within the last 1,500 years. Scotland is broadly divisible into three physical regions: the Highlands, the Central Lowlands and the Southern Uplands. The effects of glacial erosion and deposition are very marked upon these primary structural units and there is also much coastal evidence for late glacial and post-glacial changes in sea level.

The intricate juxtaposition of the physical and cultural elements which comprise Scotland's unique landscape has appealed to many writers, scientists and artists during the last two centuries. Many natural historians have described the contrasts between eastern and western Scotland, both in physique and cultural landscapes. Higher precipitation in the west of Scotland during Pleistocene times led to much more severe glacial erosion there than in the east: hence today, in the western Highlands there are serrated ridges, deep valleys and sea lochs penetrating far inland. These contrast with the moorland plateaux and more regular coastal forms in the east, with rounded whaleback hills, broader valleys and fewer sea inlets, usually shallow firths lined with mud-flats. Climate becomes progressively harsher with altitude throughout Scotland, notably above 300 metres, with frequent frost and raw winds. Moreover, the widespread occurrence of tors (eg on the granite mass of Bennachie in Aberdeenshire) and tracts and faces of rotting crystalline rocks suggest that mechanical and chemical weathering was much more active in pre- or inter-glacial times than today.

Much of Scotland is underlain by Palaeozoic rocks, and there are striking scenic differences between areas developed on gently dipping sediments and those on highly folded or contorted sediments or on igneous and metamorphic rocks. Generally speaking, strongly folded sediments occur in the Southern Uplands, metamorphic rocks in the Highlands and simple-structured sediments in the Central Valley and other peripheral lowlands. Within each of these regions there are igneous intrusions and spreads of lava of varying size, sometimes producing marked local landscape features.

In late Silurian and early Devonian times, sediments that had accumulated in a great geosyncline extending through Ireland and north Britain to Scandinavia were squeezed up into mountains, perhaps as high as the Himalayas today. The North-West Highlands and Outer Hebrides are a fragment of the north-west foreland of this trough. During this Caledonian orogeny the characteristic orientation of rock structure from north-north-east to south-south-west was introduced, or further accentuated, throughout Scotland, resulting in great fractures and thrust planes. Most prominent of these are the Great Glen and the faulted limits of the Central Lowlands rift valley, of which the Highland fault-line scarp is one of the most distinctive landforms in Britain. The southern boundary fault is much less distinct, since hilly areas developed on volcanic rocks along this fault-line merge their rounded forms with those of the adjoining Southern Uplands. The structural grain of Scotland was re-endorsed in Permocarboniferous times by repercussions of the Hercynian orogeny (which formed the Pennines and hills of south Wales and south-west Ireland) and again in the mid-Tertiary period when outer shock waves of the Alpine storm caused the Minch to founder, as a rift valley, separating the Long Isle from the North-West Highlands. The latter forces led to considerable volcanic activity, which was comparable with that of Carboniferous times in the Central Lowlands. This Tertiary vulcanism produced the great dyke swarms and lava plateaux of the Inner Hebrides and neighbouring mainland, which are often prominent local relief features. Also, repeated movement along major fracture zones preserved the main upland blocks and the intervening Central Valley.

In the Outer Hebrides and between Glenelg and Loch Eriboll along the North-West Highland coast, some of the most ancient rocks in Scotland outcrop in a narrow strip. These include the Lewisian and Torridonian formations, the massive Torridonian sandstones lying unconformably on the partly exhumed land surface of Lewisian gneiss. This gneiss, outcropping as heavily ice-abraded knobs and hills, forms the bare knuckles distinctive of the far north-west and Long Isle landscapes, its grey-pink coloration alternating with thousands of hectares of green-brown peat moorland and innumerable small lochans and bogs.

The Lewisian and Torridonian rocks are overlain unconformably by Cambrian quartzites, which giving a striking, snow-like cap to some of the strange inselberg-like hills (eg Ben Stack, Quinag, and Suilven) in north-west Sutherland, primarily developed in Torridonian sandstones. Further south, in Coigach and Wester Ross, the Torridonian sandstone becomes much thicker and more massive, giving rise to the very distinctive peaks of Ben More Coigach, An Teallach, Ben Slioch and Ben Eighe and the Applecross, Torridon, Ben Damph and Coulin Hills. Ben Eighe and Ben Slioch are also capped with white quartzite screes. Other Cambrian strata in the north-west include the Durness limestone, underlying small areas of Karst around Smoo Cave and Inchnadamph Caves: these support a flush of rich green grass contrasting with the surrounding acid peat moorlands. These Cambrian strata are separated from the Moine metamorphic complex by the Moine thrust plane. The Moine series are older than the Cambrian rocks: like the Dalradian series, which underlies much of the central and eastern Highlands, they are probably of Pre-Cambrian age.

Rocks of Cambro-Ordovician age appear along the southern margins of the Highlands and overlook the Devonian sandstone of Strathmore (with its distinctive red drift soils) along the Highland fault-line scarp. The metamorphic rocks of the Highlands comprise quartzites, schists and gneiss and relatively rare bands of crystalline limestone. Very locally, as in the Tingwall valley in Shetland, the latter gives rise to tracts of richer grazing and land better suited to arable. Large granite intrusions of Devonian age break the continuity of the metamorphic structures in the eastern Highlands and form the high plateau of the Cairngorms (Ben Macdhui, 1,322m) — the largest contiguous area over 600 metres in Britain. In the western Grampians, near Fort William, granites, lavas and breccias comprise the huge, truncated, dome-like mass from which Ben Nevis (1,355m), Britain's highest peak, is formed.

However, the igneous intrusions of the Highlands do not always form high ground. Considerable lowland tracts in Aberdeenshire and Banffshire are developed on less competent granites; indeed, within the Highlands massif, the monotonous, peaty basin called the Moor of Rannoch is formed of the same granite as some of the surrounding mountains. Glencoe and Black Mount are developed upon very resistant volcanic rocks of similar age. The complexities of the igneous and metamorphic rocks are seldom evident in the relief, though the resistant quartzites of the Dalradian series frequently stand out as ridges, eg at the Pass of Killiecrankie, near Pitlochry and the isolated hills of the north-east lowlands, including the Hill of Mormond and Binn of Cullen. Conversely, the Atholl basin and Howe of Alford are developed on relatively weak schists. Close to the Highland edge a line of rugged hills, notably Ben Ledi (876m), Ben Vorlich (983m) and Ben Lawers (1,220m) rises above the general level of summits because of the greater resistance of the grit of which it is formed. Competent granite underlies Ben Cruachan (1,160m) near Loch Awe in Argyllshire and resistant strata form Carn Eighe-Mam Sail (1,190m) — the highest peaks in the North-West Highlands.

In the Inner Hebrides, Tertiary basalts form the columnar cliffs of Staffa and the steep, dark cliffs of Skye, Raasay, Canna, Eigg, and parts of Rhum and Arran, the Ross peninsula on Mull and neighbouring islands. On Skye, Waterstein and Dunvegan Heads rise to 305m. Many of the Inner Hebridean basalt cliffs start as terrace-like profiles in the hillside, below which they drop in a precipice to the sea. These basalts also underlie the huge rolling moorlands covering much of Skye, Mull, Raasay and Arran. The serrated crests of the Cuillins of Skye and Rhum (1,100m and 850m respectively) are developed in gabbro, whilst the Red Cuillins of Skye are lower, conical and more rounded, formed in somewhat weaker Tertiary granite. Ben More on Mull (970m) and Goat Fell on Arran (876m) are underlain by resistant Tertiary volcanics. Locally, in Skye, the Small Isles, Mull, Ardnamurchan, Arran and Kintyre cliff and beach profiles and moorlands inland are influenced by upstanding low ridges related to numerous Tertiary dyke swarms.

South of the Devonian and Carboniferous sediments of the Central Lowlands, and separated from them by the fault running between Girvan and Dunbar, lies the dissected plateau area called the Southern Uplands. This consists of Ordovician and Silurian strata of marine origin, which were highly folded at the end of the Silurian, the axes of the main folds following the Caledonian trend. There are two main folded zones: a great synclinorium between Portpatrick and Dunbar and a complementary anticlinorium between the Mull of Galloway and St Abbs Head. Their complex structure contrasts with the apparent simplicity of the rock outcrops, both in the field and on the geological map. Although igneous intrusions are less widespread than in the Highlands, there are many outcrops of volcanic rocks and intrusive granites of Devonian age and a great outpouring of basaltic lavas took place in Roxburghshire and Berwickshire during the lower Carboniferous period. The Eildon Hills are a conspicuous feature developed on a trachyte intrusion and, with the granite of the Cheviot Hills, they give rise to some of the most attractive touring countryside in Scotland. More generally, in the Southern Uplands, the plateau-like surface which bevels the steeply dipping Ordovician and Silurian strata stands in strong contrast to local tracts of more massive granite terrain, eg the Merrick and Cairnsmore of Fleet in Galloway, and Criffel, south of Dumfries, and with the prominent hills which remain as the eroded necks of ancient volcanoes and lava flows. Indeed, hills like the Pentlands and Tinto Hills (Carboniferous volcanics) rival the Southern Uplands in height and, although geologically north of the boundary fault, they and the hills on the Ayrshire-Lanarkshire border cannot morphologically be separated from the uplands with which they imperceptibly merge.

In the downfaulted Central Lowlands, sedimentary rocks of Devonian and Carboniferous age occur widely. These are all aligned with their main axes following the Caledonian trend and parallel to the faulted margins. However, to call this rift valley the 'Central Lowlands' is something of a misnomer, since it is neither geologically central in Scotland nor is it largely lowland: besides the moorland landscape continuity between the Tinto and Pentland Hills and Southern Uplands, the dominant relief is often that of steep-sided, tabular volcanic outcrops, the greater resistance of which has resulted in isolated hills and tilted plateaux arranged in a north-east/south-west direction. Chief among these are the Ochill (max. 720m) and the Sidlaw (max. 376m) Hills – both of the lower Devonian age – and the Campsie Fells (max. 586m) and Kilpatrick Hills (400m) – both of lower Carboniferous age. These are continued as outliers, eg Berwick Law and Bass Rock (both volcanic plugs), Arthur's Seat (remains of volcanic neck), Edinburgh and Stirling Castle rocks (volcanic outcrop), Ailsa Craig, off Girvan (volcanic plug) and Inchcape, Isle of May, etc (islands in the Firth of Forth). The effects of this vulcanism has been to produce discontinuous belts of high ground separating well-defined sedimentary lowlands, of which the most notable is the Forth valley-Strathallan-Strathearn-Strathmore valley corridor. In Strathmore (Gaelic: Big Valley), this lowland is a synclinal vale lying between the volcanic Sidlaw Hills and the crystalline rocks of the Highlands. However, a band of lower Devonian basal conglomerate (composed of large stones brought down by torrents when the Highlands were of Alpine dimensions) intermittently outcrops to form a broken line of hills running along below the Highland fault-line scarp, their coarse, acid soils often planted up with stands of conifers. Strathfinella Hill (400m) near Stonehaven and the hills between Callander and Crieff (rising to 625m to form a spur of the Highlands in Glenartney Deer Forest) and the Mentieth and Dumbarton Hills are all developed on the conglomerate, which runs to the sea in cliffs south of Stonehaven.

Sedimentary rocks of Devonian age also outcrop in parts of the eastern Borders, the North-East and along the Moray Firth coast from the mouth of the Spey to Caithness and in the Orkney Isles. In many places along the coast they give rise to spectacular cliff scenery. Inland, they often take the form of tabular hill masses and conical hills, but, where much eroded, these rocks usually correspond with lowland basins or broad lowland areas, as in the Black Isle, where the synclinal structure is reflected in a marked inversion of relief. Orkney and north-east Caithness are flat, windswept and treeless, save for some conical sandstone hills on Hoy (max. 480m) and smaller, local eminences. The coastal lowlands of Galloway, and transition zone of low hills and plateaux, rising towards the broad, flat-topped, convex-sloped fells inland, are apparently planated and underlain by Ordovician shales and grits in the west. Further east, near the Solway estuary, and in the lower Nith and Annan valleys, these rocks are overlain by Carboniferous and Permotriassic rocks which, in turn, are mantled with glacial drift.

Fracturing and faulting is of considerable importance in determining the major structural divisions within Scotland. The topographic expression of these faults is often strongly marked, as along the Highland boundary fault between Helensburgh and Stonehaven and in the north-east section of the Southern Uplands fault where weaker sediments in East Lothian abut against the more resistant rocks in the south (Lammermuir). In the south-west section of this fault-line there is no conspicuous scarp, though there is a marked alignment of valleys parallel to the strike.

Within the Highlands, the most prominent fault-line is that along the Great Glen, which has been opened out by rivers and ice to form a great gash across the country. The continuation may be traced into Mull and along the cliff-line of the Black Isle and Tain peninsula to Tarbat Ness. The presence of other fracture zones in the Highlands, aligned parallel to the Caledonian trend, is revealed in the straight sections of valleys. Loch Tay, for example, is bounded on its western side by a pronounced fault which can be traced north-east into Glen Garry and eventually into the remarkable straight valley of Glen Tilt, near Blair Atholl, which continues into upper Deeside. Another fault-line is the Loch Awe-Glen Strae-Loch Ericht axis, excavation of which by ice has produced the two long, finger-like forms of Lochs Awe and Ericht. Loch Long, Loch Fyne, the Clyde estuary between Dunoon and the Cumbrae Isles, upper Loch Etive, Loch Shiel, Loch Carron, the upper Cromarty Firth, Kyle of Tongue, Loch Eriboll, Loch Laggan and Glen Affric follow similar trends. Other localised faults are aligned east/west,

eg the many cross-Highland valleys: Glen Lyon, Rannochside,
upper Deeside, lower Loch Etive, Loch Leven, Loch Sunart,
inner Lochs Hourn, Nevis, Torridon and Glen Torridon, etc.
Still other faults are aligned in the north-west/south-east
direction, especially to the west of the Great Glen, where the
Loch Ewe-Loch Maree fault is very prominent: upper Loch
Duich, Little Loch Broom and Loch Broom, Loch Laxford and
lower Lochs Hourn, Nevis and Torridon also follow this trend.

In the Central Lowlands, there are many faults aligned
parallel to the edges of upstanding hill masses: of these, the
Ochill fault-line scarp, facing south, is the most spectacular,
rising very steeply from the Forth haughlands east of Stirling.
There are also groups of faults arranged in east/west and
south/north directions which outline other blocks of higher
land in the Central Valley. In the Southern Uplands faults are
less prominent, although sections of some rivers suggest some
structural control, eg Glen App in south Ayrshire, and some
of the V-shaped notches or 'cleughs' in the upper valleys.
However, the complex geological structure of the Scottish
mainland and Islands plays a less important role in the relief
than might be supposed. Glacial erosion has emphasized the
main relief features, although these were initiated by pre-
Pleistocene fluvial agencies in response to an intermittently
falling sea level. Indeed, the drainage system is remarkable in
its disregard of structural variations. After Bremner and
Linton's work,[1] however, it is now generally accepted that
consequent drainage was superimposed on to the complex,
underlying structure from a now-vanished sedimentary cover,
probably Cretaceous. Drainage had predominantly a west/
east alignment.

The major features of the uplands in Scotland, notably in
the Highlands, have been produced by long-continued erosion
under varying climatic conditions which have resulted in a
multicyclic landscape in relation to successive, eustatic
changes of sea level. Viewing the Highlands from the top of
Ben Nevis, both the summits of the long whaleback hills of
the central and eastern Highlands and those of the much
more dissected North-West Highlands seem to accord: indeed
much of the Grampians appear as a plateau, with varying
degrees of dissection, occasionally topped by somewhat higher
summits, like the Ben Nevis range, the Cairngorm summits,

Ben Lawers, Mount Keen, Beinn a Ghlo and many other hills that could be residuals, or monadnocks, possibly related to remnants of a series of high-level erosion surfaces. However, Linton and King[2] have suggested that downwarping has occurred in the eastern Highlands and the secondary orientation of drainage towards the Moray Firth (eg of the Deveron, Spey, Beauly, Findhorn etc) enhances this thesis. Various theories also exist for the Southern Uplands, which also have many accordant summits, but it is not yet possible to describe the stages by which the pre-glacial relief of Scotland, as a whole, evolved. Certainly, the accordant summits of the Highlands and Uplands represent the gently sloping remnants of erosion surfaces, which bevel the structures of rocks with different resistences to erosion. Also, at lower levels, there appear to be marine platforms along both the North Sea and Atlantic coasts.

The remnants of the proto-drainage systems are found in river alignments like those of the Isla-Deveron, Don, Dee, Lyon-Tay and Tummel-Esk. Further south, other west/east streams were forerunners of the Fifeshire Leven, Forth and Tweed. According to Sölch and Linton,[3] the line of Scotland's pre-glacial watershed lay between Ben Cruachan and Cape Wrath, the deep valleys through this line believed to be the result of glacial breaching. South and east of this watershed, as the sedimentary cover (Cretaceous) was eroded, exploitation of lithological and tectonic zones of weakness allowed tributaries to cut back along the line of strike to dismember the proto-drainage streams, creating longitudinal valleys, like those of the Spey and upper Deveron. In the Tweed basin, the destruction of the earlier system is far from complete, despite glacial modification. However, in the Highlands, the characteristic enclosed and marginal basins seem to owe little, in most cases, to structural control, eg the Moor of Rannoch. Likewise, the Howe of Cromar in Deeside is partly developed on the same granite batholith that forms Morven and the Cairngorms several kilometres to the west. The neighbouring Howe of Alford is underlain by schists of considerable resistance. Many of the larger straths, like the Spey and Findhorn valleys, comprise a series of basins connected together by narrower defiles, or consist of long, narrow basins, like those of Lochs Shin and Naver in Sutherland. The origin of these basins is still rather unclear.

The landforms developed in the Tertiary era were drastically modified by the Pleistocene glaciations and the results of the erosional and depositional activity of ice are to be seen in all parts of the Scottish landscape. Greatest snowfall and ice accumulation occurred in the wetter west, and there an ice-shed appears to have developed in each glaciation roughly along the Pre-Pleistocene water-parting in the Highlands. From Rannoch Moor, the Cairngorms and the North-West Highlands and a subsidiary ice-cap in Galloway, ice either fanned out in sheets, causing erosion and much local deposition, or was restricted to valleys with much more, canalized, erosive power. Most glacial landforms in Scotland seem to date largely from periods corresponding to the Riss and Würm glaciations in the Alps.

Glacial erosion is pronounced in the upland areas of Scotland, notably in the Cairngorms and western Highlands, where there are deep, ice-gouged troughs. Many of these troughs contain lochs of various sizes, with lochans in some of the high corries. There are features resembling hanging valleys, with waterfalls, in some parts, eg the Falls of Glomach in Kintail, the Grey Mare's Tail in Dumfriesshire and the Falls of Glencoul and Falls of Mesach near Ullapool — but the glacial abrasion and overdeepening was generally not as severe as, for example, in western Norway. Hence really high waterfalls, sheer valley and fjord sides and well-formed hanging valleys are absent in Scotland, even in the western Highlands. The larger lochs of the Highlands are formed in rock basins dammed up by retreat moraines and/or delta fan debris, and a number of them have had their water level artificially raised in hydro-electric schemes. On the other hand, where a post-glacial river has eroded down the morainic lake dam, extensive peaty areas may remain on the former bed of a lake which has naturally drained away.

Geologically, lakes are but temporary landscape features. The largest and longest Highland lochs are rock basin lakes, eg Lochs Ness, Maree, Shiel, Awe, Tay and Lomond. Where glacial troughs, especially those leading to the west coast, have been drowned by the post-glacial net rise in sea level, they form long sea lochs, eg Loch Sunart (42km), Loch Fyne (50km), the upper Firth of Clyde, Loch Etive, Loch Linnhe,

Loch Leven, Loch Hourn, Loch Duich and Loch Broom. In many parts of the Highlands, ice overrode the shoulders between valleys to breach local water-partings and form cols, which became important as passes in the drove road network by the early eighteenth century, eg Rannoch Moor and the Feshie-Geldie valley. Away from the Cairngorms and the western Highlands glacial troughs are not common, although most of the Highland valleys have evidence of roughening and scraping on their sides (often masked by post-glacial slumping of moraines and other glacial debris, post-glacial deltas, weathered material, soil creep etc) and *roches moutonnées* were formed on the valley floor. The edges of the remaining high plateau areas are extensively scalloped by corries.

In the lowlands, the most prominent examples of glacial erosion are found in central Scotland, where volcanic plugs standing in the path of moving ice underwent severe abrasion: for example, Castle Rock in Edinburgh, where grooves were gouged out at the sides and a tail of debris added beyond the crag by ice as it rode over the feature. Such crag and tail landforms are common in the Central Lowlands. The Ochill Hills and other of the larger igneous and volcanic masses in the Central Valley were also modified by ice, which overdeepened the cols to give through passes, eg Glen Devon and Glen Farg. Also, the river Forth is a gross misfit in its present valley, owing to reduction of its headwaters through glacial breaching and/or to the great enlargement of its valley by glacial erosion. The Southern Uplands show a much more subdued form of glaciation with broad, flat-topped fells and smooth, convex ridges and hills. There was some widening and steepening of pre-glacial valleys into long, deep-cut dales, and in Galloway, where local glaciation was more severe, cauldron-like valley heads were formed, sometimes cut by post-glacial streams into notch-like valleys, or cleughs. However, few of the hills are pitted by corries and there are very few corrie tarns and rock basin lakes.

Glacial deposits are, by contrast, much more widespread and uniform throughout Scotland. Most of the lowland areas have a thin covering of till or glacio-fluvial sands and gravels, which locally may give rise to a wide range of soil types and colorations, eg the rich, red till derived from old red sandstone outcrops in Strathmore. Drumlins, however, are comparatively rare, except over the site of Glasgow (where they created local constraints on nineteenth-century development), West Lothian, the lower Tweed valley (Merse) and across the Galloway lowlands eastwards towards the Solway Firth, the last two examples being among the best in the British Isles of the classic 'basket of eggs' topography, accentuated by the layout of enclosure farms, fields and roads. The Lowlands exhibit many ice recession or decay features, meltwater channels, dead ice hollows, kames, eskers, post-glacial lakes, plugged valleys and drainage diversions. These features are found in profusion in the Central Valley and include the great kames of Carstairs and the stagnant ice basin, formerly occupied by a lobe of the Forth glacier, which is now partly covered by Loch Leven, in Fifeshire. Lochs Davan and Kinnord, on the Muir of Dinnet in Aberdeenshire, have a similar origin. Several rivers in the Central Lowlands and the North-East have had their pre-glacial channels blocked by boulder clay and the stream has cut a new valley. Sometimes, these may be gorge-like, closely wooded and picturesque, but they may once have been serious obstacles to road builders. The lower Don gorge and Nigg Bay valley (north and south of Aberdeen) and, inland, the former Dee spillway just north of Ballater were formed in this way.

Moraines are prominent in Strathmore, near Laurencekirk and in Strathallan, near Gleneagles. The North-East and the Moray Firth lowlands show evidence for the spread of glaciers from the Cairngorms and from the hills west of the Moray Firth. Great spreads of glacio-fluvial material and substantial kame terraces play an important role in the morphology of Highland valleys. In the wider parts of the Highland straths, accumulations of kames and eskers indicate the downwasting of detached ice masses, eg the Howe of Cromar on Deeside and Glenmore (Loch Morlich) on Speyside. The lower valley sides are often strewn with the debris of lateral moraines which sometimes link up across the valley floor with recessional moraines to form crescentic loops of moraine, now breached by the river. These are hummocky, with small pools and swampy ground impounded in the numerous hollows. Whin and broom give a golden colour to such rough, sterile ground in Highland valleys during the summer. Also, boulder clay is exposed occasionally in lightly coloured gashes on the valley sides after heavy spates.

In Highland valleys, kames (ie terraces of water-sorted debris formed by water flowing between a shrinking glacier and the valley sides) have often slumped down to form hummocky grass, or heathland reclaimed for pasture around modern farms and crofts on the valley floor, or they form rough grazings scattered with the unroofed ruins of former settlements, indicating the significance of such land in past centuries. Quite often, a road skirts the base of the kame terrace and, below it, the ground falls towards the pebble-bedded river by a series of river-eroded terraces. The lowest level is called the 'haughland' which, despite local embanking, is little used apart from intermittent pasturing, owing to the frequent risk of flooding in spates. Recently formed marshy deltas are often found at the entrance of rivers into Highland lochs: elsewhere, talus cones, footed by alluvial fans, stony and seamed with water courses, are formed below steep slopes and are sometimes large enough to have formed sites for valley settlements, since these could obtain a water supply away from the haughlands liable to flood.

In both Highland and Lowland Scotland meltwater channels frequently lace the low-lying areas and are also arranged in suites within the higher valleys. These channels are important local landscape features, eg the Burn of Vat channel near Dinnet Muir in the eastern Grampians, an enormous dead ice pothole. The Slochd channel near Carrbridge, which carried meltwater from the Findhorn drainage basin to that of the Spey, is another conspicuous spillway, rivalled in landscape impact by the Glen Saugh channel near Cairn o'Mounth in the eastern Grampians. A remarkable feature in the western Grampians are the Parallel Roads of Glen Roy and Glen Gloy, and partly, along Glen Spean, near Fort William: these 'roads' are lake beaches corresponding to a sequence of falling lake levels maintained temporarily by a pre-glacial lake during which time it sought successively lower outlets over cols which were revealed as the ice-front back-melted. In the Southern Uplands, alongside a range of valley glacial deposition features, Sissons[4] and

5   The Great Glen (Glen Mhor) from the Fort William end, looking north-eastwards. The snow cover picks out the marked accordance of hill summits: between them the ice-gouged Glen Mhor, along a major tear fault zone, forms a major through-valley. The Caledonian Canal was first used in the 1820s. Scrubby remnants of the once extensive native forest lie below the bleak, open, plagio-climax moorlands: beyond are large Forestry Commission plantations. Foreground: the crofting township of Corpach, and estates of paper mill and aluminium workers' houses.

John Dewar Studios: Caledonian Canal at Fort William end 3393/5

6   The Cairngorm Mountains (Eastern Grampians). Much less ice-carved than the Western Highlands, these rounded, whaleback granite hills, scalloped by corries and separated into blocks by glacial troughs, form a bleak, treeless moorland which constitutes the largest contiguous area above 600m in Britain. The accordance of summit levels in the middle and far distance is very noticeable.

Cambridge University Collection: Nature Reserve, Cairngorms, Glen Dee, looking north from O.S. reference 543/975950, Number AGP 6.

7   Aberdeenshire/Kincardineshire: The lower Dee valley. This view, westwards from the latest housing developments of Aberdeen, gives a good impression of North-East Scotland. In background are the rolling, heather-covered grouse moors whose summits — often in granite — form the eastern outliers of the Grampians. On low ground, an undulating patchwork of fairly small, stone-dyked square fields, shelter belts, plantations, solid granite farmhouses and a number of substantial baronial-style mansions. These, very largely, are the legacy of nineteenth-century agrarian Improvements. Post-1945 planning strives to keep the detached, largely commuter settlements of Cults, Bielside and Peterculter (middle distance) and neighbouring villages and hamlets as communities physically detached from the expanding city of Aberdeen.

John Dewar Studios: Aberdeenshire, Dee Valley: Number 3713/6

8   The Perthshire landscape of bare, rounded hills and wooded glens, punctuated with small settlements and mansions and shooting lodges, is here characterized by Blair Atholl. All the woodland in the view has been planted since the mid-eighteenth century, when the Murrays, Dukes of Atholl, first remodelled the ancestral castle and its policies (grounds). Landscaped arbours of native and exotic conifers in the home paddocks contrast with the beech avenue along the entrance drive, now fully mature. Beyond the mansion and home farm is the re-sited nineteenth-century estate village of Blair Atholl, on the A9 and Highland Railway. In the background, the large stone-walled square fields of the estate tenant farms, shelter belts and plantations — all a nineteenth-century creation — rise up to the moorland summits managed for sheep, deer and grouse.

John Dewar Studios: Blair Atholl, Perthshire Number 3860/8 others have plotted a great number of meltwater and overspill channels. The advance and retreat of the glacier in Scotland were marked by periods in which sub-Arctic conditions existed over ice-free areas. Hence there is much evidence for the creation of a range of micro-landforms, eg the smoothing of slopes by solifluction and, in the Highlands, wide expanses of frost-shattered rock arranged in sheets or as lobes of stones: the latter are well-formed on the slopes of Lochnagar and the Cairngorms. These, and all the other glacial and peri-glacial features mentioned above are, as we see them today, substantially the legacy of the last ice advance and the effects of post-glacial weathering.

Important side-effects were produced by the onset and decay of the ice-sheets along the coasts of Scotland: raised beaches are well developed all around the coastline through isostatic changes in sea level resulting from the recovery of the land from the weight of the vanished ice. Along the shores of the Moray Firth, and the Firths of Tay and Forth, these beaches are well developed (now, eg as the reclaimed haughlands of the lower Carse of Gowrie and the lower river Forth, the legacy of nineteenth-century Improvements). These beaches, which range in height from *c* 35m to 1.34m above sea level, show clear evidence of the warping which accompanied the isostatic readjustment of the land mass. Locally, this movement is further evidenced by the wooded 'denes' used by streams falling into the North Sea in cliffed sections of the coastline between Berwick and Caithness: roads are locally obliged to bridge these little rejuvenated valleys or make a hairpin detour, eg the A92 between Dundee and Aberdeen and the A9 from Golspie to Caithness.

Raised beaches and related features are conspicuous along both the west and east coasts of Scotland. The most remarkable of these, apparently of late-glacial origin, occur in parts of the Inner Hebrides where they often comprise broad abrasion platforms and conspicuous cliffs. The oldest beaches stand at about 32·5m OD in Islay and Jura, 32·52m OD in Mull and at progressively lower altitudes away from the area of greatest post-glacial isostatic recovery of the land, centred on Rannoch Moor. Similarly, the main post-glacial shoreline, considered to have gradually formed between *c* 6500 and 3500 BC, exceeds 11m OD along the shores of Lochs Linnhe,

Etive, Fyne, Long, the Kyles of Bute, together with neighbouring shores and islands and the western Forth valley — but also falls away in all directions from the centre of greatest uplift. It stands at *c* 9-11m on Arran and the peninsula of Kintyre, at a maximum of *c* 8m on the Solway coast, 6-8m on parts of the Fife and Lothian coast and *c* 5m in the Outer Hebrides, Caithness and Buchan, whilst being only 1-2m above high water in parts of the Berwickshire coast and not found at all, so far, in Orkney and Shetland.

In several areas, eg Kintyre, Islay and Jura, degraded cliff lines, sometimes with stacks and caves, can be seen lying among fields and meadows in a coastal strip now often followed by the line of a road, improved farmland and settlement. On the main post-glacial beach were built many coastal towns such as Helmsdale, Brora, Golspie, Inverness, the old part of Stonehaven, Arbroath, Carnoustie, St Andrews and Dunbar, and the golf courses adjoining a number of east coast settlements are frequently laid out upon it. Around the coasts of the Highlands and Islands, this beach feature locally forms, with small river deltas, the level sites of crofting settlements, routeways and small ports, eg Ullapool, founded in 1788, but it is not always easily discernible in coastal landscapes.

There is a great difference between the configurations of the east and west coasts of Scotland: the west coast has numerous sea lochs and offshore waters studded with over 5,000 islands and islets, whilst the east coast has few major inlets and a much simpler shoreline. Locally, post-glacial erosion and deposition, together with a slight submergence during the last four milleniums, has led to the growth of spits and bars along bays and river mouths, eg the Ythan in Aberdeenshire. This has helped to regularize the east coast.

From the mouth of the Tweed to Caithness, the east coast is a succession of finely sculptured cliffs alternating with low, sandy, dune-backed beaches. Imposing, geo-fretted cliffs, sometimes topped with glacial material, are cut in both sedimentary and crystalline rocks: the conglomerate cliffs by Dunnottar Castle near Stonehaven contrast with the granite and metamorphic cliffs south of Aberdeen and near Peterhead and with the old red sandstone (Devonian) cliffs near St Abbs Head in Berwickshire and near Gardenstown in

Banffshire and the spectacular cliffs of Caithness, the last backed by monotonous moorlands or a windswept plateau of rectangular fields. The cliff scenery and farming chequerboard is continued in Orkney, where the combination of land and sea is nowhere better seen than in the large almost landlocked harbour of Scapa Flow. On the low sections of the east coast, eg Berry Links, Tentsmuir, Culbin Sands and the Sands of Forvie, there are locally some fine examples of dunes in various stages of growth, movement and fixation. Marram grass is now used to fix such dunes, but occasionally in the past they have moved to cover wide tracts of farmland and villages. Notable for this were the Culbin Sands in Morayshire, now extensively planted by the Forestry Commission, and the Sands of Rattray, near Buchan Ness, now a nature reserve.

On the north and west coasts, great cliffs, teeming with birds, alternate with long, penetrating sea lochs and bays with long strands of white shell sand and dunes, backed by machair. In Shetland, Foula, Fair Isle and St Kilda, the bare, windswept moors often fall scores of metres into the sea (St Kilda and Foula 400m) providing some of the finest cliff scenery in Europe, fretted with geos and blow holes, and alternating with sheltered inlets, called voes, and bays of blown sands, eg St Ninian's Isle. This pattern is repeated in the cliffs of Hoy in Orkney and all along the north mainland coast, culminating in Whiten Head, Smoo Cave, Cape Wrath and Sandwood Bay in the remote north-west corner of Sutherland. The coasts of the Minch are intricate, rocky and barren, with long inlets like Lochs Broom, Eriscort and Seaforth, but the west coast of the Long Isle, backed by the deeply glaciated granite hills of Harris and elsewhere by the huge lochan-studded lowland peat moors, comprises long stretches of shell sand and machair. The latter, where the sand has blown across on to the peat moor behind, provides the crofting communities strung out along the coast with their best grazing and arable land.

Similar shell strands, backed by windswept, treeless moors, alternate between rocky and cliffed shores and sea lochs on the mainland west coast, although south of Loch Broom, increasing mildness allows tracts of native deciduous trees and planted conifers to flourish along the inner sheltered shores of the sea lochs, with rhododendrons often growing semi-wild nearby. The low cliffs and shell strands of the windswept Isles of Coll, Tiree and Iona contrast with the black basalt cliffs of Skye, the Small Isles and Mull, and with the bare rocky Isles of the Sea (Garvellachs), Luing and Scarba. These, with the Paps of Jura, the low coasts and chequerboard landscape of Islay, the slightly raised beaches of west Kintyre, the sheltered wooded shores of Lochs Craignish and Creran and west Loch Tarbert and finally with the diversity of mountain backdrops, sea lochs and shorelines of the Firth of Clyde district form one of the most interesting and diverse coastal landscapes in the world. Lastly, there remains to acknowledge the distinctive coastal forms of the south-west corner of Scotland: these begin with the cliffs and small bays south of Ayr and Girvan, looking out towards Ailsa Craig, Kintyre and the peaks of Arran, and fronted quite often by a narrow raised beach — which merge, further south, into the raised shoreline along the hill-backed coast of Loch Ryan. A rugged, cliffed coastline with small beaches and harbours (eg Portpatrick) lies to the west of Stranraer around the Rhinns, but across the tidal flats of Luce Bay the narrow raised beach, backed by low degraded cliffs, phases in again round into Galloway Bay, also largely filled with sand flats. Further east, a varied, highly indented coastline, comprised of alternating raised beaches, rocky headlands, wooded inlets, salt marshes and sandy coves continues to Arbigland Point, locally including exposures, in low, eroding cliffs, of the main post-glacial beach deposits and wave-cut platform. Then eastwards, from below Criffel and the Nith outfall, this beach merges into the salt marshes and vast expanse of tidal sands in the Solway estuary.

Describing the form of the ground is like building the foundations for a house, or painting the backcloth for a play. The remaining chapters outline the making of the cultural landscape of Scotland which blends, in a multiplicity of ways, with the great diversity of physical landforms to produce the accretion, the synthesis of natural and human elements, which contributes the unique scale, variety and intimate assemblage of features that form the character of the Scottish landscape. In essence, of course, there is only one landscape, although, for the purpose of this book, it is easier to consider the cultural, ie man-made, landscape veneer as a separate entity.

2 The prehistoric, Roman and dark age legacy

Between 9,000 and 8,000 years ago, when the first mesolithic hunters arrived in Scotland, the land was significantly lower in relation to sea level than it is today. Sea level was rising, river estuaries were broad and some penetrated far inland. Later, c 6500-3500 BC, low borders of the main post-glacial raised beach emerged around the coasts of Scotland, which provided the fairly light, sandy soils used locally by some of the first groups of neolithic colonists, although some tracts overlain by marine clays were not brought into continuous cultivation until the eighteenth and nineteenth centuries: even today some of these remain intractable. Inland, the form of the ground was basically the same as today, but landforms of glacial and glacio-fluvial origin were much rougher and sharper: frost shattering, scree slopes and mature soil profiles had yet to develop. Lakes and boggy areas were much more frequent than today, and the rivers larger, being swollen with meltwater from residual snowfields on the highest Highland summits — the last remnants of the Loch Lomond re-advance. Scotland was then a densely forested country, although the ancient Caledonian Forest was not likely to have had a continuous cover, notably over upland and coastal areas exposed to bleak, windy conditions and, near sea level, to the effects of 'salt burn'. Today, were it not for human interference, the tree-line would probably rise to c 610m in the eastern Grampians — but remain at sea level, effectively, on exposed parts of the west coast.

Much evidence about the early extent and character of the forest cover comes from analysing pollen samples from peat bogs in different parts of Scotland. Opinions differ on certain details, but it seems that oak woodland, birch, alder and Scots pine had re-colonized the Highlands and Lowlands during the Boreal period, characterized by relatively warm, dry summers, before 5200 BC. In the previous interglacial, spruce had been the climax tree over much of the Scottish uplands, but its return was thwarted by the breaching of the land bridge with the Continent and the Scots pine re-colonized without competition. Spruce was not introduced again into Scotland until the plantations of conifers in the nineteenth and twentieth centuries. As the climate became more humid in Atlantic times (*c* 5200-3000 BC), the forests spread still more: oak and birch became abundant in the Lowlands and Highland valleys. In the Lowlands, mixed deciduous forest dominated on the claylands and in the wetter, milder west, and deciduous forest, mixed with Scots pine and heathland, on the sands in the east. However, there must everywhere have been a good deal of intermixing, corresponding with the erratic distribution of glacial drift. In this drift, irregular hollows occurred frequently, filled with marsh and thickets of alder and willow.

During the Atlantic period, the damper climate appears to have encouraged the spread of vast natural areas of peat, particularly in the west, covering the stumps of the Boreal birch and pine forests. However, in the following sub-Boreal period, *c* 3000-750 BC, in which summers appear to have been somewhat drier than in the Atlantic phase and to have reached a post-glacial maximum in warmth, the forests spread upwards again to levels *c* 300m higher than the tree-line would naturally be today. Then, from about 750 to 500 BC, the climate steadily became cooler and wetter into what is styled the sub-Atlantic phase — which has continued, subject to certain fluctuations, until today. Woodland again retreated downhill, and peat began to develop on ill-drained soils on shallow gradients, especially at higher altitudes, although oakwoods appear to have remained in western coastal areas and the Highland glens: also, today, it would naturally remain, with birch, alder and beech, throughout the Central Lowlands, the southern coastlands of Scotland and the straths of the Southern Uplands. Thick deposits of peat have accumulated during the last two thousand years over wide areas of the Highlands and hills of southern Scotland, particularly in the west, this process much hastened through attrition of the forest by man. Peat erosion, or cutting, often exposes ashen stumps of the Scots pine as evidence of forest where there is now hardly a tree. In contrast, on the well-drained, exposed seashore areas, the flora has never differed greatly from that which naturally occurs today.

Today, looking at the highly cultivated, urbanized and industrialized Central Valley, traversed by busy roads and railways, with extensive areas of sprawling suburbs, with massive port installations, airports, the new towns, and areas pockmarked with flashes and bings — or looking at the huge chequerboard of enclosed fields in the eastern Lowlands, studded with large farmsteads and mansions in ornamental grounds — or looking at the great open sheepwalks of the Southern Uplands and the huge plagioclimax of tussock and bog in the Highlands (both now being assailed by regimented stands of the new Wood of Caledon) — it is extremely hard to visualize the Scottish landscape of *c* 4,500 years ago, soon after the first farmers arrived. At that time, in response to the sub-Boreal climate, the Scots pine forests had spread almost to the higher Highland summits and Scotland still had most of the indigenous fauna and flora that had re-colonized from the Continent before the Dover Strait was breached (*c* 6000 BC). Also, by then, the original, peri-glacial Arctic fauna had either adapted itself or become extinct over the previous millenniums, during which Scotland had become a land of forest, with open hilltops and considerable tracts of natural meadowlands, not unlike some parts of eastern Norway or Norrland in Sweden today. Irish elk, wild horse, wild ox (aurochs), hares and lemmings lived in the grassland areas, whilst the lesser elk, red deer, wild boar and beaver took to the forests for food and shelter. The European lynx, brown bear, wolf, fox, stoat and weasel were the main predators on the varied and abundant flora. Bird and marine life was also abundant. Many of these animals have either disappeared or been greatly diminished in numbers over the succeeding millenniums as a result of human impact. The most profound landscape change has been extensive deforestation: indeed, man's interference has been so great that there is little, except on some remoter coasts and the highest summits, that is truly natural left in the Scottish landscape.

The extension of cultivation and pasturage, from pre-historic times, made big inroads into native forests, although such inroads must have been very limited until the increase of population in the Iron Age and the acquisition of sharper, tougher axes. Later, in the Dark and Middle Ages, much more use was made of timber for building and domestic fuel: also, considerable tracts of forest were burned through raiding, or to remove cover for outlaws and later — from the seventeenth century — to provide charcoal for iron foundries in various parts of the Highlands. Once the Scots pine was burnt or cut over, it was unable to regenerate itself, both for climatic reasons and through the depredations of browsing cattle and sheep. By the fifteenth century, the Lowlands and Highland straths were almost bare of trees, and legislation was belatedly, and often ineffectually, introduced to curb or halt the destruction of remaining forests. Later, in the first half of the eighteenth century, further attrition of the largest remnants of the native forests, in the Highlands, notably Speyside, came through the activities of speculative English companies, although large tracts of woodland also remained east of the Cairngorms, the inner Moray Firth lowlands, the Perthshire glens and parts of mainland Argyll, together with certain woods in Nithsdale and some of the Border valleys.

As detailed in later chapters, the Highland forests were finally destroyed through large-scale burning to extend sheep-runs in the late eighteenth and early nineteenth centuries: thereafter natural regeneration was hindered by the selective grazing of sheep and red deer. With overgrazing, and no protective forest litter, downwash and peat formation increased; and coarse matgrass (*Nardus stricta*), with bracken, spread rapidly, neither checked any more by the coarse feeding habits and trampling of the clansmen's cattle. Today, the huge moors of the Highlands and Southern Uplands, flamed with rusty-gold spreads of bracken in autumn and purple carpets of heather (maintained for sheep and grouse) in the Grampians and Uplands in late summer, convey to many suburban tourists the illusion of natural wilderness, although in reality all these areas are managed in a very delicate state of ecological balance. Nevertheless, remnants of native oak can still be seen in well-drained tracts in eastern valleys, and sometimes scattered in sheltered sites at higher levels, and along the inner shores of west coast sea lochs. The pine can be found in scattered stands or lone trees growing on peat in the east and west Highlands, whilst birch now grows on moraines and outwash material in most of the places where pine and oak formerly grew, reaching up to 600m in the Cairngorms. Hence most of the woodlands we see today are not natural: as we see later, many are the result of plantations of Scots pine and, more commonly, exotic conifers, by improving landlords in the Highlands and Lowlands during the last two hundred years, though, since 1919, the chief contributor to the new Caledonian Forests, alongside private and company planting, has been the Forestry Commission.

The earliest farmers apparently settled first in Galloway and then in other areas around the west coasts of Scotland *c* 3200-2700 BC. These neolithic people probably confined their settlement and shifting cultivation practice to the raised beach areas and clearings inland in lightly wooded areas up to *c* 160m. They left no substantial landscape legacies, although their large chambered, or megalithic, tombs are locally significant. Their seasonal movement of herds from lower woods and pastures to upland grazings, accompanied by firing of the ground for hunting and clearing for tillage, probably constituted the first organized attack by man on the primeval landscape which produced clearings of more than a temporary nature — although earlier mesolithic groups may well have set fires to flush out game that may have accidentally spread. The first real evidence for permanent coastal settlement comes from carbon 14 dates *c* 2950 ± 150 BC. Remains of neolithic houses and graves occur up the west coast as far as Shetland: accompanying them are sometimes one or more small fields, up to 18m by 80m in size. These houses and nearby chambered tombs seem to cluster in groups, although in Orkney, which apparently had a much more pastoral economy at that early time, settlement was more dispersed. There is, however, a marked absence of neolithic settlement sites down the east coast of Scotland and field evidence suggests a continuation of the neolithic culture in the remoter Highlands and Islands until the early centuries BC. The best-known chambered tomb complex is that of

Skara Brae in Orkney, which has revealed much about the life of those times.

About 1800-1500 BC, a new people began to settle along the eastern and northern coasts of Scotland, with a bronze culture, originating from the Rhine delta area and central Europe. Like the neolithic farmers, they took up sites in coastal areas and, inland, tended to clear the lightly wooded areas on sandy or gravelly morainic or outwash material. Pollen analysis suggests the spread of birch and weeds over abandoned clearings on such lands during this period. These were followed by Scots pine, although the succession was probably delayed where stock grazing occurred on abandoned clearings. This was certainly a practice in later centuries. Moreover, since these earliest, simply equipped farmers opted for the more easily cleared areas of intermediate and lighter soils, despite their lack of fertility, the heavier claylands of eastern and southern Scotland were avoided at this period in favour of areas of light loams on middle slopes above frost hollows and floodable areas which often had southerly aspects. As with the neolithic peoples, evidence of early Bronze Age settlement comes mainly through burial sites, with very little landscape impact, although later, cairns and hut-circles came into Scotland: these are well scattered throughout the eastern half of the country and can sometimes be identified from the air. Certainly, although the forest was little eroded before the Iron Age, it is quite possible that the earliest farmers first induced the spread of heathlands away from their natural ecological occurrence, aided by the slow regeneration of the forests in the cool temperate climate.

The Iron Age came to Scotland about the second century BC and lasted throughout the period of Roman influence from the south between the first and fourth centuries AD. This culture phase contributed a much more substantial landscape legacy than earlier times. In Fife and Strathmore, there were promontory forts on the coast, and the grass-covered remains of hill forts can be seen on the Sidlaw and Ochill Hills and the foothills of the Highland line. Later, in the east and north-east, stone footings were introduced, as evidenced by a number of coastal forts and souterrains, or earth houses, inland. The souterrains consist of a long underground passage of dry masonry roofed with massive lintels of wood or stone, but their exact dating and function is uncertain. These earth houses occur, notably, in the Howe of Cromar in Aberdeenshire, perhaps dating from the period contemporary with Roman occupation in the south.

In late Iron Age times, crannogs or lake dwellings, built offshore for protection, on a massive raft or low piles on a muddy shoal or islet, were developed in Loch Kinnord and the Loch of Leys (now drained) in Aberdeenshire. Such crannogs were also built in many other parts of eastern and southern Scotland at this time, and later into the Pictish period. They continued in use in the Highlands right up to the sixteenth century. Today, their landscape legacy, distinctive in Scotland, is sometimes a low, tree-topped, half-submerged islet, built up of mud around the now-vanished piles and tree roots. Later, as on Loch Awe, Loch an Eilean and Loch Leven, castles were sometimes built on such sites, if footings were suitable, stressing their continued defensive value. Among the most prominent Iron Age relics in the North-East are a group of massive hill forts, generally built of stone, although one or two are earthworks. It seems that these hill forts in central Aberdeenshire may either have been built by the local inhabitants to counter the Roman military expeditions or during local clan disturbances, or may have served some kind of dual function. One of the best-known of these forts crowns the Mither Tap of Bennachie: its main rampart, 4.5m thick, includes a regular wall-walk parapet. This seems to have been in imitation of Roman engineering practice and in at least two cases, Dunnideer and Tap o' North, the hill fort is vitrified, ie large portions of the dry-stone masonry, probably tied together with frameworks of combustible logs (fired perhaps by the Romans?) have been wholly or partly fused by intense heat.

As the Pax Romana was imposed in the south, so displaced peoples moved northwards into the areas commanded by the inland hill fortifications already built by the people in occupation, and into the areas around the coastal forts built by sea rovers. This movement, too, may have been partly responsible for their continued use. The Iron Age peoples frequently occupied cultivable land near a coastal haven and also settled along natural routeways, such as Loch Awe-side and the straths of Sutherland and Caithness. On the coasts, notably around the northern and western coasts and isles, stone look-out towers or *brochs* can be seen in varying states of decay: they originally consisted of a circular, dry-stone tower, with passages in the massive wall faces. Not many of these, or kindred structures, occur south of the Highland line, although a number of *duns* are found in Arran, Argyll and Bute, with similar galleried walls. Also, in the Southern Uplands, a number of fortified settlements appear to have been built by the local population either during or after the temporary Roman occupation of that region, notably multiple-rampart hill forts and fortified homesteads. Hill forts were placed on eminences (generally lying between the 200m and 300m contours) and cluster quite markedly in Lammermuir, the upper Clyde basin and in the Tweed basin, where more than 150 are known (eg the prominent fort on the top of the Eildon Hills). There are also some hill forts of the 'Gallic' type, similar to those in the North-East of Scotland, overlooking the fertile areas of Lorne, Kintyre and Bute. Of the *brochs*, well over a hundred sites are known in Shetland (where after the first century AD they were replaced by wheel houses and open settlements) and some of the best-preserved of these structures are now found at Scallovaig in Glenelg, with a nearly complete specimen at Mousa in Shetland. These structures may have been refuges against raiders collecting slaves for the Roman markets. The more spacious 'Gallic' forts, however, could have been the normal home of people tilling land nearby or grazing livestock on adjoining hills. However, our knowledge of the exact functions of many of these features is uncertain, as is the extent of forest clearance at that time. No doubt iron tools greatly assisted the clearing process, as did the winning of wood for fuel and timber (although at what stage the digging of peat for fuel began is uncertain, before it became active in the Middle Ages). It was not until *c* AD 800-1100 that the first major inroads were made into the forests, according to the consensus of evidence now available.

Compared with England, the Romans, during their short occupation of southern Scotland, left relatively little evidence of their presence in the landscape. For them, the Lowlands and Southern Uplands were a military frontier, never properly

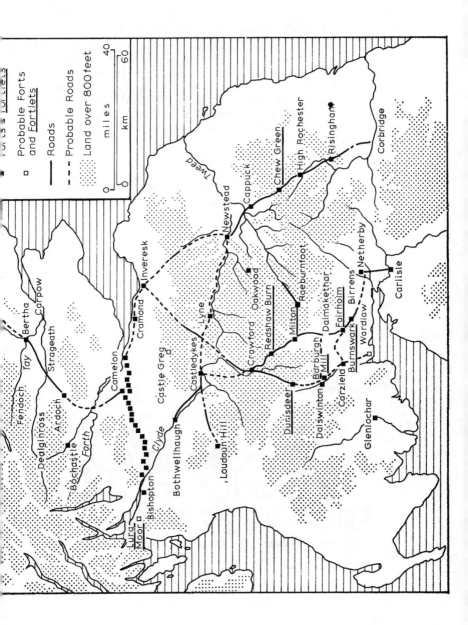

Fig. 1
Roman
Scotland

9   The medieval Palace of Scone, in its landscaped grounds, overlooks the river Tay: downstream is the major road and rail crossing and city of Perth, set in an Improvement landscape dating from the late eighteenth and nineteenth centuries. In the backgound, successively, are Kinnoull Hill, the Moncrieff Hills, the Ochill Hills and the Lomond Hills, all of Palaeozoic volcanic origin. Perth was much remodelled in the late eighteenth and nineteenth centuries and has expended considerably in the last hundred years. Stone-built, Scottish Victorian style villas contrast with new housing estates on the perimeter.

Cambridge University Collection: Panorama, Scone Park, looking south to Perth from O.S. Reference 563/111270 Number GO 79.

10   The spring snow highlights the prominent volcanic scarp of the Ochill Hills and the fault-line scarp and fronting old red sandstone-age ridges of the Highland front beyond. In the intervening vales is the rich, fertile, patchwork of fields, shelter belts and plantations, the legacy of eighteenth- and nineteenth-century Improvements. Loch Leven (foreground) is a legacy of glacial deposition: drumlins and other depositional and glacio-fluvial features are also discernible in the fields. The policies of Kinross House adjoin the centre of the medieval burgh of Kinross (rebuilt in the eighteenth and nineteenth centuries). A motorway now sweeps around the western (farthest) side of the town, linking Edinburgh with Perth.

John Dewar Studios: Fife: Ochill Hills Number 3859/1

11 This view of the mining landscape near Pumpherston, West Lothian, typifies the mining area of the Central Lowlands. Red shale heaps (bings) and colliery tips and patches of derelict ground intrude into the original, high farming Improvement landscape, together with spreads of rather bleak-looking nineteenth- and twentieth-century miners' housing. Oil was originally extracted from the shales (note the small refining plant in foreground) but that industry is now defunct and the plant associated with it demolished, left derelict or adapted to other uses.

John Dewar Studios: Pumpherston, West Lothian Number 3285/2

12 Along the east coast of Scotland, rocky coves and headlands alternate with broad, shallow sandy firths, long, smooth stretches of sands and tracts of dunes, often now stabilized by grass and plantations. Dunnottar Castle, near Stonehaven, perched on a massive cliff of Palaeozoic conglomerate, was one of the key medieval strongholds of Scotland, guarding the route north. Inland, the fertile Improvement landscape leads into the Howe of the Mearns and Strathmore: the distant hills are low outliers of the Grampians. Stonehaven – once an active fishing port – is now a small seaside resort and commuter settlement for Aberdeen.

John Dewar Studios: Kincardineshire: Dunnottar Castle Number 4079/4 colonized: it was a marchland between the warlike Picts and the more settled communities in the military and civil zones south of Hadrian's wall. Agricola, in his campaigns, recognized the strategic importance of the Forth-Clyde isthmus, although he did not use it as a frontier, but as a temporary halt-line on his way north to the victory of Mons Graupius in AD 84. In south Scotland, however, the Romans held the Agricolan forts until about AD 100. It seems that Agricola's scheme of conquest was considered practicable for a while after his campaigns of AD 80-85, and his roads and forts into Scotland were kept in commission. The roads followed two main routes from the south: one via the Cheviots, the Tweed valley and Lauderdale, to the Forth; the other up Annandale to Clydesdale. Roman forts, ramparts, ditches, road surfaces and other constructions have been identified, aided by aerial photography, along these routes: locally, Roman road alignments were later followed by drove roads and footpaths, local field and estate boundaries and occasionally modern roads (eg the Carter Bar road from Corbridge to Newstead). In other places the road has disappeared, although the general line of communication continued in use over later centuries. Air photography has also revealed several Roman camps in Kirkcudbrightshire and Dumfriesshire. The Romans probably mined local ore bodies in the Southern Uplands, but evidence for this is very scanty.

The Romans never really gained a hold on Scotland, although fragments of Roman road are claimed as far north as the Vales of Strathallan and Strathmore. However, evidence of Roman military penetration into the North-East remains in a series of rectangular marching camps up the Vale of Strathmore, through the Howe of the Mearns into Aberdeenshire, at Banchory, and as far north as near Keith in Banffshire; their outlines are often clearly visible from the air. These entrenched bivouacs were temporary bases for legionary expeditions and appear to be of two types, the larger of which was between 37 and 49 hectares, enough to hold 12,000 men. The Romans probably used them on several expeditions into the north, the two more certain of which are that of Agricola and the punitive expedition of Septimius Severus in AD 208-11. The camps appear to have been strategically sited to maintain supply lines and avoid being outflanked by tribes from the adjoining southern Highlands. We also gain, from the voyage of the Roman fleet around Scotland under Agricola's orders in *c* AD 82, the first crude map of Scotland, its axis mistakenly rotated from north-south to east-west, as it has come down to us in Ptolemy's map, showing the Roman names of the tribes, inlets and promontories.

There was so much unrest on the northern frontier of Roman Britain that Hadrian's wall was begun as a permanent barrier, or *limes* between the Tyne and the Solway (116 m) in AD 122. In AD 142 a Roman army invaded Scotland and established a new frontier-line as the Antonine wall (named after the Emperor Antonius Pius). This ran from Bridgeness on the Forth to Old Kilpatrick on the Clyde — a distance of 56km — clinging mostly to the southern slopes of the isthmus valley with a clear view towards the threatening hills to the north. It was built mainly of turf, on a stone foundation 4.28m wide, with a great ditch, or vallum, 13m wide and 4m deep, on its north side and a military road running along the south side. There are nineteen forts at intervals of two Roman miles along the wall, most of them occupying sites previously selected by Agricola in AD 81 with some intermediate stations. The Antonine *limes* was maintained through various reverses until it was given up by the Romans *c* AD 186 or 196 in favour of the more strongly fortified Hadrian's wall. However, several of the forts gained civil annexes: in fact, like Hadrian's wall, the Antonine system may have served as much as a customs barrier as for defence. Indeed, the Roman road system to the south offered convenient routes for travellers for several centuries after the Romans departed. The alignment of the Antonine wall can still be traced throughout its length: moreover, with the marsh and forest tracts nearby in Roman times, eg near Grangemouth, Cumbernauld, or at the western end, submerged by the expansion of Glasgow — all along cleared and drained and now sometimes covered by houses and factories — the original *limes* would seem much more formidable to an attacker than its degraded remnants would suggest today.

During the first centuries of the Christian era there was a considerable movement of peoples in Scotland. The original inhabitants of Iron Age Scotland were the Picts, who had a

Celtic language and culture. Bede distinguished between the Southern Picts, converted to Christianity by St Ninian, and the Northern Picts, whom St Columba converted. However, this pattern is complicated by the immigration of the Scots from Northern Ireland, the Angles from Frisia into Northumberland and south-east Scotland and later the Norsemen, first as raiders, then as settlers, around the coasts, especially in the west, north and the Islands. All these immigrant groups contributed language and culture traits and laid the basis for regional distinctiveness.

The term Pict was probably a tribal name and the traditional march of Pictland coincided with the Antonine wall. In south-west Scotland, the Britons of Strathclyde ruled from Dumbarton what is now southern Argyllshire, Buteshire, Ayrshire, Galloway and Lanarkshire. Then, in the fifth century, after sporadic earlier colonizing from Ireland into central Scotland, the Scots founded the Kingdom of Dalradia in the central and south-west Highlands, with its key points at Dunadd and Dunollie. This was a salient well into Pictish territory and it seems, from a record of Athfotla (= Atholl = New Ireland) in AD 739, that the Scots had penetrated beyond Dalradia. However, when in 843 Kenneth Macalpin, King of the Scots, also became King of the Picts, the two groups became united − with the resulting extension of Celtic missionary and language influence throughout central and northern Scotland. In the south-east, the incursion of the Angles from Northumbria in the sixth, seventh and eighth centuries was checked in the ninth century. As the Pictish kingdom became united, with the peaceful penetration of Gaelic-speaking settlers from Argyll and Galloway (the Britons' kingdom) into the north and east, the Norse (Viking) raiders were descending into the Northern and Western Isles and mainland coasts. At first they came to plunder, but the Picts were heavily defeated and weakened by the Norsemen in 829 so that the Dalraidic Scots were able to take over the throne. From then on the name Scotland can be applied to the whole country, although, for much of the land, it meant a nominal sovereignty of the Irish Scots, who were strong in the Central Lowlands, over a Pictish population.

Later, in the tenth and eleventh centuries and thereafter, the Norsemen came to settle around the coasts of Scotland:

their legacy is very evident in place-names, eg voe, firth, wick, fell, 'uig' (gaelicized 'vik' meaning harbour), ness, eg Stromness, kirk instead of church, eg Kirkwall, and 'ting' (meeting place), eg Dingwall (Ross) and Tingwall (Shetland). In Shetland, 'satter', 'gaard , 'gord' and 'land' names appear. These names contrast sharply with the Gaelic names that are strongly residual throughout the Western Isles (but not so in the Northern Isles or lowland Caithness, then under strong Norse influence) and throughout the Highlands and quite often, too, locally in parts of the Central Valley, North-East Scotland, Galloway and the Borders. Also, one clue to the earlier extension of Pictish influence in post-Roman times occurs in the legacy of 'pit' place-names, eg Pitourdrie, Pitarvie, Pittendarvie, Pittenweem, which are distributed throughout eastern Scotland as far south as Fifeshire. Outliers of these names south of the Forth-Clyde valley and into the central and Western Highlands suggest colonizing or else place-names not submerged by later people. In the fertile areas of the Lothians, the Merse, Glendale (Northumberland) and adjoining valleys in the uplands of south-east Scotland, the characteristic place-name elements of 'inge' or 'ingehame', 'ham' and 'ton' are found as a legacy of Anglian settlement. The endings 'inge' and 'ingehame' generally signify the earliest Anglian sites, 'ham' and 'ton' indicating a secondary phase of colonization. On the ground, the prominent earthwork in Roxburghshire called the Catrail is believed to be the line on which the Anglian colonists, pushing up the Teviot valley from Bernicia, temporarily established their position. Like the Devil's Dyke in north Dumfriesshire, it is considered to be a boundary bank, filling in gaps between natural features such as bogs and forest — features which may no longer exist today, leaving curiously discontinuous lengths of the earthwork on the open hillside.

From the early Pictish period, although their exact date is uncertain, are a number of 'ring forts' built on prominent sites in the valley of Highland Perthshire. Another legacy scattered about the area of the former Pictish kingdom are many standing stones, dating from the pagan and early Christian period. The earliest of the strange designs on these stones are apparently pagan, dating from the late eighth century, but a later group of such standing stones (AD

800-1000) have symbols, undoubtedly reflecting Irish, Anglian and other influences, which are associated with a Christian Celtic cross design, with both cross and symbols carved in relief and enriched with Celtic ornament. The final development was apparently when the symbols pass out of use, and only a great Celtic cross graven in a slab remains. In Galloway, the west coast and the Western Isles fine Celtic crosses locally survive, strongly resembling those found in Ireland. In southern Shetland, the Jarlshof (so named by Sir Walter Scott) gives us a continuous record of occupancy from the Bronze Age through the *broch* period and its settlement as a Norse family homestead to a medieval jarl or lord's house or fortified stone dwelling. Other Norse house sites have been discovered in the Orkneys on Birsay and at Freswick in Caithness. Around the coasts, Viking settlements probably occupied every bay head where farming and beaching facilities were available, with farmsteads on the west mainland coasts and islands grouped into both tightly knit and scattered communities.

Further evidence of migration and settlement during the Dark Ages came from the finding of the St Ninian's treasure in Shetland in 1955, in an excavation of an early monastic settlement by the late Professor O'dell of Aberdeen University. There was also the early monastic settlement on Hi, or Ioua (misread Iona) in the Inner Hebrides (a misreading of Latin *Ebudae*). The Columba monastery lay 400m north of the restored Benedictine monastery, founded in 1200. Other early Celtic missionary outposts were founded at Whithorn (Wigtownshire) and Lindisfarne (Northumberland). However, Christianity, with its later legacy of cathedrals, churches and abbeys, did not pervade Scotland until the Anglo-Norman period when the whole country came under the Church of Rome.

The contrast between Anglo-Saxon place-names in southeast Scotland and those of Celtic and Norse origin in Galloway reflects the early communication difficulties imposed by relief in the Border area. It is only in Northumberland, the Merse and the Lothians that the form of the English village is properly seen in Scotland, presumably once associated with some form of open field cultivation. For a long period after the Roman withdrawal, southern Scotland

and northern England were controlled alternately from the north and the south: indeed, the Border with England today is neither a clear-cut physical or cultural entity. Although the Tweed-Solway line became the recognized frontier between the Scots and the English as early as the eleventh century, conflict between the two kingdoms was to continue for another 500 years.

Meanwhile, between AD 800 and 1100 the first great phase of deforestation in Scotland proceeded steadily. Most notable was the Viking plundering, burning and raiding of the forests in the north in the eighth and ninth centuries. Similar destruction took place in the lowlands and straths of the Highlands and Southern Uplands through hunting, wasting and cutting for fuel and timber — and also for the extension of cultivation and pasture. The deforestation went on largely, often wholly undocumented, in a manner very similar to that later recorded in documents for many parts of continental Europe. With the destruction of the woodland went much of the fauna and flora associated with it. The forest was not simply destroyed by cutting or burning: browsing animals, notably cattle and pigs, did very considerable damage to the native woodland since they were left to forage freely in the forest on the edge of the cultivated lands at this time and until the sixteenth and seventeenth centuries.

3 Medieval and post-medieval Scotland: c 1100-1707

On the geographical and cultural periphery of Europe, Scotland saw only a slow diffusion of medieval influences and ideas: hence the medieval period, in terms of social and economic history and landscape evolution, can conveniently be extended until the late seventeenth and early eighteenth centuries. A suitable end-point is the Act of Union in 1707. From c 1100 onwards, the church and civil powers worked to break down the isolation of Scotland and weld the country into a political whole. Castles were built, ranging from the simple towers of local landowners to substantial royal strongholds, and monasteries and bishoprics were established, notably in the Lowlands and North-East. Local markets were established and trade gradually expanded. However, many parts of the Highlands and Islands lay beyond the direct influence of Lowland government, and there the Gaelic culture and a subsistence economy lingered until the mid-eighteenth century. Indeed, it is remarkable how far new ideas did percolate, even into the most isolated districts as, over the centuries, the ruling and trading power of the South became stronger. Nevertheless, even by 1700, after several centuries of gradual unification, many districts in Scotland had a very marked regional character and consciousness.

The Glendale area, Belford Gap and Carlisle Gap were the most heavily defended parts of the Border and they still retain a higher density of medieval fortified buildings of various kinds (including church towers) than anywhere else in Britain. Carlisle and Berwick upon Tweed commanded strategic crossing places on the Eden and the Tweed: Berwick changed hands several times, finally falling to the English in 1482. It is now in the anomalous position of being the only Scots town in England. Across the two narrow necks of lowland where rivers were the only suitable boundaries, parts of the Border remained debatable until the Union of the Crowns in 1603. By the eighteenth century, the Border area had become huge open sheep pastures and wastes, with local remnants of forest in the valleys that had escaped clearing, or the depradations of border raiding, over the centuries. Indeed, because of the unrest, there was very little permanent settlement in much of the Borderlands.

Although they cannot be accurately dated, numerous short lengths of earthworks, known as cross-dykes, are found on' both sides of the English Border. These were probably medieval and were intended to check raiding parties encumbered with sheep and/or cattle. They are most frequent on the Scottish side of the Border. One such dyke extends across the Border-line itself, high above Catcleugh, to block the narrow ridge giving access to Redesdale (Northumberland). Others occur along one of several ancient trackways across the Border-line, which was used as a drove road.

The Solway Firth cuts off the ancient province of Galloway, west of the Nith valley, from direct contact with England: hemmed in on the north and east by a fairly continuous upland rim, it has, since the Middle Ages, retained a greater degree of isolation from the mainstream of Scottish affairs than the rest of southern Scotland. Open to wide tidal inlets of the Irish Sea, some of its most important cultural contacts have been with Ireland and the western peninsulas and islands of Scotland. Although subjected to the Norse invasions from the north-west, it largely escaped Anglian penetration from the east and resisted Norman subjugation for longer than did the rest of southern Scotland. The resulting cultural landscape contrasts between Galloway and the Border country to the east stand alongside pre-existing variations in land forms to endorse their regional distinctiveness.

David I (1124-53) first encouraged Anglo-Norman infiltration and settlement in Scotland, with its associated developments of feudalism and the expansion, through new bishoprics, of the organized Church of Rome. Fortunately, these newcomers recorded details about land ownership and legal judgements which give some record of the life and landscape of those times and which help us to clarify the significance of certain relict features of that period, eg ruined castles, abbeys and early burgh foundations, which are seen in the modern landscape. Between the twelfth and fifteenth centuries, the Scottish kings contested two marchlands: that of the northern and western Highlands and Islands with the Norwegians and that of the Solway Firth lowlands, the Cheviots and Merse-Glendale area with the English. In the former, a legacy remains in many gaelicized Norse place-names, and scattalds and 'udal' tenure arrangements in Orkney and Shetland. From the time of Edward I (of England) the southern boundary was more actively defended, by means of marcher wardens and a line of castles on the Scots side of the Tweed. However, this frontier remained an unruly marchland, with feuding and raiding between the Percys and other families in Northumberland and the Scottish marcher lords until the seventeenth century. On both sides of the Border-line, and east of the river Nith, the west, middle and east marches were organized for defence, governed by their respective wardens, and subject to a particular code of Border Laws. The Scottish marches, east of the river Nith, today retain their regional name of the Borders, while the eastern marches remain known as the Merse (old Scots for marchland). Isolated from the main centres of law and order in England and Scotland, the Border dales became the strongholds of powerful and frequently rival families.

The legacy of castles and fortified houses

During the late eleventh and twelfth centuries, pressure from the Normans in their harrying of the North drove Saxon nobles as refugees northwards onto Scotland and these were followed by Norman adventurers seeking estates. Some of these immigrants were acceptable and were given grants of land, sometimes displacing native chiefs who had not been totally loyal to the policies of the Scottish king. The most common defensive structures at that time were *mottes* or *mottes with baileys* which were earth mounds, dykes and stockades thrown up hurriedly by the incoming Anglo-Norman vassals for the protection of their households and the local population. These mottes appeared rapidly, by the score, all over the Lowlands and North-East Scotland, notably in the Solway lowlands, the Central Valley, Strathmore and the area around Aberdeen. The keep, made of wood, was the lord's residence: likewise, the household buildings in the bailey. In the landscape today, these mottes stand up as grass-covered mounds, their woodwork long rotted away, in fields, woods, or the parks of some market towns.

In the North-East, the Bass of Inverurie, Peel of Fichlie, Peel[1] of Lumphanan and Doune of Invernochty are good examples of mottes, the Doune ranking with Duffus Castle in Morayshire and the Mote of Urr in Galloway as the three best examples of Norman military engineering in Scotland. Later, in the relatively peaceful times of the thirteenth century, such castles were thrown up to hold lands reclaimed as the Norman frontier advanced into the Highland zone.

Several more substantial castles among these were royal – but intended for control purposes, not as residences: they mark attempts to extend royal authority beyond the Grampians. The Celtic mormaors were subdued and Norse influence reduced by feudal nominees and the royal castles. At the end of the twelfth century, William the Lion erected Edindour and Dunskaith Castles in Ross-shire, Urquhart and Inverlochy Castles to control the Great Glen and Dunstaffnage to secure Argyll. In 1220, Alexander II built Eilean Donan Castle (now restored) on Loch Duich, facing Skye. These were on the march between the Scottish Crown and the Norse Lord of the Isles and emphasize how little of northern Scotland was under Scottish control at that time. Nevertheless, Scone (8km east of Perth) became a royal castle in the twelfth century, and, with the aid of several other royal castles in the region, was for a time maintained as the royal capital in central Scotland. In the east, in the thirteenth century, Dunnottar was defended on its splendid coastal vantage point near Stonehaven to command the route north to Aberdeen, and later, Brechin and Edzell Castles were raised in Strathmore, overseeing routes along the vale and across the Mounth. Further north, the great royal stronghold of Kildrummy, with its circular towers and curtain walls, was built in the second half of the thirteenth century to guard the cross-roads of an important route north, over the Mounth, towards Strathbogie and the Moray Firth lowlands, with the Don valley routeway in Aberdeenshire. Considerable sections of this castle remain. In the south-east Tantallon Castle was built, like Dunnottar, on a cliff-top site, to guard the coast route south from the Lothians to Berwick.

Over the rest of the country, the Normans also built their castle keeps very strong and strategically located to control a whole district. In hilly areas, it was logical to place a castle on a height or edge of a cliff, with the keep on the highest and most defensible point, eg Stirling and Edinburgh, on volcanic crags; whilst on the lowlands, water and marshes aided defence. Looking at the modern landscape, it is sometimes difficult (except for instance, with the later much remodelled castles of Stirling and Edinburgh, or Kinross, now a ruin, in Loch Leven) to appreciate the strategic significance of fortified sites in the medieval period. Marshes have been drained, land reclaimed and enclosed in great square fields, medieval ports have become silted up or very much diminished, rivers canalized and once-huge forests and bogs, then of much military value, have largely or entirely disappeared. Where the earliest earth and timber mottes were rebuilt in stone, ie as a ring wall defended by towers and a stone keep, this generally proved enough to protect the lord and his family and retainers until the introduction of siege artillery in the fifteenth century. However, no Norman keeps of this type survive in Scotland, although Carlisle and Norham provide two fine examples from the twelfth and thirteenth centuries just over the English Border. Also, the ruined castles and rectangular peel towers (for look-out and family defence), which are distinctive landscape features on both sides of the Border, are a tangible reminder of the former marchland function of that area. From the fifteenth century, vassal lords' defences merely became strong enough to allow small garrisons of trained men to resist a raid: only royal castles remained as large, fortified units.

In the later Middle Ages, there was a general development towards fortified towers and houses throughout Scotland, a number of examples of which, notably in the east and north-east, survive today. The plans of castles built by noble vassals reveal variations according to defensive needs and the wealth of their builders. During the impoverished times of the English wars, in the fourteenth century, the simple keep was common — but later, in the fifteenth century, a tower was often added to make an L-shaped plan. Some more wealthy owners added a courtyard. After the Scottish Reformation, proprietors rich from seizing church lands, and wealthy merchants, built defensible mansions which had a second wing added, with firing points for small arms, called Z-plan castles. In the sixteenth century demand for yet more comfort gave rise to the E and T plans, of little use for defence.

A considerable wealth of castellated domestic architecture in the North-East arose in the period of rivalry between local families on a large number of comparatively small estates or baronies (eg between the Gordons and the Forbeses) which followed the collapse of the royalist Earldom of Mar at the time of the Reformation. The period saw the building of castles like Corgarff and Glenbuchat (now ruined), Castle Forbes and Castle Fraser. Crathes Castle (Burnett of Leys, now National Trust for Scotland) and Glamis Castle are two good examples of residential castle architecture of the late sixteenth and early seventeenth centuries in which defensive needs were minimal. The Keith stronghold at Dunnottar was remodelled, as was the great residence of the Gordons of Strathbogie at Huntly. As finally constructed in the seventeenth century (though now only a ruin), Huntly Castle became one of the finest examples of Renaissance building in Scotland; likewise, Fyvie Castle is a very good representative of the period, along with Midmar Castle, Craigievar Castle, Castles Fraser and Tolquhon, Balbegno Castle, the sixteenth-century ruins of Edzell Castle, and the exterior of Muchalls and Arbuthnott Houses (sixteenth and seventeenth centuries). These buildings form very attractive historic elements in the tourist landscape of North-East Scotland and Strathmore, although the best-known baronial castle, Balmoral, dates only from 1855.

Many fortified houses from the fifteenth, sixteenth and seventeenth centuries remain as crumbling ruins over the Lowlands and straths of Scotland. Some of these were sacked, others just abandoned, others vacated in favour of a more comfortable, fashionable eighteenth- or nineteenth-century mansion nearby. Some others have been maintained, enlarged or restored as private houses. Some earlier houses have become embedded in later structures, leaving no external traces today. Still others have entirely disappeared through centuries of stone robbing for field dykes, or new mansion or farm buildings or cottars houses, nearby.

The legacy of cathedrals, monasteries and churches

Many monasteries and bishoprics were founded during the reign of King David I (1124-1153). Some cathedrals were built in the centres of former Celtic sees, eg at Glasgow, Whithorn, Dunkeld, Dunblane and Brechin. Between the twelfth and fifteenth centuries, the Roman Church gradually asserted itself, even in the Celtic north and west. The building of cathedrals like Kirkwall, with its fine Romanesque work, which survives today as a parish church, shows not only the power of the church, but also, along with the vassal castles, how architectural ideas diffused northwards. Collegiate churches, notably St Andrews (founded in the fourteenth century) and King's College, Aberdeen (late fifteenth century) were used for teaching and were usually founded by rich landowners through endowments. Also, there are some large burgh churches, eg St Nicholas, Aberdeen, with endowed altars, that were often semi-collegiate, yet also associated with the burgh council.

Most of the monasteries founded in the twelfth to fifteenth centuries were in the south, where the King's writ ran most strongly, eg Scone Abbey, 1120; Melrose Abbey, 1136; Arbroath Abbey, 1178; Lindores, 1191, and later Perth, 1429. In the Borders there are the ruins of the great medieval abbeys of Dryburgh, Melrose, Kelso and Jedburgh, and in Galloway those of Glenluce, Dundrennan and Sweetheart. Some of the first monastic foundations were Benedictine; later in the twelfth and thirteenth centuries came the Cistercian communities. These abbeys introduced sheep farming into Scotland — a practice that was later to have a big role in the making of the modern upland landscapes. The centuries of deforestation and sheep grazing over the South-

13 Scott's View in the middle Tweed valley illustrates well the main features of the Border landscape. The prosperous farming country is a patchwork of large, square, hedged and dyked fields, with copses, shelter belts, game coverts and plantations — the legacy of eighteenth- and nineteenth-century Improvement. Prominent are the Eildon Hills, in Palaeozoic volcanics; the skyline, even-summitted sheepwalks and grouse moors of the Southern Uplands, with large Forestry Commission plantations on their flanks. In the middle distance are the burghs of Melrose and Galashiels. The attractive, wooded, incised meanders of the Tweed complete this well-known view, with the fine viaduct of the Borders rail line (now defunct).

John Dewar Studios: Tweed Valley and Borders: Scott's View: Eildon Hills Number 4604/9

14 The small burgh of Kirkcudbright, a medieval foundation, fronting on to a tidal creek and backed by a landscape of planted woods, stone-walled pastures and white farmhouses leading up to the distant fells, typifies the Galloway countryside. The town was rebuilt and remodelled in the eighteenth and nineteenth centuries, as evidenced by the characteristic house styles of the Improvement period fronting directly on to the streets. On the periphery, postwar council houses and private housing form a clearly contrasting townscape from the older houses, churches and schools in the centre.

John Dewar Studios: Kirkcudbright Number 3734/A5

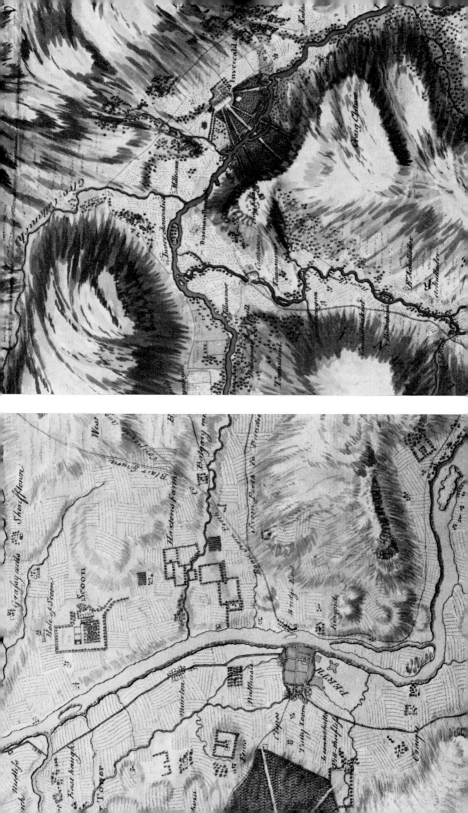

15 Plates 15 and 16 are two selected extracts from General Roy's
& remarkable, semi-pictorial survey of Scotland, made between 1747
16 and 1755, scale (approx) 2 miles to the inch (1.2km to 1cm). The
illustrations are shown at half scale. Plate 15 shows the area around
Invercauld House and Braemar in upper Deeside (Aberdeenshire).
There is no sign of the village of Braemar, erected in the early
nineteenth century, but the early planting around Invercauld
House is clearly seen, together with the drove road south, over the
Cairnwell. Very little native timber was left at the time of the
survey. Both in this extract and Plate 16, run-rig cultivation is given
a generalized symbol suggesting the peasant rigs. Around Perth, the
landscape is fairly typical of the Lowlands at that date: a few early
Improvements are seen, mainly as hedges, enclosures and plantations around substantial farms and mansions. The unimproved
roads converging on Perth are clearly shown, but there was then no
bridge across the river. Roy's map gives a remarkably good picture
of the Scottish landscape before the coming of Improvement to
lowland areas and the clearances for sheep and deer in the
Highlands.

*British Museum Copyright: General Roy's Military Survey of
Scotland.*

ern Uplands have resulted in a considerable loss in soil fertility and stability. Assisted by the tradition of *muirburn* this has led to the spread of coarse hill grasses and, notably in the drier east, heather moors, together with a general increase in soil erosion on many of the steeper slopes. Similar trends followed the introduction of sheep and of deer forests into the Highlands in the eighteenth and nineteenth centuries. However, a number of the abbeys in the south of Scotland managed their pastures for wool, which was important as a trade item between Britain and Europe in the later Middle Ages. Both these abbeys, and those in the Central Lowlands such as Paisley, Cambusnethan, Dunfermline and Hadding-ton, were the earliest agents of large-scale agricultural exploitation. Lowland abbeys, like Paisley and Arbroath, used the better soils and coastal raised beach deposits. In the north David I founded Urquhart Abbey in Morayshire *c* 1136 on the march of his kingdom and the Cistercians founded New Deer Abbey in Aberdeenshire. The Norse Lord of the Isles founded the Benedictine Abbey on Iona and the Cistercian House at Saddell in Kintyre in the early thirteenth century; and Pluscarden Priory, near Fochabers (Morayshire), Beauly Abbey near Inverness and Ardchattan Priory, north of Oban (Argyllshire) were founded later in that century. Nunneries in Scotland were few and poor, but hospitals (note the modern place-name legacy 'spittal' or 'spital', eg Spital of Glenshee, Spital of Glenmuick) were created for the care of travellers and the sick, chiefly in the Central Lowlands and North-East Scotland.

What is remarkable, however, following the thorough politico-religious Reformation in the mid-sixteenth century in Scotland, is that so many of these churches and abbeys have survived as relict features in the modern landscape, eg Kirkwall Cathedral (twelfth century), St Machar, Old Aber-deen (rebuilt of granite field boulders with defensive towers 1424-40), Dunkeld, Dunblane, Glasgow and Edinburgh Cath-edrals, and the university foundations of St Andrews and King's College, Aberdeen. The centres of learning continued, and the cathedrals were adapted as churches for town worshippers, whilst the monasteries, often wealthy and remote from the people, as in England, were despoiled, robbed of their best building stone over later centuries for nearby mansions, cottages and walls, and just left to decay. Even Elgin Cathedral, turned over for lay worship, was later left to become a noble ruin, because of the cost of repairs. Some abbeys, priories and hospitals have disappeared altogether, although Grange, Spittal, etc in field or farm names may sometimes allude to their former existence. Others, like the abbeys of the Borders and Galloway, together with bishop's palaces like Linlithgow (West Lothian), have their remaining massive walls and delicate vaulting placed in the care of the Department of the Environment.

Very noticeably, however, the Scottish rural landscape lacks almost entirely a feature characteristic of the English scene — the medieval parish church. There are isolated examples, eg the fine Norman church at Monymusk in Aberdeenshire and the church at Fowlis in Angus, both built in the twelfth century, the fortified towered church of Greenlaw in the Merse, and the fifteenth century church at Kincardine o' Neil, Deeside (with its hospital at one end) — and there were certainly many more such churches before the Reformation. However, the main reason for their relative absence from the Lowlands appears to be that the largest part of the agricultural land has come into cultivation since the Middle Ages, mainly in the eighteenth- and nineteenth- century Improvements. Against the lack of medieval churches as focal points in Lowland landscapes might be set the aesthetic compensation of the rationally planned, efficient layout of large square fields, farms, roads and new settlements of the last two hundred years. Hence the structure of the Scottish rural landscape differs considerably from its English counterpart: the rectangularity, the scattered settlements and planned villages, with isolated kirks of the presbyterian, episcopalian or roman catholic denominations, with their graveyards around them, often serving a scattered rural population within a four to five kilometre radius. Free churches, built after 1844, and other dissenting chapels are likewise situated, or else often on side streets in nearby small and large burghs. Most of these buildings date from the time of the Improvement or a little later: after the Catholic Emancipation Act of 1829, the spires of the presbyterian, episcopalian and roman catholic churches locally competed with one another in height and ostentation in the country districts and small burghs, often contrasting sharply with non-conformist architectural simplicity. Similarly, in the large burghs and four largest cities, the towers of huge, ornamented and often grimy churches — frequently in red or grey local stone and baronial or gothic style — compete with one another and with the latter-day towers of mammon (chimneys, flats and office blocks) to form distinctive features of Scottish townscapes.

The legacy of town growth between the twelfth and early eighteenth centuries in the modern landscape

Between the mid-twelfth and the mid-fifteenth centuries, many small market centres were founded by the king (royal burghs) or by vassals (burghs of barony: either lay or ecclesiastical), although there continued to be a considerable number of burgh charters granted between the mid-fifteenth and mid-eighteenth centuries. In North-East Scotland, Aberdeen, Inverurie, Kintore, Banff and Cullen were founded as royal burghs; Ellon and Newburgh were burghs of barony and Old Aberdeen was an ecclesiastical burgh. In eastern Scotland, Dundee was founded by William the Lion c 1180 and Perth by David I in 1120: later came burghs of barony, eg Kirriemuir, founded by the Earl of Angus in 1459, and Glamis, early sixteenth century; also, Auchterhouse, East Haven, Fettercairn, Kincardine, Arbuthnott and Strathmiglo, and Pitlessie in Fifeshire — to mention but a few. In the east, St Andrews, Perth, Dundee and Montrose grew to be of most significance by the sixteenth and seventeenth centuries whilst others enjoyed very varying success. Some did not survive, eg Kincardine, whose market was transferred to nearby Fettercairn in 1730. In the Moray Firth area, Dingwall, Inverness, Elgin, Nairn, Fochabers, Keith and Huntly were founded as market centres in the thirteenth century by the advancing Anglo-Norman vassals; but they grew only very slowly until turnpiked roads, then railways, opened up the area in the nineteenth century, after which modern county and educational functions stimulated further growth.

Burgh foundations between the twelfth and seventeenth centuries were most numerous in the Lowlands, reflecting the concentration of medieval local and regional trade in that sector of the country. In consequence, the visitor today may be amazed at the number of settlements called 'small burghs' in southern and eastern Scotland. Coastal burghs, stimulated by seagoing trade, fared well in the Lothians, Fife, Angus and Ayrshire, as did those in their agricultural hinterland. Generally, royal or barony burghs often grew up under the protection of a nearby castle or abbey, in a time when trading monopolies, rigidly defined by royal decree and lack of transport facilities, determined the sphere of influence of a particular town and contributed to its importance as a local and regional centre. In this context, despite the vicissitudes of war, the Galloway-Borders area early became an area of economic importance, a fact which accounts for the surprising number of burgh foundations in this part of southern Scotland. As elsewhere, some of these burghs failed to survive or maintain their importance, but the remainder owe their survival and relative size and importance to sites commanding, or having access to, the principal routeways through the south of Scotland, such as Nithsdale, Annandale, the coast route between Gretna and Stranraer and the Tweed valley. Hence the early distribution pattern of towns remains virtually unchanged in this area, eg Lockerbie, Moffat, Annan, Dumfries, Wigtown, and Kirkcudbright. In the eastern Border area the most important towns cluster around the historic and still important routeway of the middle Tweed valley, eg Peebles, Selkirk, Kelso and Jedburgh which, founded in the twelfth century, are amongst the oldest towns in Scotland. Likewise Haddington in East Lothian grew up around the great twelfth century abbey. These towns, and the adjacent abbeys, reflect the strategic and economic importance of the contact zone between upland dale and lowland march.

The Merse still reflects, in its absence of towns, something of its former marchland vulnerability. The administrative Border has, since the late fifteenth century, deprived the Tweed basin of a natural focus lying within Scotland, and the impressive Elizabethan (English) walls and small harbour of Berwick upon Tweed are reminders of its former function as a garrison town and as an important medieval seaport for eastern Scotland. In the western Border area, Dumfries is an important route focus from the coast and dales: it is the oldest and still the most important of the medieval burghs which, like Annan, Moffat, Lochmaben and Lockerbie, defended the Scottish marches. Dumfries was once the major port of south-west Scotland, but it was situated far enough away from the Border to escape the fate of its eastern counterpart, Berwick. In contrast to the Border towns, those of Galloway reflect its greater isolation and its former dependence on sea communications. Its oldest burghs, eg Wigtown, Kirkcudbright, Whithorn and Stranraer, are coastal and, together with many small abandoned harbours, are a reminder of the once greater coastal trade in the whole area.

Whereas in England there is often a fairly clear distinction between town developments of medieval and Renaissance origin, the former often characterized by an irregular street pattern, lined with strip-like burgage plots and with a main street widened into a market place, there is no such parallel in Scotland. In contrast to most of Europe, where the majority of town nuclei had been laid out by the thirteenth century, the founding of towns in Scotland continued actively, with few major breaks, until comparatively recent times. Although the origin of a street and plot plan and the granting of burgh status are by no means always contemporaneous, it is likely that some Scottish towns underwent important formative changes during the sixteenth and seventeenth centuries. However, the resulting layouts adhere much more to medieval than to Renaissance precepts, a reflection on the slow diffusion of prosperity and fashionable ideas into this corner of Europe. Formal, classical town planning did not appear in Scotland until the time of increased trade and travel (the Grand Tour, etc) and agricultural and industrial innovations in the eighteenth century: moreover, when they came, these changes were telescoped much more closely together in time than they were in England. Indeed, it may have been quite common for medieval town plans in Scotland to remain stunted until gradually augmented by later developments. Medieval town plans are almost exclusively confined to the Lowlands and valleys of the Southern Uplands (as these are preserved today in street patterns, together with occasional, listed historic buildings), whereas new town plans are few in the Southern Uplands and Central Lowlands but do occur sporadically in the North-East, in

Strathmore and in straths in the Highlands. Within the Central Lowlands too, there are contrasts, the medieval (ie pre-seventeenth century) plans generally having a more easterly, and later plans a more westerly, distribution — reflecting the retarded development of the western part of the Central Valley until the Industrial Revolution and the growth of trans-Atlantic trade from the Clyde.

A notable problem in discussing the forms and origins of elements of early town layouts which have become part of modern town plans and fabric in Scotland is the lack of academic literature on the subject. Whitehand and Alauddin[2] identified two basic types of medieval town plan in Scotland, the first consisting of a single street and its associated plots, and the second of two parallel streets and their associated plots. However, there appear to have been many variants and hybridizations of these forms in different settlements as they developed over the centuries; besides which, some early town plans have now decayed beyond recognition, and in quite a few others modern redevelopments and realignments are taking their toll. Moreover, some town high streets, especially the longer and narrower ones, appear transitional in character between medieval and later plans and may, in large part, date from the sixteenth and seventeenth centuries when, certainly, a number of such towns attained burgh status. Over half the single-street plans are bounded partly or entirely by back lanes. Such back lanes are especially characteristic of the plans of towns granted burgh status before 1250, eg in Hawick, Jedburgh, Haddington or Lauder, in south-east Scotland. Plans without back lanes are often those of 'transitional' character and are more common in the west Central Lowlands (eg Kilmaurs and Kilwinning in Ayrshire). Further, as other types and elements of town plans are studied, the distinction between the east and west lowlands becomes more evident. The parallel street system identified by Whitehand and Alauddin has an almost entirely east coast distribution, with twelve such town plans situated around the Firths of Forth and Tay. Although a higher portion of these than of the single-street plans date from before 1250 and are royal burghal foundations, such parallel plans may also derive from strong medieval and early post-medieval trade contacts with the Low Countries. Moreover, in Scotland, compared with planned towns on the Continent, close inspection suggests that the parallel street plan has resulted from subsequent additions to an original single-street plan, as at Auchtermuchty and Crail (Fifeshire) and Coldstream (Berwickshire).

In contrast to the basically linear single and parallel street layouts is the convergent street plan, in which a number of streets may meet at a focal point, usually the market place: however, this last type is uncommon in Scotland and has a scattered distribution. Irregularity appears to be characteristic and there is no suggestion of overall planning, eg Strathhaven, Cumnock and Coupar Angus. It is perhaps significant that all ten burghs with plans of this type were late in attaining burgh status, most not doing so until the sixteenth and seventeenth centuries. This convergent plan may, in fact, be a hybrid or composite of the street and parallel street layouts and/or with modifications and later additions. Generally, in towns having one, or a hybridized form, of the street plans mentioned above, many of the original cultivated plots associated with houses facing on to streets have long since been built over and often no more than approximate alignments of most, or parts, of the original streets are preserved in the modern town fabric. Indeed, save for a handful of accidentally preserved, but now carefully 'listed', traditional buildings, all the present buildings of large and small towns in Scotland date from the eighteenth, nineteenth and twentieth centuries, having been built on the sites of earlier, long decayed, or demolished, often much less substantial houses, barns, etc. Local building stones are still very much in evidence, notably in the small burghs, eg granites in the North-East, mellow red sandstone in the Lothians, Fife, Strathmore, the Moray Firth lowlands, and the Borders; gritstones in the Highlands and parts of Galloway, together with a general use of roofing slates.

Forms and origins of rural medieval settlement and their legacies in the modern landscape

Certain of the rather similar settlement forms of Atlantic Europe, including the Scottish clachan, may have their origins in prehistory. The clachan, or fermtoun, consisted of

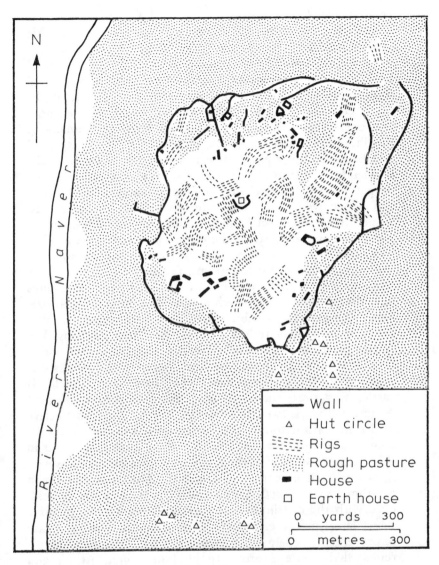

Fig. 2 Plan of a pre-clearance clachan (excavation), Rossal, Strathnaven.

a small hamlet of people engaged in joint farming, run-rig agriculture: the term clachan is of Highland origin, that of fermtoun of Lowland derivation. Neither of these forms of settlement remains in its original state, except as ruined footings in some of the Highland glens, as a result of the sheep clearances in the eighteenth and nineteenth centuries and occasionally, in a very modified form, as hamlets of smallholdings between tracts cleared for new, improved farmlands in the eighteenth century in fertile parts of the Lowlands. Sometimes these 'touns' on the Lowland remained on patches of land that were distinctly marginal for farming and hence were not much affected by the Improvements. Sometimes a small settlement would develop with a church and the manse and, often, the *glebe*, or minister's farm. This was often sited at a cross-roads, or some point accessible to the population of the fermtouns, forming a *kirktoun* – the religious centre of the parish. However, many such kirktouns have disappeared or are much modified or diminished in size; hence the present distribution of such settlements can only very approximately reflect that of the earlier clachans. The Gaelic place-name *clachan* – literally 'stones' – often indicates a former kirktoun, perhaps because the one stone building in the medieval landscape, apart from the lairds castle, was the church. A few, like Fowlis in south-west Angus, with its twelfth century church, form distinctive landscape features today. The *castletoun* was in some ways the secular counterpart of the *kirktoun*, but, as shown earlier in this chapter, the role of the castle was more varied. However, the early twelfth century mottes in the Lowlands, notably in Strathmore, the Forth valley and Fife, have much coincidence with the distribution of rural settlement sites. In some cases, later, in the eighteenth or nineteenth century, estate improvement separated a rebuilt village from a laird's remodelled castle nearby, eg at Longforgan, Atholl and Glamis.

The medieval milltoun was another widespread settlement form right up to the eighteenth century in some areas, finally being erased by the Improvers. Many mill sites are of great antiquity in the Lowlands, some linked with major religious houses. Milling was of greatest significance near the larger rural settlements where small, easily-managed streams abruptly left the hill country for neighbouring basins or straths, eg Strathbogie, the Howes of Alford and Cromar or along the inner edge of the Carse of Gowrie where water power was one of a number of advantages enjoyed by the braefoot villages of the glens. Milling was widely distributed, but the true milltoun was nucleated by its mill, sometimes with a smiddy and a school. Often old corn mills were later adapted to other uses, such as small factories. The tweed mill at Killin (Perthshire), for example, stands on a site occupied by a succession of mills. Moreover, the mills, although often not associated with a milltoun, have been amongst the most distinctive and persistent elements in the Lowland rural scene, many surviving into this century. Another variant of the old clachan, or fermtoun, was the cottoun: only a few, much altered, remnants of these survive, eg in southern Angus (as Brighty, Letham and Gardyne) and rather more examples in the North-East. Originally, these were small, loosely grouped settlements of cottars economically dependent, as labour, upon nearby farms.

Occasionally, on the initiative of the Crown, or more often a local noble vassal, certain kirktouns or castletouns between the twelfth and seventeenth century acquired a market function, sometimes of sufficient importance to be given, or later raised to, burgh status. Also, in the Lowlands, there has been a long tradition of farming in some of the more fertile areas since the twelfth century, notably on grange farms in the Lothians, Fife and Strathmore, originally linked with monastic foundations, eg Grange of Conon. Grange of Airlie and Grange of Coupar in Angus. Moreover, in Strathmore, names incorporating muir, bog, moss, pow, carse, haugh etc suggest that the vale was not without its difficulties for medieval farmers, despite its fertile, red drift soils. Elsewhere, these names appear in less well-endowed areas — particularly the North-East and Moray Firth lowlands, indicating the assessments made by medieval farmers of the ill-drained, moraine-covered terrain. K.Walton (1963),[3] looking at the Garioch in Aberdeenshire, using the list of pollable persons from 1696, noted the preference of settlements for the well-drained, gentle slopes, especially those facing south: the settlements were located on swellings of the boulder clay cover and show a clear relationship to the deep, freely-drained pockets of fertile soil weathered from the parent material. In the Firth of Tay area, probably all the flat haughlands of the straths, howes and the Low Carse of Gowrie (beside the tidal flats) were initially avoided by medieval farmers. These and other sections of raised shore-lines in the lower Forth Valley were only colonized in late medieval times and in the eighteenth- and nineteenth-century Improvements. The 'inch' settlements of the High Carse of Gowrie, correlating with occasional sandstone outcrops that gave firm sites above the clays, are suggestive of the former untamed conditions, In parts of the Highlands and Southern Uplands (see chapter 4 below) there were scattered shielings for use in midsummer pasturing of livestock above the wintertouns (clachans) in the valleys. In the second half of the eighteenth century, some of these were amalgamated into hill sheep farms with permanent steadings of stone instead of wood and turf huts, eg at Dalnaspidal, an old 'Spittal' site on the A9 road, above Blair Atholl.

On the rivers and coasts in the Central Lowlands and other low-lying areas, there were many ferry settlements before the coming of expensive road bridging in the eighteenth and nineteenth centuries, as at Boat of Garten on the Spey and Eastferry, Boat of Carputh and Meikleour on the lower Tay. The latter were replaced by Telford's bridge at Dunkeld in 1809 and other bridges downstream, but in the unbridged section of the lower Tay between Kinclaven and Perth, Waulkmill and Burnmouth, ferries operated until quite recent times. On the east coast, certain fishing hamlets are thought to have origins in the Dark Ages, eg East Haven and Angus, possibly settled by the Frisians, who were related to the Angles. Arbroath, also, was a medieval fishing harbour; likewise Crail in Fifeshire. Local place-names may also indicate the existence of quite a number of coastal salmon fishing stations which have now disappeared.

The clearing of the land: 12th to early 18th centuries

Before the first concerted attack on the Caledonian Forests in the Dark Ages, perhaps half of the land below 600m was covered by woodland. Between *c* AD 800 and 1100 the most serious inroads were made into the Lowland forests, and elsewhere, notably on the coasts, depredations had accompanied the Viking raids. By the time of the Anglo-Norman infiltration, in the twelfth century, limitations were being placed on the taking of fire and domestic animals into the woods, but this may may have been due as much to the desire of the Crown to protect the hunting for itself and the nobles as to protect the forests *per se.* From 1424, numerous Acts were passed ordering trees to be planted and making it an offence to destroy trees in bloom, but little attention was really paid to them. In the lowlands and, latterly, in the largest remaining reserves of timber in the south, east and central Highlands, trees must have been wilfully destroyed on a great scale for fuel since, as in England, coal only became used when timber became scarce. Local timber was also used extensively in house building notably before stone quarries were opened up and roads suitable for haulage had been built. Forests were also destroyed along routeways, as in England and continental Europe, because they harboured thieves lying in wait for travellers and sheltered fugitives from the law. Also, wolves found refuge in the Highland pine forests, which were sometimes deliberately burned to try and flush them out, together with other game considered vermin. Timber used industrially was mainly burned by blast furnaces or coastal salt pans.

When iron smelting was exhausting the English forests, the iron masters turned to Scotland. Hence, in 1607 a large ironworks was established at a place now called Furnace on the east shore of Loch Maree. Some local bog iron ore was used but haematite was also worked at Edderton in Ross-shire. Peat, as well as charcoal, was used for smelting. The remains of this furnace, and several others like it scattered about the Highlands, can still be seen: some were exposed, on a hillside, for draught, whilst others, larger and more successful, were sited beside rivers giving power for the bellows. Streams in well-wooded country were often favoured sites for such furnaces. The Letterewe furnace is the earliest known ironworks in Scotland. Built of Torridonian sandstone and brick and now very much vitrified, it stands on the north bank of the Furnace Burn flowing into Loch Maree. Remains of the oakwoods from which it obtained fuel still line the eastern shore of the loch. Clearly, some primitive drove or track-way system must have existed before the time of General Wade to carry the materials to the site, but with the opening up of the Highlands a hundred years later, after the 1715 and 1745 rebellions, many more such ironworks were established which hastened the destruction of the remaining Highland forests. In the Lowlands, coal-measure iron ores were smelted with charcoal until the late eighteenth century, and the toll on the remaining woodland was likewise very great.

Locally in the Highlands the attrition of native timbers continued through the eighteenth century and even into the nineteenth century and very few quasi-natural stands of Scots pinewoods remain today. The great woods of native (sessile) oak which formerly existed on the west Highland coasts and the inner islands and on the southern and eastern Highland margins has also largely disappeared. What deforestation began, cattle, and latterly sheep and deer grazing and muirburn, have finished in the Highlands, so that today the region is one huge moorland tract of heath, boulders and peat bog — the latter particularly in the damper west — in which the last remnants of native flora, and various modifications of it, like birch scrub and bracken-covered hillsides, remain in glens where there were once dark forests. In the Lowlands too, trees had become a rarity by the early eighteenth century, the run-rig farming system, involving common pasturing of stock, effectively preventing regeneration of seedlings. Generally, all over Scotland, the destruction of the forest was a process of attrition, through cutting, wasting and the indiscriminate pasturing of stock, that left a bare, open landscape, which in its turn, over the last two hundred years, has seen more rapid and extensive changes than in any previous period.

4 Scotland in the 18th century: the rural landscape before Improvement

It is very difficult to assess the changes which had occurred in various parts of the Scottish countryside before the mid-eighteenth century because documentary evidence is often scanty. Much of the land belonged to a small group of influential lairds but the tenant farmers had not, over the preceding centuries, acquired customary rights like those of the English villagers. Indeed, except in the south-east, the village was a very late development in Scotland, and with a very different function from its older English counterpart, in having a planned form, often together with some kind of industrial or trade development promoted by an Improving landlord.

A wealth of documents is available from the late seventeenth century, from the time shortly before the Act of Union (1707), during which new ideas for trade, industry and agricultural improvement were belatedly diffusing into Scotland as the country became increasingly orientated towards the commercial and governing influence of England. From such records, it seems that a very considerable number of medieval farming practices survived, together with the field patterns and settlement forms associated with them. Much regional variation undoubtedly occurred, but there was a substantial uniformity in rural occupancy over both the Highlands and the Lowlands. Some evidence for the pre-Improvement landscape order comes from the First Statistical Account of Scotland, published in the 1790s and containing the edited observations of parish ministers throughout the country at a very interesting period of landscape change.

17 This view of Callanish (Isle of Lewis, Outer Hebrides) shows a typical example of the crofting landscape of the west coast of Scotland and the Islands. Clearances during the nineteenth century for sheep, then later for deer, resulted in the remaining crofting population being grouped into settlements on the coast, sometimes in scattered crofts or smallholdings but mostly into very distinctive, linear townships like those in the photograph. Many of the houses have since been modernized or rebuilt in a distinctive Highland style (stone, slate roofs and dormer windows or modern bungalows) but a few old-style houses and many ruined steadings (indicating emigration) also remain. Below the bare, bleak, gneiss hills, between the peat bogs, patches of land are still tilled by hand or small cultivators, eg for oats or potatoes, but yields in this treeless, exposed, acid-soiled terrain are often poor. The famous prehistoric standing stones nevertheless indicate continuity of settlement in this remote Gaelic-speaking realm over the past four millenniums.

John Dewar Studios: Callanish (Lewis) Number 4135/5

18 Around the coasts, notably along the east coast, many fishing villages were built, rebuilt or enlarged during the eighteenth and nineteenth centuries, often as attempts by Improving landlords to promote fishing as an alternative livelihood to the land. Findochty, in Banffshire, shows three phases of growth: first, the old town, eighteenth-century and earlier, with gable ends facing the gales; second, the new expanded settlement with houses characteristic of the eighteenth- and ninteenth-century Improving period; and lastly, on the periphery, houses in the early twentieth-century, inter-war, and postwar styles, including a row of prefabricated seaside chalet-type homes. The harbour offers little protection and fishing is now defunct. Note the raised beach fragments on both flanking headlands and the Improvers' fields inland.

Cambridge University Collection: Findochty, Banffshire, town and harbour: No GS45

19 Accompanying the agricultural improvements in the second half of the eighteenth century and the nineteenth was the building by landlords of many planned new or rebuilt villages. In the fashion of order and enterprise of the times, these settlements were neatly laid out with the house plots around a square, or a grid of streets, or a single street, with houses and cottages built of local stone and facing straight on to the street. Garden plots were allotted behind the houses and attempts made to introduce textiles and/or a market function as an alternative to agricultural employment. Grantown on Spey, laid out by Sir James Grant of Grant in 1776, is one of the best examples of the planned village in Scotland. Nearby are the bridge over the Spey, also a legacy of Improvement, large areas of private plantations and a patchwork of improved fields on the terraces and haughlands of the Spey valley. The moorland-covered hills are outliers of the Grampians.

John Dewar Studios: Grantown on Spey, Morayshire Number 4537/P4

20 With the new rectangular field patterns, farmsteads, planned villages and rebuilt mansions in their landscaped policies, the Improvers created a new dimension of scale, order and dignity in the Scottish countryside. The view over the magnificent Adam mansion of Hopetoun House (late eighteenth century) looking towards the Forth bridges, near Queensferry (West Lothian), demonstrates the new focal points in the Improvers' landscape created by the grand mansions of the landlords made wealthy by agriculture and new industrial enterprises. The wooded grounds, the terrace gardens, lakes, fountains, stables, home farm and enclosed fields together form a landscape of fashion and efficiency. The Forth railway bridge was built 1883-90, the road bridge opened in the early 1960s.

John Dewar Studios: Hopetoun House: Number 4209X/P

However, there are also numerous large-scale estate surveys dating mainly from the second half of the eighteenth century, prepared for Improving landlords as a first step towards reorganization. Some plans are very well drawn, showing the actual measurements of houses and individual rigs; others seem to have been rather casual in this respect, as though the surveyor knew that many of the old settlement and farming patterns were soon to be replaced. Indeed, the existing system of land tenure was so complicated and the changes so radical that it was common to have at least two estate surveys, the first plans showing the old, unimproved terrain and the second the new geometry of field-grids, roads and other features. We thus have a unique, detailed and remarkably accurate representation of a landscape of medieval origins.

During the late eighteenth and early nineteenth centuries, many of the old agricultural hamlets (fermtouns) on the Lowlands were modernized out of recognition: indeed, the rural landscape of today is substantially the product of this agrarian revolution. No great difficulties were experienced by the landowners in enclosing the common fields: the tenants on the old Scottish joint (or group) farm, under the laird's middlemen, called tacksmen, rarely held their lands on more than a year's lease. In contrast to England they had no protection against eviction.

The legislation empowering the landlords to sweep away the fermtouns and their open run-rig fields, and to enclose and rearrange their lands as they pleased, came as a series of Acts passed by the Scottish Parliament between 1661 and 1695. So thorough was the obliteration of the old order in the Lowlands that sometimes not even a cottage marks the position of an old fermtoun settlement. In the Highlands, however, pre-eighteenth century patterns survive as the tumble-down ruins of clachans in many glens cleared for the sheep graziers in the late eighteenth and early nineteenth centuries, or deserted through depopulation or deer forest clearances in the second half of the nineteenth century. Since then, much marginal land below the old head dyke has gone out of cultivation and most of the dykes are on sheep walks or deer forests. Both these, and a number of possibly medieval villages sites in the Lothians and south-west Scotland, would doubtless reward systematic excavation.

It was not until the second half of the eighteenth century that farming practices, firstly in the Lowlands, began to be modified — and even there a number of changes were delayed until the nineteenth century. However, *c* 1750 is a convenient point from which to glance back on the old order in the Scottish landscape and then forward, in the next chapter, to the making of the modern Lowland and Highland country-side.

A most remarkable semi-pictorial impression of the landscape of mid-Scotland comes from William Roy's military map of Scotland 1747-55, surveyed at a scale of 1,000 yards to one inch and edited at 4,000 yards, or roughly two miles to the inch[1]. The original maps are now in the British Museum. Roy's work was as much a military survey as a product of the eighteenth-century fashion for scientific observation. No comparable maps for England exist until the Ordnance Survey First Edition one-inch-to-one-mile maps were published in the early nineteenth century, none of which has the pictorial vividness of Roy's work. Roy gives us a general picture of the post-medieval Scottish landscape in which run-rig cultivation predominated, with huge, mostly treeless upland moorlands and lowland heaths. Scattered throughout the landscape, however, notably in the Lowlands, were many hedged mansion policies (grounds) — a vanguard of the changes to come. His maps, incidentally, do not include Orkney and Shetland, nor information about the Western Isles. But, together with the Statistical Accounts some forty years later and the estate surveys, these maps give for Scotland data about an important formative stage in the making of the rural landscape. Roy's map shows relief by hachuring, the rivers and lochs, formalized ridges of land in run-rig, distinguishes between heathland, peat-moss and marsh, shows woods, forests, enclosures and plantations, together with settlements and communications. It is interesting to compare a map of land use prepared from this survey with the land-use maps of L. D. Stamp in the 1930s and of Alice Coleman in the 1960s. Only then do the latter, plotted from Ordnance Survey plans showing all the Improvers' field dykes, farmsteads and roads, give adequate emphasis to the change that has occurred in the landscape during the last two centuries.

Before the mid-eighteenth century, arable land in Scotland had become divided into infield and outfield: this was a reflection on the often poor quality of the land and the limited availability of fertilizer. Indeed, an integral part of this field system was the seasonal movement of stock and the use made of their manure. There appears to have been rather an irregular distribution of infield and outfield within the territory of the joint farm, and the arable in the infield was further subdivided, with tenants holding individual strips, called 'run-rig', which were periodically reallocated. In addition, tenants held rights in an area of common grazing. Transhumance enabled most distant grazings to be utilized and shielings (rough huts) associated with distant pastures in the Highlands and other upland tracts gave rise to a scatter of very isolated, seasonally used settlements in such areas.

In both the Highlands and the Lowlands, the multiple tenancy, or group, or joint farm was the characteristic, nuclear form of agrarian settlement: it seems generally to have consisted of from three to eight tenants, working their holdings under annual leases granted by middlemen, called tacksmen, who in turn rented their holding from the feudal landlord. These group tenants were supplemented by a few cottars working as farm labourers. Rents took the form of payments in kind or, in the Highlands and Islands, military service to the local clan chief. The 'clachan' of the Highlands (called a 'fermtoun' in the Lowlands) contained up to twelve dwellings, loosely grouped and irregular, with no recognized focus. It was, in function, strictly agricultural and had nothing corresponding to the social organization of the English village. Joint farms were generally sited on the most favourable lands on an estate. A good illustration of this comes from an early Improvement plan of the Monymusk estate in Aberdeenshire, the home of the famous Improving laird Grant of Monymusk. Generally, if the growth of a fermtoun beyond six to eight tenants occurred, the tenants began hiving off into new communities nearby. This is not just a reflection of the terrain, for the Lowland straths and Highland glens could often have afforded room for a more extensive community: at least, this was true in the Highlands before the population explosion of the eighteenth century.

Tradition, it seems, was important in controlling the size of joint farms. But both the size and siting of the fermtouns was flexible to some degree: sometimes the dwellings formed a cluster in the middle of the infield, and sometimes they were distributed in several clusters in the outfield, or at other times strung around the edge of the infield. A very useful account and discussion of the nature and development of infield-outfield in Scotland, based on research in the Borders and challenging — in the light of new evidence — many traditionally held views, is now in the literature.[2]

In the Highlands, there was a great deal of ploughing in the glens and straths and in the coastal belt: the latter, although not continuous, reflected the distribution of low raised beach and sea loch-head sites along the west coast. In contrast, the lowlands of Caithness and the Moray Firth area show a more restricted arable area before *c* 1750 than at the present time. These gaps in Lowland cultivation which appear on Roy's map were, generally, coincident with swamps, stony moraine and outwash areas that were later to be enclosed and improved. Since leases in the mid-eighteenth century were either very short or non-existent, this militated against any improvement of the land. A prime agency in the Improving movement was the introduction of the long lease of between nineteen and thirty-one years, which gave farmers greater incentive to improve their lands in ways which would profit both them and the landlord. In the North-East, Strathmore, Fife, the Central Valley, the Lothians, Merse and Galloway, it would seem that the arable area in the mid-eighteenth century was much the same as today — although organized, of course, in a radically different way.

For all the changes of the past two hundred years, including much technical improvement in farming, one common factor remains within Scottish agriculture as the constraints exercised widely by relief, altitude, bad drainage and acid soils — notably in the Highlands, but some parts of the Lowlands, too, continue intractable. Another element of continuity survives in the far North-West Highlands, the Outer Hebrides and Shetland, where the division of land into small, elongated, unfenced and sometimes periodically redistributed holdings still survives locally — usually in a somewhat modified form, eg Hougary in North Uist, Sheigra in Sutherland and Gloup and Midbreck in Yell (Shetland). Here, instead of the old joint farms being let to a single tenant, these farms often became (or were sometimes later restored to) crofting townships, with part or all of the cultivated land divided and consolidated into narrow lots. The sandy machair land, facing the Atlantic in the Outer Hebrides, has in many cases remained in some form of run-rig. The common pastures are still shared by the tenants of the lots or crofts. However, very few townships, such as Sheigra, still practise complete run-rig, drawing lots annually for the strips.

The most obvious link with the old agrarian order that survives throughout Scotland is the feature incorporated into the Improvers' landscape as the *head dyke*. This is found everywhere upland meets lowland, marking the division between land in permanent use and the moorland above. It runs along the hillsides in a strath or glen, separating the arable land, meadows, woodland and permanent pasture on the lower ground from the rough, seasonally used grazings on the higher slopes. The head dyke does not indicate the upper limits of all agricultural practices, but acknowledges, throughout Scotland, the abrupt change in climatic conditions with altitude, particularly on the wetter western side of the country exposed to the raw Atlantic winds. There, the division between the prosperous farms on the vales and the peat moorlands above can be as low as 130m in some places.[3]

Willam Marshall, in his *General View of the Agriculture of the Central Highlands of Scotland* (1794), noted the use of the moor above the head dykes for pasturing horses and sheep, whilst patches of better-quality grazing above the dyke were used on a daily transhumance basis for cattle, to keep the lower valley pastures for the autumn. In Marshall's time, the height of the dyke varied between *c* 380m in the drier, eastern moors of the Southern Uplands and the Grampians, and *c* 200-380m in the west Highlands and Galloway, but was only 30-60m in exposed parts of the Outer Hebrides and Northern Isles. Generally, these limits still obtain today, although in some upland areas the modern head dyke may be somewhat downhill of the crumbling remains of its predecessor, owing to depopulation and the contraction of farming during the last century, eg in the north-east of

Scotland.

Under the old run-rig system, each cultivated field consisted of seven or eight ridges, each 6-12m wide, often crooked into an S-shape. These ridges were leased by individual tenants from the tacksmen, and all the arable land was divided into either infield or outfield. The infield was the ground nearest the farmsteads and usually comprised about a fifth of the arable land in the township. This infield was always cultivated, growing bere (a poor quality barley), then oats, then bere again in an annual rotation. The ground was usually manured before the first planting. The outfield was divided into two unequal portions, the smaller, usually of about one-sixth of a hectare, called the 'folds' and the larger called the 'faughs'. The folds were divided into ten parts, one of which was cultivated each year, the name 'fold' coming from the practice of folding cattle on this land the year before cropping. For the purposes of folding, a temporary turf-walled enclosure was built to contain livestock, then the manured fold was sown for oats for as long as it would bear cropping. After this, it was left fallow for five or six years. The faughs were never deliberately manured — only wandering cattle did that — but nevertheless, they were cropped like the folds until they could scarcely return the seed. Sometimes additional farmland was available, notably where toun lands included sections of flood plain. This moist, low-lying meadowland, called 'haughland' or 'laighland' according to its situation by a stream or damp hollow, was invariably ploughed for three years for oats and then left to grass without manuring for another three years. These lands were fertile, but most liable to crop failure as a result of river floods. Higher up the valley slopes were the 'brunt lands' — managed in the same manner as the laighlands. These were areas with peaty soil — usually in basins or depressions — and the turf, when ploughed up for cropping, was gathered into heaps and burned. Bere (barley) was then sown in the ashes, followed by two crops of oats, this being typical of the shifting cultivation practised in Scotland before the mid-eighteenth century.

Since the oats and barley took a long time to mature, and needed little attention between sowing and harvesting, time was left to tend the cattle and sheep. Throughout the

example, small black cattle were the trad-
of stock rearing: moreover, since the system of
encouraged a large tenant population, with cattle
realizable form of wealth, the local grazing land was
overstocked. Likewise, Galloway was cattle country
a stocking problem, although the climate was milder and
pastures more lush than in the Highlands. Generally, the
upland pastures of Scotland were coarse: many hill farmers
depended entirely on this grazing, together with some hay
from the damp valley meadowlands for winter fodder, and
portions of pastures near the steading were ungrazed from
September to November to eke out the autumn grazing.
Generally, the number of cattle surviving the winter depended on its severity, but stock in the milder western Highlands
and Islands and the south-west were better off than those in
the east, although winter feed in Strathmore, Fife and the
Lothians was usually more plentiful than in the west.

In the Highlands and (before the early eighteenth-century
advent of the sheep graziers) in the Southern Uplands,
pastures near townships could not support large numbers of
cattle so it was necessary to search farther afield for natural
grazing. In the eastern Highlands, the valley benches and
upland moorland surfaces, especially in the drier Cairngorms
and Monadliath Mountains, offered suitable stretches of grass
mixed with heather. Here the families left their growing crops
in the glens and moved, with their stock, to temporary
summer shielings. But such transhumance was not confined
to these parts of the Highlands: in Wester Ross, for example,
cattle were driven from Lochalsh for 30km to shielings on
the high ground of Monadh Aillseach, west of Loch Monar,
where each township had an area allocated for summer
grazing. In some places, however, such as parts of Lewis and
western Sutherland, the shielings were close to the townships.
In fact, most Highland and Lowland localities could offer
additional rough grazing on nearby moors or mosses or
uplands to augment restricted glen and strath pastures in this
way, eg the Carse of Gowrie farmers used the Sidlaw Hills
lying immediately to the north. Occasionally, eg in certain
lights and seasons, the much degraded footings of shielings
can still be seen on the open hillsides, as, for example, on the
flat surfaces above the Quoich burn in upper Deeside, some

of the Perthshire glens, parts of the Southern Uplands and parts of the Campsie, Sidlaw and Ochill Hills.

The Cairngorms in the mid-eighteenth century illustrated very well the pattern of Highland land uses at that time[4]. After the centuries-long deforestation of upper Deeside and Speyside, local cattle-grazing areas were well established and prized over the mountain flanks by the sixteenth century, and through and around this area ran several important drove roads. A good deal of timber remained in the Dee and Spey valleys however, to be exploited by the iron smelters in the seventeenth and eighteenth centuries — and, as in many other parts of the Highlands, the cattle economy remained until the end of the eighteenth century. About 1750, the tree-line was effectively *c* 400-500 metres in the Cairngorms: the cattle were grazed in the high and low valleys around the massif, the rest of the high plateau being used on a very informal basis for the lairds' deer hunting. It seems the landscapes of the area today are the result of a combination of factors: cattle grazing and a deterioration of climate between the sixteenth and nineteenth centuries initially upset the delicate balance on the timber-line over the area, as in other parts of the Highlands. Added to these, the iron smelters and timber speculators cut over the best remaining timber in the Abernethy and Rothiemurchus Forests between *c* 1720 and 1780, whilst the surrounding scrub forests had been worked over, on a free-for-all basis, by the local people from the sixteenth to eighteenth centuries for fuel, timber and birch bark (for tannin), notably by the tenants in Strathspey. Finally, repeated muirburning, coupled with grazing, spread the heather moors and inhibited regeneration along the forest edge.

The building materials of the old nucleated clachans or fermtouns were stone, lime and thatch; boulders were used in Lewis, old red sandstone flagstones in Caithness, Orkney, the Moray Firth areas, parts of Arran, Strathmore and parts of the Central Lowlands. Locally, eg in Argyllshire or the Foundland district of Aberdeenshire and in parts of the Southern Uplands, slates replaced thatch. We know, for example, from records of the Monymusk estate in Aberdeen shire, that the houses of tenants were very primitive. Generally, where ploughland was sporadic and sparse, the townships were always sited on ground which was too infertile to be cultivated. In the glens and straths of the Highlands, they were often sited on the undulating kame terraces on the edge of the bluff overlooking the arable on terraces below, as evidenced by the many ruined townships to be seen in such situations today, eg in Glen Esk, Glen Clova, upper Tayside and upper Deeside.[5] On the Lowlands, they were often located near peat mosses for fuel and always, in both Highland and Lowland areas, above haughlands or laighlands liable to flood. In the North-West Highlands, western coasts and Islands and the south-west, the raised beaches were favoured settlement sites, together with the low ground at the head of sea lochs or fan and delta areas which gave a small stretch of arable ground. In Orkney, the settlements were set down by the seashore on the edge of the best arable land: similarly, in the Long Isle, the edge of the machair was often most suitable.

It is in the Highlands that the most evidence for pre-eighteenth-century settlement types and distribution remains: change there came late, and was apt to be dramatic.[6] Overpopulation in the eighteenth century swelled the size of the old clachans before the improved techniques of farming could provide any solution to the problem. Then, from the late eighteenth century, came the clearances. On some of the old Highland clachan sites, occupation in a much modified form lingered into this century, but more generally, and notably in Sutherland where whole glens were cleared for sheep at one time, the ruins of old townships can be seen, little disturbed for a century and a half, in the midst of the open hillsides. This type of deserted settlement in the Highlands appears to be unique in Europe. Certainly, it evokes a nostalgia amongst many visitors and residents in Scotland today, who have perhaps, too little regard for the landscape of Improvement on the Lowlands, and even for the sheep walks and deer forests of the Highlands which displaced this outmoded form of occupancy, and which often combine to provide the most attractive and diverse elements in the modern Scottish countryside.

5 The landscape of Improvement

During the second half of the eighteenth century, a series of changes began in Highland and Lowland Scotland which were to contribute substantially to the present appearance of the countryside. Slowly, during the early eighteenth century, ideas about new crops, better tillage and improved stock breeding began to diffuse northwards from England, although a precocious initiative had been shown by the Laird of Glenorchy, Sir Duncan Campbell, more than a century before. Sir Duncan, who died in 1631 after forty-eight years as laird, built mansions and constructed flood banks along the water of Orchy (Argyllshire); he also planted the policies (grounds) of Balloch, Finlairg, Glenlochay and Glenorchy Houses with fir, birch and oak, and even enforced an old Scots law which enjoined the planting of a few trees around every dwelling in what was then a largely bare, treeless tract of moor and glen.

The changes of the eighteenth century, however – notably those following the collapse of the Highland clan system after 1745 – symbolized the ascendancy of the Lowland Scots and the English order over the whole country. In both the Lowlands and the Highlands the old clachans and run-rig farming were swept away and replaced in the broad straths and Lowland vales by a more or less regular pattern of large square fields in individual holdings. Hedges, sporting coverts, ornamental woodlands and shelter belts were laid out by Improving lairds who often vied with each other in their planting activities. Some hedges have subsequently been neglected, but generally the many kilometres of dykes (walls), fences and quickset hedgerows that characterize field boundary patterns today are well maintained and, locally, fine mature ornamental hedges and mature tree avenues of beech can be seen, although beech is probably not indigenous to Scotland. In the Lowlands, large farmhouses standing amid their rectilinear fields, steadings and workers' cottages form a very impressive agrarian landscape; settlement is largely dispersed, and the largest farms, in the eastern lowlands, range from 80 to 100 hectares. The countryside is here substantially planned, in contrast to some parts of England where field patterns sometimes contain pre-Norman elements and some farm houses date from Tudor times.

Changes in Scottish agriculture involved changes in land tenure, Improvements, in particular, depending on the granting of long leases. Land came to be divided amongst tenant and owner-occupier farmers on a more equitable basis. Besides timber planting and enclosures, the ground was drained, limed and manured. Crop rotations, made possible by introducing the turnip, better cereals, other root crops and sown grasses, both improved the character of the soil and supplied winter fodder for the livestock. Animal husbandry was transformed as the emphasis was shifted from cattle to sheep in the wetter and more exposed north and west and as more scientific feeding and the breeding of cattle developed in the eastern and central lowlands and parts of the south-west. Improvements in roads, the building of bridges, and the introduction of canals, then railways, allowed for local specialization in agricultural production. All these changes also involved a redistribution of population, usually marked by migration to the industrial towns and cities or emigration, and a substantial change in the character and distribution of rural settlement.

Although in the mid-eighteenth century there was still a large amount of uncropped land in the lowland areas of the North-East, the Central Valley, the Merse and Galloway, the distribution on Roy's map of localized tracts of farmland, already enclosed, shows that the Lowlands were then the most agriculturally advanced region in Scotland. Indeed, the new Improving techniques were even beginning to appear in occasional instances as far north as Aberdeenshire and the southern shores of the Moray Firth. However, in the

Highlands *c* 1750 such innovations were exceptional north of the Great Glen, and occurred only occasionally in the straths of the Grampians. On Roy's map it is possible to pick out enclosures at Blair Atholl and beside Loch Tay. In Strathspey, early Improvements and enclosures took place in the lower, northern section of the basin, almost all of these around the mansions of Improving landlords, where they were often accompanied by plantations aimed at beautifying the estates. Otherwise, such plantations maintained a Lowland distribution, rarely penetrating other Highland straths and glens. The Highland valleys, however, together with the upper valleys of Dumfriesshire and Galloway, still contained sizable tracts of indigenous woodland.

In the Highlands after the 1715 rebellion few Scots wished to buy up properties forfeited by some of the oldest families, so most of these were bought from 1719 onwards by a speculative London concern known popularly as the York Buildings Company, although many were sold off again in 1764, 1777 and 1782 through mismanagement of its affairs. This company in 1728 leased the Abernethy pine forest on Speyside from Sir James Grant of Grant and started to build a charcoal-fired iron foundry on the river bank nearby. The best timber was floated downstream to Speymouth for ship building. The adjoining Glenmore and Rothiemurchus Forests were similarly exploited. Today, thanks to nineteenth and twentieth-century replanting, some regeneration and protection, glades in Abernethy and Rothiemurchus Woods still remain in a semi-natural state. The York Buildings Company later leased and opened up the Strontian lead mines in Sunart (north Argyllshire) which still have shafts visible today. Nearby, the early eighteenth century Improver, Sir Alexander Murray of Stanhope (in the Borders) bought the whole peninsula of Ardnamurchan (population was 1352 in 1730). There, he created a settlement called New York in which many of the inhabitants were English, brought in to work the Strontian mines, at first as quarries, then later for the lead, by shafts. The York Buildings Company was one of several speculative enterprises to contribute to the destruction of the Highlands' remaining reserves of native timber. It was not until the opening of the Carron Ironworks at Falkirk (1787) and similar coke-smelting furnaces that the old

Highland charcoal furnaces, eg at Abernethy, Invergarry, Furnace and Bonawe, were closed.

Meanwhile, in the eastern lowlands many small changes on the land took place in the eighteenth century, especially changes in organization. Run-rig began to fall into disuse about 1760 on the more enlightened estates. Rosalind Mitchison, in her biography of Sir John Sinclair of Ulbster[1] — an energetic late eighteenth- and early nineteenth-century Improver on his Caithness estates, describes the scene there, similar to many parts of the eastern lowlands, before and after the Improvements took place. Before Improvement, the Caithness landscape was open, bleak and treeless, with poverty-stricken hamlets, open, ridged fields, with emaciated stock wandering over the mosses and stubbles and great moors rising inland. Today Caithness and many other areas of north-east Scotland are still bleak and treeless, but a very different landscape of square, enclosed fields (by flags in Caithness; by wire, granite boulders and, occasionally, hedges in Aberdeenshire and Banffshire) can be seen. There, as further south in the Central Valley, it is difficult to grasp the transforming impact of the Improvers in the Lowlands during the last two hundred years: a new landscape of geometry, reason, fashion and efficiency emerged.

The first Agricultural Society in Scotland was founded in 1723, very much in the spirit of the times, and from this date the Improving movement gathered momentum. Landowners acted both as a body and as individuals, with their own fancies of layout and management — but always effecting change out of conscious choice. Acting for these landowners was a band of variously qualified, sometimes amateur, land surveyors. These had to have the ability to measure land, use instruments, and present results accurately, to draw maps, and often make value judgements as to the quality of the land, all this requiring skills of high order. Men of this calibre were not plentiful and for many years during the Improving period land surveyors were drawn from a variety of backgrounds, including architects, schoolmasters, farmers, gardeners and nurserymen. At the simplest level, the surveyor recorded the existing landscape to enable the proprietor and his factor to plan future developments. However, many such plans go beyond merely recording the landscape. Besides often evaluating the quality of the ground, the surveyor in certain instances made recommendations as to the course that improvements should take. The dated plans are the only dependable means of tracing the spread of the enclosure movement in Scotland. The earliest plans were produced about 1720, usually on small well-appointed estates whose owners had achieved sufficient capital for effecting improvements through either the fertility of their lands or wealth made in industrial or trading enterprises.

Land surveyors flourished only for a brief period in Scotland: from being practically non-existent in the early eighteenth century, their numbers grew rapidly after 1740, but they found themselves redundant a century later with the coming of the Ordnance Survey in Scotland. By the 1780s most of the Lowland Improvements had been effected and the surveyors then found further work in the first quarter of the nineteenth century with the widespread building of turnpikes, with canals and, by the 1840s, railways. It has been estimated that in about a century more than 30,000 plans were produced in Scotland, and with these the proprietor and the land surveyor first practised planning in something like the modern sense of the word.[2]

On an estate, the tounship, group, or joint farm in run-rig, was put into the hands of a single tenant as the holdings became vacant. This new tenant not only obtained a nineteen-year lease but also was often bound by it to adopt Improving methods, such as fencing, dyking, manuring or sowing green crops and regular rotations. In the mid-eighteenth century, whilst Improvements were actively being planned on many central Lowland estates (notable examples being those of Lord Gardenstone, of the 9th Earl of Strathmore and on the 950-hectare estate of Delvine in Perthshire), the estates of Garden of Troup, Grant of Monymusk, Ferguson of Pitfour and the Earl of Cawdor, all on lands in generally good condition, were the leaders in the North-East. In the Highlands and Islands, stimulus was given by the government after 1745, when the commissioners appointed to manage the forfeited estates began to reform the agrarian system. On the forfeited Lovat, Cromarty, Mackenzie and Macleod estates, leases of up to twenty-one years were granted, sub-tenancies were eliminated, enclosures

21   The medieval street pattern of the burgh of Biggar (Lanarkshire), with the main street widened to form a market place and back lanes behind the burgage plots, is still clearly evident — although the houses now date largely from the late eighteenth, nineteenth and twentieth centuries. Note the three churches, very close to one another, of different styles and denominations — reflective of Scottish ecclesiastical history. Beyond, enclosed, Improved, farming landscape, with market gardening near the town. Some post-1945 housing is for car commuters to Edinburgh (30 miles, 50km).

John Dewar Studios: Biggar, Lanarkshire, Number 3552/7

22   The medieval burgh of Haddington (East Lothian) developed in close association with the local abbey, the nave of which is still used as the parish church. The line of the old High Street, widened for a market, is flanked by a very attractive grouping of seventeenth-, eighteenth- and nineteenth-century houses focusing on a classical style church: this area has now been restored as an urban conservation area. Industrial enterprises have taken over riverside sites formerly occupied by mills.

John Dewar Studios: Antiquities: Haddington Number 4521/12

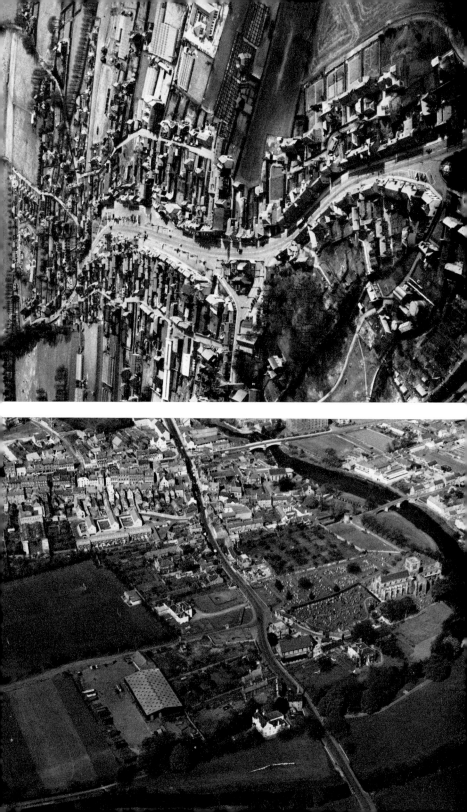

23 Berwick upon Tweed, 'the only Scottish town in England', was heavily fortified against cannon siege in the style of the day in Elizabethan times after this medieval port and guard point on the coast route south had finally fallen to the English in the late fifteenth century. The defensive works are clearly seen, as are the medieval street pattern and bridge (1624), the eighteenth-century classical style church and eighteenth- and nineteenth-century Scottish house styles. The elegant Victorian railway viaduct (1849) across the Tweed is just visible, as is the modern relief road bridge (1928).

John Dewar Studios: Berwick upon Tweed Number 6236/3

24 The view of Edinburgh looking west from Calton Hill shows the Old and New Towns divided by Princes Street Gardens and Waverley station (on the site of a drained loch). The medieval castle — later much modified — crowns the volcanic plug in the background; the old High Street leads down from the castle esplanade past St Giles Cathedral towards Holyrood Palace. Both the High Street-Castle area and New Town (to right, north of Scott Memorial and Princes Street Gardens) have been declared conservation areas, with the aim of ensuring a measure of harmony and continuity in their respective townscapes in future redevelopment schemes. In the background, the Victorian episcopal cathedral.

John Dewar Studios: Edinburgh: Calton Hill West, Number 3007/1 legally enforced and new tillage and herding arrangements (for cattle and sheep) introduced.

In 1770 an Act was passed enabling proprietors to give leases up to thirty-one years, and in such long leases provision had to be made for fencing, so that within thirty years all the lands had to be enclosed. These famous long leases were themselves the incentive for Improvement.* Rent (ie interest on the capital of the land and improvements on it or to it) was to be the only form of payment between landlord and tenant. The proprietors could be the creditors to succeeding heirs of entail for three-quarters of the money laid out in making these improvements, provided the amount did not exceed four years' rent. They could also exchange land to make holdings more convenient to work. The Act accounts for the great increase in estate surveys just before 1770 and afterwards (c 1765-75), and was of prime importance in stimulating the Improvement of laggard estates.

Slowly at first, but with increasing momentum after 1770, the landscape was modified and agricultural production increased. However, the new farming made its impact in a rather piecemeal fashion, much depending on the exposure and drainage of the land, the condition of the soil, the local patterns of ownership and the wealth and personal initiative of owners. Furthermore, whilst the old fermtouns were generally easily removed, the ploughing out and levelling of the ridges and baulks of the old group farm was not always so easily accomplished. Besides, the layout of new farmsteads, fields, hedges and dykes proved a very costly business which bankrupted many tenants. Landlords with large estates and capital reserves (eg for loans to tenants) had the best capacity to reorganize.

In the reclamation of the land, the major items involved were the removal of stones and the application of manures and fertilizers. Moreover, on the eastern and central Lowlands and on the Merse and the Highland straths, there was much glacial deposition, with a preponderance of boulder clay and outwash, which complemented the heavily glacially eroded scenery of the Highlands and Southern Uplands. In

---

*Long leases had been given since the 1620's in South-east Scotland.

the North-East, for example, the problems of removing stones, sometimes boulders, from the fields were considerable. There, the building of stone dykes and the removal of boulders and stones from the soil went on side by side. Sometimes, particularly in Aberdeenshire, the dykes assume such a size that the name 'consumption dykes' has been given to them. Simply because they are so difficult to remove, they locally remain an impressive feature in the North-East landscape today, eg the very substantial dyke at Kingswells, 8km west of Aberdeen. Throughout the North-East, dykes are often wider than they need to be in an area strewn with metamorphic and granitic glacial erratics from the Highlands. The removal of granite boulders from the fields (eg for the walls of St Machars Cathedral and the rear and side walls of houses in Old Aberdeen and other settlements in the North-East) also established the use of granite for building in Aberdeenshire. The use of quarried, dressed granite for house fronts, mansions, public buildings and harbours developed from the late eighteenth century.

In the North-East, the only major gaps in the pattern of dykes occur in the old lake basins, where the fields on the relatively stone-free floors are divided by fences. Moreover, since these areas were often marshy, they were drained late, in the nineteenth century. In addition, a number of acid heathlands over granite outliers, or lowground mosses and areas of infertile gravels in the North-East, have never been reclaimed at all and are left as outliers of scrub or rough grazing in a landscape of relatively small, square, stone-led fields. Occasionally, eg near New Deer in the 'driftless' zone of Buchan, hedges planted for shelter and amenity by Improvers can still be seen. In the North-East, many minor engineering projects were undertaken in swamps, lochs and haughlands — but some, like the Loch of Auchlossen near Lumphanan on Deeside, and the Loch of Strathbeg between Peterhead and Fraserburgh have never been successful. Along the rivers of the North-East, such as the Dee, Don, Spey and Findhorn, and in the Central Lowlands, beside the Clyde, Forth and Tay, embankments were made to prevent crops and stock being washed away in spates, thus bringing good valley land into permanent use. However, deep drainage of hill pasture and Lowland farms has increased the rapidity of run-off and rendered such river lands more liable to flood than before.

Farmers in the Central Lowlands had similarly to gather up stones and drain bogs, besides clearing away remaining scraps of woodland. The Central Valley contains extensive tracts of low-lying land that had to wait for treatment using modern drainage techniques. The Forth Carselands were drained in the eighteenth and nineteenth centuries, but many small peat mosses still remain undrained, eg Flanders Moss, which is now being reclaimed and planted in a piecemeal fashion by the Forestry Commission. Also, some of the Forth and Tay haughlands have locally resisted attempts at drainage. Often, a dry spell reveals widespread patches of peat-staining in ploughed fields which recalls the enormous amount of drainage and reclamation which has been needed to overcome the chaotic conditions left by the retreat of the last ice.

In Strathmore, the Carse of Gowrie, Howe of the Mearns, Howe of Fife, Strathearn, Strathallan and the Forth valley, Ayrshire and the Lothians, Improvements between 1740 and 1840 were aided by the occurrence of superficial deposits better suited to the new course rotations and grazing regimes. There were far fewer boulders and bogs to contend with compared with the North-East, hence the marked contrast between the smaller, stone-walled fields of Aberdeenshire and Banffshire and the great chequerboard of enclosures on the rich, red-brown drift soils of Strathmore and the Howe of the Mearns, with many more hedges, copses, and coverts and square, red and grey stone farmhouses and yards set in the midst of their fields. The Central Lowlands comprise some of the finest high farming landscapes in Europe. Moreover, the initially large fields have been considerably less subject to enlargement to take new farm machinery introduced in the last fifteen years, compared with smaller fields laid out in the areas of England affected by parliamentary enclosure. The Scottish landscape has remained more stable. In the Lowlands, many of the farms date from the second half of the eighteenth century, although rebuilding and/or extensions have usually taken place since then. For example, the farms of the Carse of Gowrie date from estate Improvements around 1780. The dwelling house was laid out with the offices and barns in a square behind, sometimes with a

Fig. 3 The Enclosure Movement: a study in Ayrshire — (top) before Enclosure; (bottom) after Enclosure (1= barony boundary, 2= pre-enclosure farm boundaries)

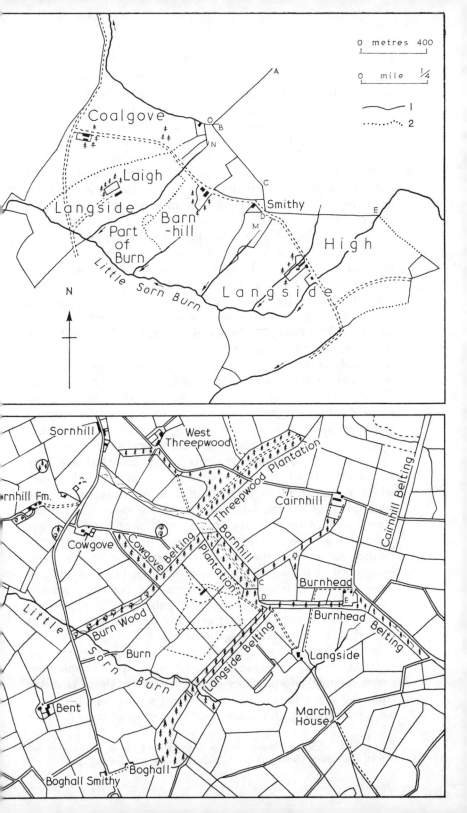

threshing mill — the latter being a relict feature of the nineteenth century when the Carse was unenclosed cornland. Yet this style of building often remains in the district, despite extensions and rebuildings *c* 1830-40.

In Ayrshire, the wetter, milder climate has aided the development of dairying, in a landscape of hedged and dyked fields, with dykes rising up on to the Renfrew Hills and Southern Uplands to enclose huge sheepwalks above the head dyke and to demarcate the boundaries over spurs and watersheds of tenanted (but now often owner-occupied) hill farms. However, in north Ayrshire and Renfrewshire, as in certain other areas like the North-East, a number of older features of rural occupancy have survived, embedded in the modern cultural landscape: such are distinguishable by the careful study of field boundaries, roads and steading patterns on old estate plans in comparison with the modern 1:25,000 and 1:10,000 maps.[3] A field dyke here, part of an old track there and, above all, the names and location of the majority of farmhouses: these are remnants of what was formerly much denser settlement. Such tounships were generally on, or very close by, the sites of steadings traceable on old maps spanning the last two centuries, which bear the original names of the fermtouns. In north Ayrshire and Renfrewshire, a mosaic of small estates and farms existed before the eighteenth-century Improvements which hindered sweeping Improvements of the type which took place on baronies which remained intact further south in Ayrshire, and of the type laid out on the large estates of the eastern lowlands. Hence change on this scatter of small properties was less radical in the Improving period than on the larger estates further south, and the present-day landscapes of this area have evolved during the last two hundred years to include many more surviving features from the pre-Improvement occupancy phase than have the substantially replanned layouts elsewhere. To greater or lesser degrees, this theme is echoed in other lowland areas in Scotland.

Within the Lowlands, there are a number of other marked contrasts in the Improvement landscape. For example, the better-drained sheep walks of the Southern Uplands differ from the moorlands of the central hill masses, which are still blanketed by bog and coarse grasses over wide areas because

Fig. 4 The Enclosure Movement: a second study in Ayrshire — (top) before Enclosure; (bottom) after Enclosure. For key see Fig. 3.

Top map labels:

Woodhead Burn
M.P. M.P.
Saarston (East Satersyke)
Wester Easter
Sawyer Syke
Glenturf Overland
Wester Overland Hill Head
Road from Kilmarnock to Mauchline
To Hill Head
Netherland
M.P.
Easter
Netherland
Craig Mill Whitell
Cessnock Water

0 yards 440
0 metres 400
———— 1
··········· 2
N

Bottom map labels:

Woodhead Burn
A
H
Satersyke
West Satersyke
Glenturf
West Overland
East Overland
B
C
R
S
Q
To Kilmarnock
Former Parish Boundary
Netherland Cottage
Hillhead
Netherland
D
Townhead
F E
G
P
To Mauchline
Whitehill
Craig Mill
Cessnock Water

0 yards 440
0 metres 400
N

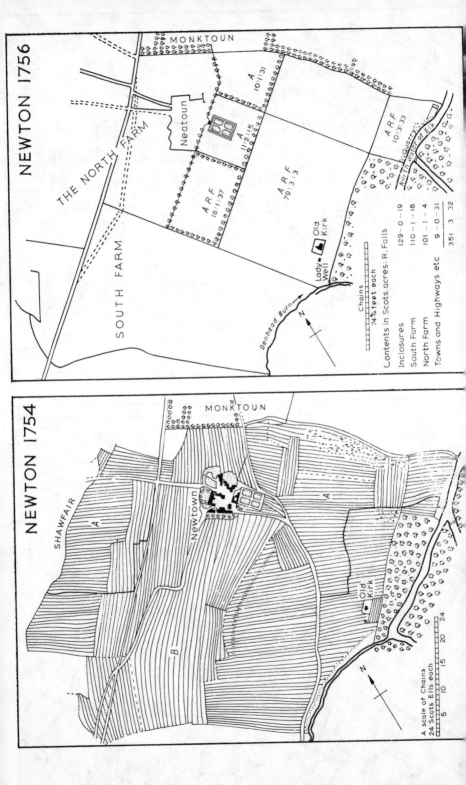

NEWTON 1754

SHAWFAIR

A

B

Newtown

MONKTOUN

A

Old Kirk

A scale of Chains
24 Scots Ells each
5   10   15   20   24

N

NEWTON 1756

THE NORTH FARM

SOUTH FARM

MONKTOUN

Neatoun

A
10·1·31

A
11·2·15

A R F
10·3·33

A R F
16·1·37

A R F
79·3·3

North Walls of Elk
Quarry

Old Kirk

Lady Well

Denhead Burn

N

Chains
74½ feet each

Contents in Scots.acres: R.Falls

Inclosures   129 .. 0 .. 19
South Farm   110 .. 1 .. 18
North Farm   101 .. 1 .. 4
Towns and Highways etc   9 .. 0 .. 31
                    351 3 32

of their tabular shape and cover of morainic drift. In Fifeshire, the Lothians and Strathmore, stock raising, geared to rotation grasses and fodder crops, developed alongside the expansion of grain (barley for malting) on the drier, warmer soils. Locally, in Strathmore, small fruit growing also developed. In contrast, Galloway, like the Highlands, received new ideas more slowly: there, today, we see dyked and sometimes hedged fields dotted with dairy and beef cattle, with sheep pastures on the moors rising up inland. The present farming landscape and economy of the south-west are largely a reflection of the terrain, soils and mild winter climate. The drift-covered lowlands of south Dumfriesshire, however, overlooking the Solway Firth, have a rectilinear 'enclosure' field pattern similar to that of the Lothians.

Such was the success of the new farming system that the reclamation process accelerated in the early nineteenth century: by the time of the New Statistical Account (1830) most of the Lowland parishes were regarded as Improved. People from the towns bought land in the Improved areas as an investment, and those who could not afford such land Improved the barren wastes and moors, pushing ever higher up the slopes of the eastern margins of the Highlands and Southern Uplands to heights where frosts and poor soils often proved too much for the colonists. As a result, the limits of cultivation have subsequently slipped back downhill, leaving the old head dyke to crumble in the moorland grazings above. In the eastern and central Lowlands, the internal colonization was completed when the interfluvial ridges, which had previously only been used for sporadic cattle grazing, came under the plough. The improvement in land management was paralleled by improvements in stock. New cross-breeding by enlightened Improvers, eg Barclay of Urie, eventually produced the Aberdeen-Angus beef cattle breed in the nineteenth century. At the same time, the modern Ayrshire dairy cattle were being bred. Both the beef and dairy markets were stimulated by the growth of railways from the 1840s. Meanwhile, the intaking of new land in the Lowlands continued until the closing decades of the nineteenth century, by which time cheap food imported from overseas came to precipitate an agricultural depression at home.

Fig. 5 The Enclosure Movement: Newton Farm, East Lothian — (left) before Enclosure; (right) after Enclosure

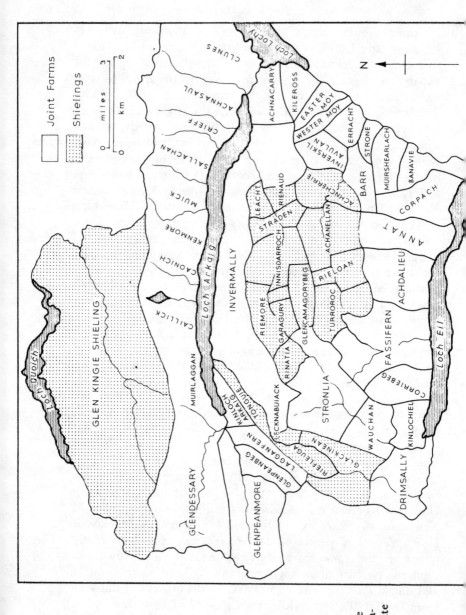

Fig. 6 The land use changes in the Highlands: Lochiel Estate pre-Improvement. Lochaber: mid-eighteenth century.

The changes in the Highlands and Islands

In many respects the years following the rebellion of 1745 saw the start of the modern development of the Highlands. In the broad straths a sequence of Improvements took place similar to those on the Lowlands to the east and south. For example, the Earl of Bredalbane had his estates beside Loch Tay surveyed in 1769 and subsequently cleared, to be laid in· farms, with sheepwalks over the hills. In the south-west Highlands, John Campbell, the famous 5th Duke of Argyll, began a series of important improvements over many parts of his vast estates. Generally, the west coast of the Highlands did not become adapted to commercial agriculture, but continued at subsistence level, crofting being supplemented by fishing, kelping and other activities. The climate and terrain did not generally favour the creation of large arable and stock farms like those in the eastern and central Lowlands. Indeed, social and economic factors in the western Highlands contributed largely to the evolution of the crofting system and the changeover from cattle to sheep grazing. In Jura, Morven and Ardnamurchan, for example, the terrain, the remoteness, the isolation from new ideas and difficulty of emigration together gave rise to overcrowded clachan communities in the late eighteenth and early nineteenth centuries. The situation prompted landlords to impose rigid patterns of reorganization in which their new, more lucrative sheep-grazing enterprises took up most of the land, with the crofting townships sandwiched on coastal tracts on their margins.

In Kintyre, however, where the climate is mild and coastal margins quite tractable, the old tacksmen were given nineteen-year leases by the Improving 5th Duke: they then sublet to their tenants who thereby were given sufficiently secure incentives for Improving the land, with none of the drawbacks experienced by the crofting communities further north.[4] Similar Lowland-style Improvements took place in the Bute estates in Bute and the Cumbraes and the Hamilton estate on Arran. In the Inner Hebrides, Islay and Gigha had the easiest access to the new Improving ideas from the Lowlands, as well as the greatest scope for emigration of landless labourers. These factors, together with fairly workable soils, enabled the Campbells of Islay to reproduce a

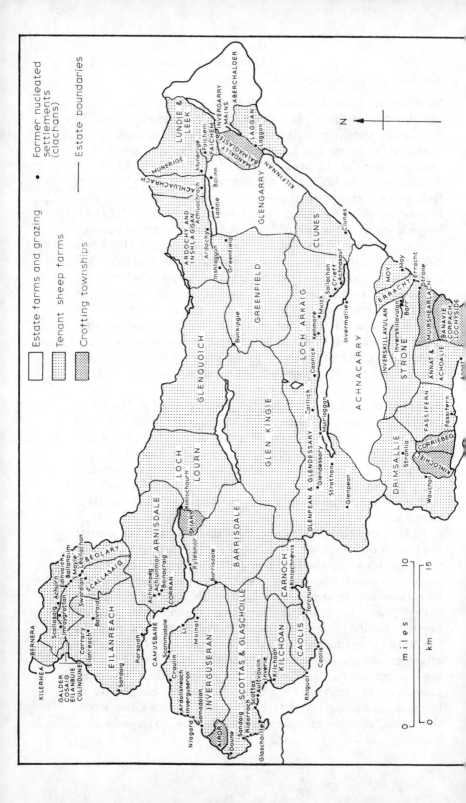

varied pattern of agricultural holdings and industrial villages (fishing, textiles and whisky) strongly resembling the Improved mainland landscapes of the Lowlands.[5] This transformation was substantially complete by the 1860s.

The 5th Duke's efforts to improve the farming on Tiree, however, met with considerable resistance from the expanding island population.[6] There was a modest improvement in communications and some progress in land reclamation and in the building of march dykes; and new crops were introduced, notably hay and potatoes. However, the technical simplicity of the islanders, the deeply-entrenched run-rig system, clan traditions and a suspicion of Campbell overlordship combined with prevailing economic factors to inhibit any further developments. In the last years of the eighteenth century the Improving Duke divided the larger tenant farms into smallholdings (crofts) on long leases designed to stimulate Improvement, which has given rise in large measure to the present low, flat, treeless, but quite closely cultivated landscape of the island.

With the cessation of clan warfare in 1746, many of the Highland lairds began to appropriate the clan lands held in their name for new, more lucrative enterprises. The Lowlander's economic, social and political way of reasoning began to permeate the Highlands: alongside the exploitation of the woodlands on their properties many lairds saw that sheep grazing could be quite a profitable use of their estates. This was the first Highland revolution: whereas in the first half of the eighteenth century the clanfolk's black cattle had dominated miles of upland and valley grazings, sheep were now found more efficient to manage on such areas, besides which, in the western Highlands, sheep were often better suited than cattle to the steep rocky slopes. The sheepwalks were leased to, or owned by, graziers according to the system originally developed in the northern Pennines and the Lake District in the seventeenth century. This spread into the Southern Uplands during the early eighteenth century and, by the 1770s and 1780s, farther north into Perthshire and Argyllshire. Indeed, the Dukes of Argyll (notably the 5th Duke) appear to have introduced large numbers of sheep into their lands as early as 1740 and by 1764 large tracts of Cowal were converted into sheepwalks. Great areas of the central

Fig. 7 The land use changes in the Highlands: the Improving Movement (sheep) Lochaber: early-nineteenth century.

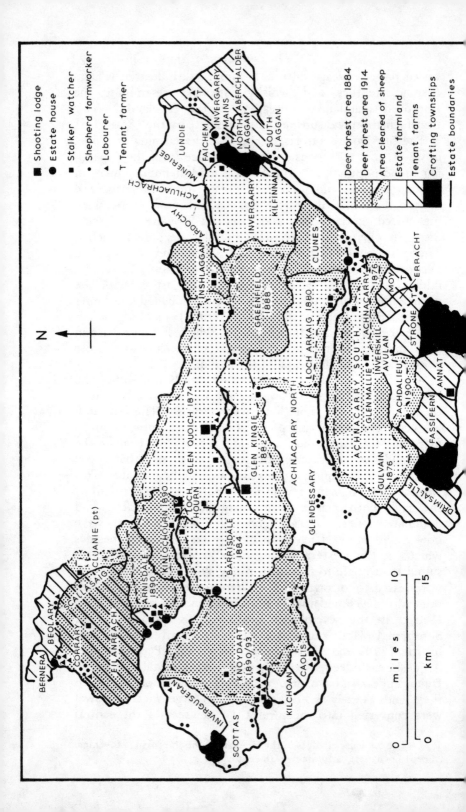

Shooting lodge
Estate house
Stalker watcher
Shepherd farmworker
Labourer
T Tenant farmer

Deer forest area 1884
Deer forest area 1914
Area cleared of sheep
Estate farmland
Tenant farms
Crofting townships
Estate boundaries

N

BERNERA
BEOLARY
CORRARY
SCALLASAIG
CLUANIE (pt)
EILANREACH
ARNISDALE 1890
KINLOCHOURN 1890
LOCH HOURN
GLEN QUOICH 1874
INVERGUSERAN
SCOTTAS
KNOYDART 1890/93
KILCHOAN
CAOLS
BARRISDALE 1884
GLEN KINGIE 1882
GLENDESSARY
ACHNACARRY NORTH
LOCH ARKAIG 1880
GREENFIELD 1888
INSHLAGGAN
ARDOCHY
ACHLUACHRACH
MUNERIGG
LUNDIE
FAICHEM
INVERGARRY MAINS
NORTH ABERCHALDER LAGGAN
SOUTH LAGGAN
KILFINNAN
INVERGARRY
CLUNES
MOY
ACHNACARRY SOUTH
GLEN MALLIE
INVERSKILLAVULAN 1876
IGULVAIN 1876
ACHDALIEU 1900
STRONE TERRACHT
ANNAT
FASSIFERN
DRIMSALLIE

miles   0   5   10   15
km   0

Highlands, Mull, Morven, Ardnamurchan, Perthshire and southern Inverness-shire went under sheep grazing by the late eighteenth century and by 1800 sheep outnumbered cattle ten to one in Argyllshire.

During the first half of the nineteenth century the North-West Highlands and Islands were largely cleared to make way for sheep. The sheep graziers could offer higher rents than the clansfolk so the lairds amalgamated the old group (run-rig) farms and let the ground for hill pasture. Accompanying the advance of sheepwalks were the clearances of the overcrowded clachans of the clansfolk remaining in the glens, events which are still some of the most controversial and emotional issues in Scottish social history.[7] Between *c* 1780 and 1830, stories of successive clearances were first recorded by romantic journalists and other travellers who made their way into the Highlands as road communications improved; however, the First (Old) Statistical Accounts of the 1790s and a few more recent works (eg Philip Gaskell in *Morven Transformed*)[8] record the events which took place with greater restraint.

During the eighteenth century, increasing population pressure, based on the traditional subsistence economy, was causing considerable hardship in many Highland glens. Famine and pestilence became increasing risks and the arrival of a heavy stocking of sheep on the hills made the position of the clansfolk remaining on a limited amount of land in the glens untenable. Formerly, cattle and sheep grazed over the same hill pastures, sheep being in the minority, resulting in a better ecological balance. From the late eighteenth century, however, these uplands were used by sheep all the year round instead of just by the cattle in the summer months. Moreover, when the infield-outfield system was discontinued, the transhumance associated with it also came to an end. A considerable amount of outmigration had already begun through overcrowding, poverty, the breakdown of the old clan system and the attraction of new factory jobs in the South before the sheep clearances actually took place. Of those who remained, many thousands chose to emigrate, the rest usually being moved to the coasts where their crofting townships remain today.

The period between *c* 1780 and 1830 saw a largely silent,

Fig. 8 The land use changes in the Highlands: the deer forest era

25 The view of Paisley (near Glasgow, Renfrewshire), shows all the features of a large, industrial, Scottish Victorian burgh. The old Abbey, still used as a church, is surrounded by central shopping, office and parking redevelopments whilst the Victorian classical style town hall with clock-tower remains, overlooking the river in grimy civic pride. Beyond the town green is an old textile mill and a confusion of other Victorian industrial buildings and rows of substantial tenement housing of the same period. Inter-war and post-1945 housing and blocks of flats in the background denote the latest phase of town growth, whilst beyond is the huge Linwood car assembly works and spreads of modern commuter housing leading up towards the Renfrew Hills (Palaeozoic volcanics).

John Dewar Studios: Paisley: Number 5985/4

26 The townscape of Aberdeen, nicknamed the 'Granite City', is substantially a nineteenth-century creation in various types of local granite stone. The medieval church of St Nicholas and the lines of Union and George Street (built early nineteenth century) and Rosemount viaduct (built 1880s) are clearly seen, together with the classical style music hall and elegant granite stone Golden Square, by Archibald Simpson — also early nineteenth century — lying immediately behind. In the background, north of the central area, is a mixture of industry, schools and solid tenement housing, whilst throughout the city the Victorian Gothic granite spires of the various churches, which used to be the focal points of a dignified nineteenth-century townscape, are now usurped of that role by the incursion of new office blocks and multi-storey flats. Several parts of the city, however, including Union Street, Albyn Place, Golden Square and Old Aberdeen have now been declared conservation areas.

John Dewar Studios: Aberdeen-Townscape: Number 3713/1

27 The city of Glasgow originally developed within the howe of the river Clyde, but has now spilled over a suburbs of new commuter housing towards the Kilpatrick Hills and Campsie Fells (background) occluding fields laid out by eighteenth- and nineteenth-century Improvers. Plantations and, near the centre, parks like Kelvin-grove and Glasgow Green, remain to relieve the grimy, densely built townscape of housing mixed with railways, dereliction and industry. Many solid Victorian tenements remain, but the photograph shows the redeveloped Gorbals area and the number of high-rise office blocks and multi-storey flats in the city centre and suburbs has increased rapidly. The new bridge and inner ring road are not shown on the photograph. Slum clearance actively continues. Downstream are the docks and shipyards.

John Dewar Studios: Glasgow-Townscape Number 4224/11

28 Cumbernauld, 14 miles (24km) north-east of Glasgow, set amid the rolling Improvers' landscape of the Forth-Clyde valley, was begun in the mid-1950s to assist in rehousing Glasgow's overspill. The town centre is sited on a hill, with distant views of the Campsie Fells and Lennox Hills, and is surrounded by newer sectors of the town and light industry, separated by strips of woodland and open space. Together with the other new towns, new motorways, oil refineries and òther large coastal installations, it represents the latest phase in the development of the Scottish landscape.

John Dewar Studios: Cumbernauld, Dumbartonshire. Number 4008/P1 but profound, social and economic change in the Highlands which laid the foundations of the modern landscape. Some of the changes on the land were undoubtedly accompanied locally by painful measures of eviction which prompted many to emigrate. More generally, these changes involved wholesale movements of population and generated great bitterness between landlord and tenant in certain districts. We hear, for example (through Prebble, in *The Highland Clearances*),[9] of the sheep clearances on the once-huge Seaforth estates in Ross-shire (notably Parc, Isle of Lewis and Wester Ross), as graziers from the Borders moved north in the early nineteenth century when the Earl of Seaforth was obliged to dispose of his land. Shortly after the Napoleonic Wars, the notorious Strath Naver and Strath Kildonan clearances occurred at the hands of the Duke of Sutherland's opportunist ex-tacksman-grazier-factor, Patrick Sellar, which certainly involved cases of hardship and injustice. Similar evictions took place in Inverness-shire and northern Argyllshire but, as in Sutherland, efforts were made to rehouse the displaced population from the glens and straths in coastal villages, where raised beaches and the sea respectively provided some farmland and fishing as an alternative means of livelihood. Some fishing settlements were put down in very poor-soiled, exposed sites.

A detailed local documentation of this period is unfortunately often lacking and several writers do not further the cause of accuracy by adding passages of unreasoned passion to their descriptions of the clearances. Indeed, 'it should be stressed that the word "Clearance" may easily lead to a misunderstanding. Many of the small tenants were undoubtedly disturbed and resettled, but the circumstances under which this took place clearly varied on different estates, and . . . there was a tendency towards later and more revolutionary changes in the North West Highlands compared with changes in the south and east [Highlands]. Hence, clearances should not be indiscrimately linked with extreme hardship and brutality.'[10]

In the second half of the nineteenth century, a measure of passion, assisted perhaps by the developing reaction to rampant laissez-faire capitalism, accompanied several contemporary descriptions about the deer forest clearances.

Fig. 9 The land use changes in the Highlands: the 1892 Commission suggestions (reallocation of holdings proposal) for Lochaber

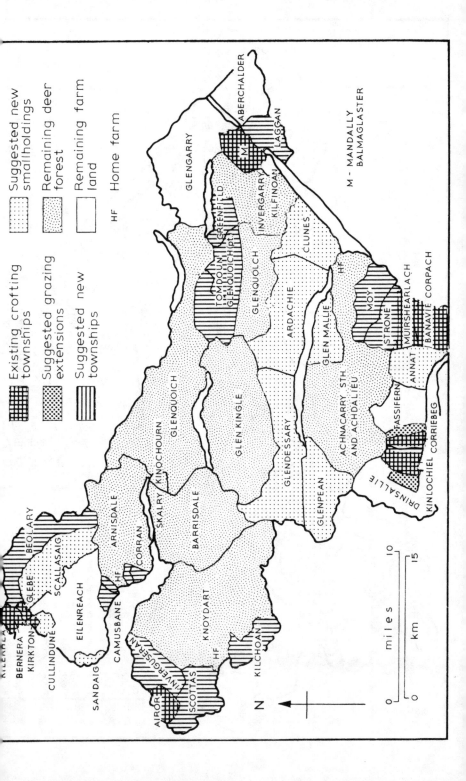

Suggested new smallholdings

Remaining deer forest

Remaining farm land

HF Home farm

Existing crofting townships

Suggested grazing extensions

Suggested new townships

M - MANDALLY
BALMAGLASTER

GLENGARRY

ABERCHALDER

M

LAGGAN

GREENFIELD

GLENQUOICH PL.
TOMDOUN

INVERGARRY

KILFINOAN

GLENQUOICH

CLUNES

ARDACHIE

HF

MOY

GLEN MALLIE

STRONE

MUIRSHEARLACH

ANNAT

BANAVIE CORPACH

FASSIFERN

ACHNACARRY STH
AND ACHDÁLIEU

DRINSALLIE

KINLOCHIEL CORRIEBEG

GLENPEAN

GLENDESSARY

GLEN KINGIE

BARRISDALE

KINOCHOURN

SKALRY

GLENQUOICH

CORRAN

ARNISDALE

HF

KNOYDART

HF

KILCHOAN

SCOTTAS

AIROR

INVERGUSERAN

CAMUSBANE

SANDAIG

EILENREACH

CULLINDUNE

SCALLASAIG

KIRKTON

GLEBE

BEOLARY

BERNERA

KILERRLA

N

miles
0   10
0   15
km

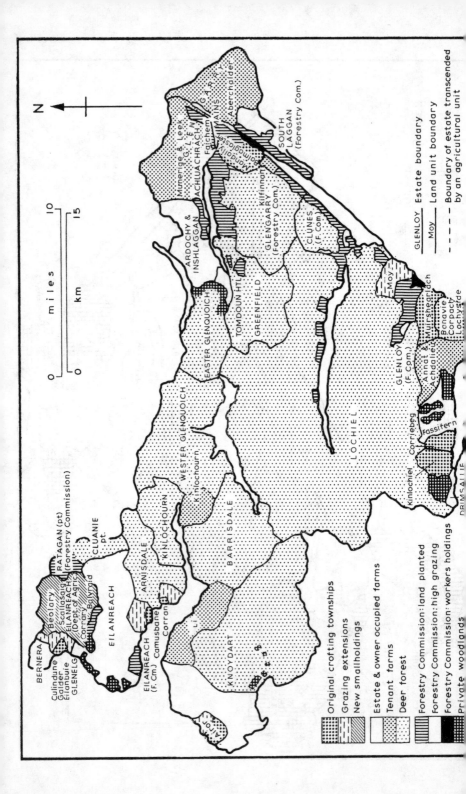

Such accounts, however, were written after the majority of clearances occurred, since it is known that the sheep clearances, fifty years earlier, caused much greater disruption to life in the Highlands than the secondary clearances for deer forests. Some writers argue that what happened in the Highlands — resulting in their being today one of the least peopled regions of Europe — was probably the best expedient of change in the developing national and international economic and political order of the nineteenth century. From the mid-eighteenth century, the clansfolk were left politically weak and undefended by public opinion of the day against the ascendency of the Lowlands and England, until at a very late stage, after the Skye clearances and the Napier Commission of the 1880s, Gladstone's ministry passed the Crofters' Holdings (Scotland) Act in 1886.[11] Even so, Mull and Jura were cleared in the late nineteenth century and elsewhere deer forests were being formed up to World War I.

Contemporaneously with the sheep clearances, many landlords in the central, eastern and southern Highlands and Moray Firth lowlands began to reorganize their holdings and to initiate the landscape managed largely on the basis of sizable estate units which still characterizes these areas today. The better-quality land on the broader straths was laid out in large square fields, like those on the Lowlands, some of which continue to be used for growing rotations of grain and fodder crops and others for fattening store cattle or for feeding sheep (on lifted turnips) in winter. However, with the little good arable land in the Highlands, the new order becoming characteristic of the Lowlands did not penetrate very far into the straths. Even so, later in the nineteenth century, the fashion for planting ornamental woodland and laying out landscaped policies around mansions and lodges became rather more widespread in the region, beginning with Straths Tay, Dee, Spey, Conon and adjoining glens.

In the far north, in Caithness and Orkney,[12] notably due to the respective influences of the Sinclair and Dundas families, the landscape underwent an agrarian revolution more closely akin to the rest of the eastern Lowlands than to the changes in the Highlands and Western Isles. Shetland,[13] however, remains in crofting tenure, since through adverse soils, climate and remoteness, Improvement never reached it.

Fig. 10 The land use changes in the Highlands today: Lochaber

In Orkney, the old run-rig farms were first regrouped in square fields in the late eighteenth and early nineteenth centuries, then later more progressively reorganized into a landscape of 'ladder' farms — so called since the field boundaries in such elongated holdings resemble ladder rungs. These are found generally with small farmsteads in their fields and with rebuilt or refurbished villages and hamlets on coasts nearby. As a result, today, the chequerboard stretching over the low treeless, drift-covered old red sandstone islands of Orkney is distinctive to the group. Many of the old estates were sold up to the tenant farmers in the inter-war years but postwar economies of scale have frequently resulted in field and holding enlargements as the holdings laid out in the nineteenth century now often prove too small. In north-east Caithness, the energies of Sir John Sinclair in the early nineteenth century stimulated the draining of mosses, liming of soils and the laying out of large square flagstone-dyked fields and farmsteads, with several planned or rebuilt settlements, like the estate and fishing village of Lybster and the burgh of Halkirk (which was never finished).

However, over much of the Highlands, the new sheep-grazing regime was already beginning to show deleterious effects in the landscape by the mid-nineteenth century. Sheep overgrazed the better pastures and it was soon found that (through increasing acidity and no adequate fertilizer) they could not carry as many animals as before. Also bracken, originally often marking areas of woodland clearing but now no longer trampled down by the clansfolk's cattle, began to spread rapidly over the hill pastures of both the Highlands and the Southern Uplands, where it remains a serious problem to this day, despite spraying, the advance of coniferous forestry and the reintroduction of cattle (eg the Luing cattle on the Lovat estates in Glen Strathfarrar). Furthermore, the steady attrition of birch and oak scrub (owing to the former extraction of the bark for tannin) and the practice of muirburning, to give an early spring bite for grouse and sheep, have both contributed to the retreat of the remaining native trees into the least-disturbed areas within the huge, open landscape of grass and bog which now covers the Highlands. Indiscriminate, or illmanaged, grazing, cutting and burning have together contributed to the devolutionary spiral in the ecology of the mountains and moorlands during the last two hundred years to produce what Dr. F. Fraser-Darling has termed a 'Wet Desert'.[14] This produces the artificial semblance of 'wilderness' that appeals to many tourists today.

In the last three decades of the nineteenth century a new use was found for the high plateaux and moorlands when the sheep grazings were turned into deer forests to gain higher rents after the prices of wool and mutton began to decline. Before this, during the first half of the century, the romanticism of nature and rural life had become fashionable among the landed and professional classes and the industrial *nouveaux riches* of Victorian Britain. As the Highlands became much more accessible, especially after the opening of the Highland Railway in 1864, rich businessmen desired to quit their town houses in grimy Victorian cities and escape to the hills in order to commune with nature. Thus began the second land-use revolution in the Highlands during which the region became a great sporting preserve.

The sport of hunting red deer was traditionally the privilege of the king and landed gentry of Scotland. On the death of James VI, however, this right passed entirely to the landowners. Deer hunting was then done on horseback, using staghounds to drive all before them over vast stretches of open country. During the eighteenth century, interest in deer hunting waned, except among a few great forest-owners like the Dukes of Atholl and Gordon and the Earls of Fife and Bredalbane, and by the early nineteenth century there were only five ancient deer forests left in the whole of Scotland. Deer, however, were plentiful and lived for the most part in the high plateau areas of the Highlands, although they had the run of the whole country before the dyking and fencing of the Improvements began. On the whole the chief's sport interfered very little with the livelihood of the crofter and small farmer.

The last Atholl hunt in the traditional style was in 1800, but that year also saw the initiation of a new era of deer sport through the letting of shootings over the Abergeldie estate in upper Deeside. Gradually, the new fashion for following the deer on foot, with a gun, developed amongst a small group of English gentry — begun, it seems, by the Duke of Bedford in 1818. Nevertheless, this was the forerunner of the sport of deer stalking which became popular amongst industrialists in the second half of the century. It was not, in fact, until after the visit of Queen Victoria and Prince Albert to Atholl in 1844 that the new sport really started to gain a wider popularity among the wealthy. In 1845 William Scope wrote the second edition of his book *Days of Deerstalking* (it first appeared in 1838), eulogizing the quality of stalking in Glen Bruar on the Atholl estates, which was read by many industrialists who followed rapidly in the footsteps of a vanguard of sporting gentry in the clamour to rent or purchase deer forests. Before 1850, deer stalking was largely a matter of 'roughing it' on the hills since there were very few estates with organized sporting facilities; many landowners then did not appreciate that their deer stocks could be remunerative.

The creation of the large modern deer forests occurred between 1870 and 1910, when most of the great sheep runs were abandoned after proving unprofitable in the face of overseas competition. The sporting era produced a substantial veneer upon the Highland countryside which remains today. The impoverished lairds rented or sold deer forests to industrial magnates with the result that by the end of World War I, 'it was not the descendant of the feudal chief, but the brewer, or distiller or financier . . . who [held] the Highlands in the hollow of his hand . . . together with the creation of deer forests there began a phase of lodge building in some of the most fantastic styles of architecture Britain can ever have seen . . .'.[15] The shooting lodges, the ornamental policies, mock baronial mansions, carriage drives, bothies, etc are now found all over the Highlands although, through the inroads of taxation, fragmentation of estates, mounting maintenance costs and vandalism, these are in varying states of repair. The Departmental Committee on Deer Forests (1922) noted that in 1912 deer forests covered a maximum of 3,584,966 acres (1,440,000 hectares) in the Highlands, ie about 20 per cent of the whole of Scotland. In 1923 Inverness had a greater proportion of its area in deer forest than any other Scottish county, namely 400,000 out of 1,040,000 hectares.[16] Moreover, throughout the Highlands, many of the hill areas surrounding the moorlands officially classified as deer forests were used as deer shootings at that time, notably in Perthshire and the eastern Highlands.

Grouse shooting and fishing also developed as fashionable forms of recreation for the wealthy alongside deer stalking. Grouse shooting is best in the drier, eastern and southern parts of the Highlands (and likewise in the Southern Uplands) where rolling heather-covered moors give good feeding for the birds. In addition, many rivers have been locally regulated and stocked by sporting interests throughout Scotland. Over sheepwalks and grouse moors, the more or less systematic burning of heather in the spring over a cycle of years accounts for the attractive mottled appearance of many eastern hillsides at that season; indirectly, this same practice promotes the vigorous growth of heather which produces the carpets of purple blossom that characterizes the hills of Deeside, Speyside, Perthshire and Angus in late summer. Later, in the autumn, the fronds of the great spreads of bracken on the Highland and southern hills turn a rich rusty gold, completing an artificially emphasized colour change in the Scottish landscape through the seasons, rendered more attractive to tourists by the ever-changing lights resulting from the maritime air masses sweeping across the country.

Another distinctive feature of the Highlands and Islands landscape that often generates much sentiment amongst visitors is the crofting township on the northern and western coasts, which are mainly the legacy of the sheep and deer clearances. 'Sometimes these coastal townships were in places of such extreme exposure and poverty of soil that after a hundred years of hand to mouth existence these crofts have gone empty . . . In other places, however, the shift to the coast has proved almost a salvation, for the people have found a mild, sheltered and early climate and natural resources in fish and seaweed which enabled them to live a much better life than they could have done in the glens.'[1][7] The population which chose to remain on the coastal fringes of the west Highlands and Islands, supplemented by people driven there by the clearances, evolved an agricultural system which today remains, although considerably modified through a series of crofting Acts in the late nineteenth century and subsequent measures, the closest to the pre-Improvement farming landscape of any to be seen in Scotland. The arable land is

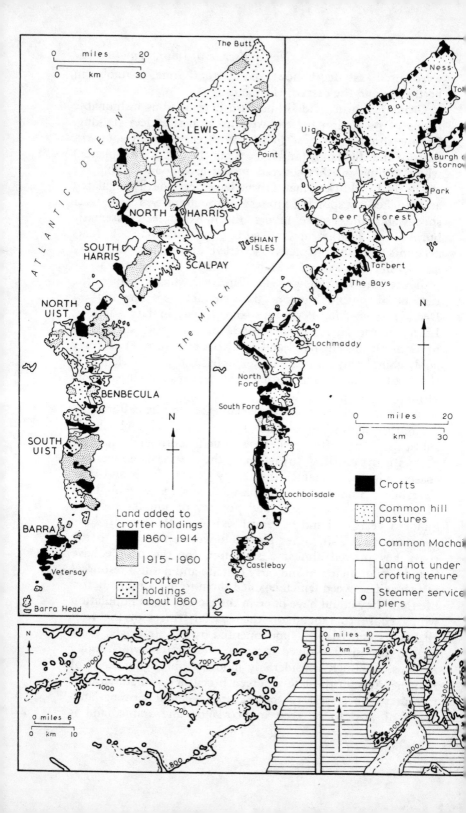

The Butt

Ness

To

Uig

Barvas

Burgh of
Stornow

Lochs

LEWIS

Point

Park

NORTH HARRIS

Deer Forest

SHIANT
ISLES

SOUTH
HARRIS

SCALPAY

Tarbert

The Bays

ATLANTIC OCEAN

NORTH UIST

N

The Minch

BENBECULA

Lochmaddy

North Ford

SOUTH
UIST

South Ford

miles 20
km 30

BARRA

Lochboisdale

Vatersay

Crofts

Common hill pastures

Common Macha

Land not under crofting tenure

Steamer service piers

Castlebay

Barra Head

Land added to crofter holdings
1860 - 1914
1915 - 1960
Crofter holdings about 1860

N

miles

km

scale markings: 1000, 700, -1000, 700, 800

0 miles 6
0 km 10

0 miles 10
0 km 15

300

N

restricted and scattered amongst rocky outcrops and peat bogs — or on the raised beaches naturally fertilized by blown shell sand (machair) and on the deltas at the head of sea lochs. The last sites offer the largest areas of cultivable ground, although soils are often stony or gravelly. Because of adverse soils and climatic conditions, the scientific farming methods of the eastern and central lowlands were very hard to apply on the west coast.

The Long Isle (Outer Hebrides) contains some of the best examples of crofting landscapes: there, in the first half of the nineteenth century, many of the clan chiefs found themselves in debt and by 1844 all of them had sold out to mainland lairds who felt no obligation to the tenants. Afterwards came the evictions, emigrations and the move to coastal settlements, so that by the time the Crofters' Holdings Act was passed in 1886, nine-tenths of South Uist's population was occupying two-fifths of the land, with the remaining best-quality land in farms. Later some of the poorest lands were converted into deer forests. The 1886 Act gave security of tenure to the crofters, together with allocations of common pastures and, in certain cases, run-rig systems on common arable machair were restored. Generally, wherever the laird's decisions had been responsible for lotting and regrouping of crofters' lands and clearance, the government's legislation restored the *status quo,* particularly in those areas designated Congested Districts (Congested Districts Board 1897).

Fig. 11 (top) The crofting landscape in the Outer Isles; (bottom) the head dyke in Scottish landscape: contrasting examples from east and west coasts (Mounth and Knapdale)

6 Woodlands in the Scottish landscape

From the plantations shown on Roy's map of Scotland (1745-55), we can see that a few attempts were already being made to redress the previous thousand years of timber wasting and to beautify the landscape. These, like the new enclosures and improvements, were born out of the spirit of enterprise and fashion for order and efficiency which developed during the eighteenth century. However, the exploitation of native timbers continued locally, especially in the Highlands, into the nineteenth century: for example, on Speyside, during the Napoleonic Wars, logs from the Duke of Gordon's forest at Glenmore were floated down river to build forty-seven naval vessels at Speymouth. Even secondary-growth deciduous forest (notably birch and oak) continued to be used for fuel and tannin extract: thereafter, grazing and burning, connected with the spread of sheepwalks, then deer forests, as shown in the last chapter, took a further toll.

The chief priority amongst eighteenth-century Lowland landowners was to plant hedges, belts and coverts for sheltering crops, stock and wild game. There was also a considerable amount of ornamental planting of mansion and lodge policies and modest attempts at plantations for fencing, fuel and building timbers, not least to meet home demands on the improved estate. Mention has already been made of the precocious but modest replanting schemes effected by Sir Duncan Campbell of Glenorchy in the early seventeenth century around Taymouth and Bredalbane, and by the late seventeenth and early eighteenth centuries most of the country houses in Fifeshire, for example, were surrounded by ornamental plantations in an otherwise treeless landscape. This early preference for amenity and shelter was continued throughout the nineteenth century with the introduction of exotic parkland and garden trees, but alongside this was developing a parallel fashion for commercial timbers.

The first species to be grown commercially, the European larch, was originally introduced to the grounds of Blair Atholl Castle in Perthshire in the early eighteenth century as an ornament. Moreover, with the Dukes of Atholl taking the initiative, it was in Perthshire that the greatest attempts were made in Scotland to plant trees during the remainder of the eighteenth century, partly because the dwindling native forests of Rannochside could no longer supply the needs of the Atholl estates. Experimentally, the 2nd Duke had planted an arbour of about thirty species, but not all were suited to the Highlands environment. The European larch, however, did well and from three seedlings planted on the Atholl Dunkeld estates in 1737 came the larch woods which later formed such an important part of the estate management. Between 1744 and 1747, Atholl estates planted over 4,000 acres (1600 hectares) of trees, mainly larch and Scots pine. Later, in the nineteenth century, a total of 15,473 acres (6,200 hectares) of Scots pine, spruce and fir woods were planted around Blair Atholl. Contemporaneously, other landowners in southern Perthshire, and elsewhere in the eastern Highlands and Southern Uplands, introduced these species around their house policies and estates.

Also, through a nineteenth-century fashion for planting exotic species, hybrid larch, Douglas fir, various pines and cedars, rhododendrons and a variety of subtropical flowering plants now ornament the grounds of many great houses and lodges throughout Scotland, notably the gardens at Inverewe, Achnashellach, Gigha and Logan, sheltered from the raw winds on the frost-free west coast, which attract thousands of tourists each year. Around many mansion policies, the rampant rhododendrons, native to the Himalayas, have often quickly established themselves, semi-wild, to produce a brilliance of bloom in early summer that is now a familiar part of the Scottish scene.

In the southern Highlands and Central Lowlands many landowners joined the planting fashion in the second half of the eighteenth century and in the nineteenth. Whereas in 1733, at Blairadam in Kinross, there was hardly a tree on the estate, by 1792 there were 1,144 acres (550 hectares) of plantations belonging to the famous Adam family of architects. Nearby, in Fifeshire, the Melville estates were particularly active at that time, as were Glamis (400 hectares), Bredalbane, Scone, Blair Drummond, Kildares and Drummond Castle estates.[1] Many authors, including those of the First and Second Statistical Accounts, described the wooded character of the Tay and Tummel valleys in the late eighteenth and early nineteenth centuries.[2] Of particular interest are the whims or preferences of different planting landowners. Until *c* 1750, shelter belts comprised hardwoods such as elm, alder, oak and birch, eg in Fife, the Lothians and Strathmore. However, the Scots pine came to be extensively planted on the Leven and Melville estates in Fifeshire and on Drummond Castle and Scone estates in Perthshire. Elsewhere at that time oak and beech were favoured by some landowners on low ground but the Atholl estates consistently favoured pure larch. Sometimes, through a careful balancing of the planting of deciduous and coniferous species, the woods of an estate could be managed on a multi-purpose basis (timber, game, shelter, amenity), although coppicing, as practised in parts of England, never developed in the same form in Scotland. Today, many broad-leaved trees on Lowland estates, notably on the hill margins, have been replaced by conifers, but a continuance of the tradition of mixed planting has allowed such woodlands to remain a very attractive feature of the Lowland and some Highland strath farming landscapes today.

The fashion for planting European larch in the mid-eighteenth century spread quickly southwards into the Central Lowlands from Blair Atholl, eastwards over the Mounth and, through the influence of the energetic Improver, Grant of Monymusk, into the North-East. Grant himself planted large areas of larch over the slopes of Bennachie and neighbouring hills on his estate. From Atholl and Monymusk, the species diffused quickly throughout the rest of Scotland to become the most popular planting species by the end of the eighteenth century. Although introduced on many lowland estates, the larch was well suited to moorland above 250m. At Blair Atholl, it was the 3rd Duke, in 1764, who first realized the value of the larch as a forest tree and began to plant the hill slopes extensively near Blair and Dunkeld. In was, however, the 4th Duke, the famous planting Duke, who developed the Atholl forests commercially for house timbers and ship building, but the coming of iron vessels on the 1830s prevented the full exploitation of the Atholl larch forests. In the 1830s and 1840s large quantities of larch were sold for sheep hurdles and railway sleepers. By the second half of the nineteenth century the European larch had become diseased, but the 7th Duke developed a resistant hybrid with the Japanese larch, which is the only variety now planted on the Atholl estates and by most other large-scale landowners in Scotland. This, being a deciduous conifer, accounts for a brilliant green of new growth in the spring and a rich gold in autumn in many parts of Scotland.

In the North-East, some fairly extensive stands of native pinewoods still exist, notably at Glentanar, Ballochbuie and Braemar in upper Deeside, together with considerable tracts of heath and birch scrub. Planting spread out from centres like Monymusk from the mid-eighteenth century, although some of the Cawdor estate woods were probably planted in the late eighteenth century.[3] The commissioners of the forfeited estates made some attempts at afforestation in the Highlands and North-East, but most planting was on private estates belonging to landowners influenced by ideas gleaned from the Grand Tour and the energetic examples of Atholl and Monymusk. Oak and Scots pine were most often planted in the North-East before 1770, and some of these woods still remain, eg the oakwoods of Darnaway and Cawdor. Later in the century, European larch became generally preferred. In the nineteenth century, planting in the region was done with Douglas fir, Sitka spruce and ornamental exotics.

Beech — probably introduced originally by the Romans — was used by the Improving lairds to produce the trimmed beech hedges and beech avenues whose rusty-gold leaf cover to protect the buds through the winter forms a very distinctive feature of the high farming landscapes of the central and eastern Lowlands, North-East and Moray Firth district today. The planting of oak was usually confined to the damper parts of the lowlands, whilst more generally, and notably in the Highland glens, the management of semi-natural birch and oak scrub for tannin bore some resemblance to coppicing in England and continued well into the nineteenth century (eg along Loch Maree-side, and in Glen Strathfarrar and Assynt).

In the Central Lowlands, many writers in the late eighteenth and nineteenth centuries commented on the bareness of the landscape and on the advantages of planting trees for shelter. The Statistical Account (1794) for the parish of Douglas in Lanarkshire, for example, noted that there was very little woodland in the district, but it also mentioned 300 acres (120 hectares) of conifers and deciduous species planted in 1774, with a further 800 acres (320 hectares) similarly planted in 1784, in both cases by the Douglas estates. The Second Statistical Account of 1845 noted that there were still only 1,500 acres (600 hectares) of woodland out of the 11,200 hectares of the parish. Naismith, in his *Agricultural Survey of Clydeside* (1794), records only 1,800 acres (720 hectares) of plantations about twenty years old in the whole Clyde valley. As elsewhere on the Lowlands, remnants of scrub forest were managed on a rotational basis for hardwood, timber, tannin and charcoal. However, during the nineteenth and twentieth centuries, a notable feature in the west Central Lowlands, besides the ornamental planting of mansion policies, was the considerable laying out of hedgerows in Dunbartonshire, Stirlingshire and Lanarkshire. But here, as in other areas, the amount of hedgerow, forestry and woodland planting and the continuing quality of woodland management rested, and still depends, on particular owners taking a personal interest in forestry.

In south-west Scotland, Inverary was another early centre of silviculture: as part of the Improvement activities of the Marquis of Argyll and his son, the 1st Earl, spruce was planted there in 1682. Later Norway spruce, Sitka spruce and Douglas fir spread over the region after initial successes on the Argyll estates in the early nineteenth century, with sizable plantations developing around Inverary, Dunoon and Kilmuir. In 1798, the Rev John Smith, in his *General View of the Agriculture of the County of Argyll,* noted that the Duke of Argyll's plantations 'may be ranked amongst the greatest in the kingdom'. At that time most of the woodlands around the Firth of Clyde coast were managed for oak, charcoal and tannin on a short rotation, together with other hardwoods on the valley floors. In the upper Forth valley however, it seems the same process was operated on a twenty-four year rotation, and on both sides of Loch Lomond this practice continued until the late nineteenth century, despite the large-scale introduction of conifer plantations by the Luss estates after 1845. Likewise, nearly all hardwoods on the Argyll estates were replaced at that time by conifers.[4]

Throughout the nineteenth century planting continued, more by some owners than others, in many parts of the eastern and southern Highlands, the lowlands and valleys of the Southern Uplands. By 1914 Scots pine forests and stands of indigenous and replanted oakwoods formed most of the timber in the Highlands, with large areas of larch also, either as pure stands or mixed with pine. Sitka spruce, Douglas fir and Japanese larch occupied relatively small areas. World War I, however, led to the felling of a great deal of the woodland, with large areas of hillside left covered with bare stumps and debris. Normally, since trees are a crop, like corn in a field (and, equally, an object of beauty, although reaped over a much longer period), stands would have been felled on a rotational basis in much smaller lots as the timber matured: as a result, cutting and replanting operations would have been relatively unobtrusive and formed one of the regular activities of the countryside. Indirectly, the mismanagement of woods over the last hundred years, and the inroads of both World Wars, have contributed to the contemporary horror expressed at forestry operations by suburban visitors to the countryside since blanket cutting and replanting has often been necessary to bring the forests back under proper management.

Indeed, after World War I, the supply of home-grown timber had become so inadequate that private estates could no longer cope with the expense of timber production on their own, so the needs for timber planting throughout Britain were placed in the hands of the government agency called the Forestry Commission in 1919. However, the Commission could only acquire land as it came on to the open market (eg as sales for death duties), and this often left the agency with either small scattered parcels or large fragments of land that tended to be poor in quality and/or at too high an altitude for planting. Very often coastal sand dune areas, acid heathland areas or old deer forests were bought by the Commission, the last type of property often including fishings, lodges, farms and deer stalking beats. Examples include the Culbin Sands, Clashindarroch, Ballindalloch, Bennachie, Tournaveen and Fetteresco Forests in the North-East, the Forests of Rannoch and the Angus Glens. Large parts of Cowal and south-west Argyll were bought up from the executors of the Argyll estates and from adjoining owners in the inter-war years. Of about 40,000 hectares in that district, *c* 14,000 are now planted.

In Cowal, the Argyll Forest Park, the first area in Britain organized to combine forestry and public leisure, was designated in 1937: a few years earlier, in 1929, the Loch Ard Forest adjoining Glasgow Corporation's catchment of Loch Katrine in the Trossachs, was purchased (covering 12,800 hectares of which 7,200 are now planted). In the 1950s this area was designated the Queen Elizabeth Forest Park. In Galloway, the largest Forestry Commission estate in Scotland was bought up from the Galloway estates in Glentrool. With further additions in the last twenty-five years this estate now totals 60,000 hectares. In Dumfriesshire, the Forest of Ae covers *c* 20,000 hectares.

Whilst large areas were needed for planting, ecological and economic constraints still caused large tracts of hill land to be left unplanted above *c* 350-450m in the eastern Highlands and 150-250m in western coastal districts — that is, much of the land above the head dyke. The introduction of the Commission's dedication scheme in the inter-war years enabled private owners to make over tracts of woodland to the Commission for management, and quite a number took advantage of the scheme. Planting between the wars, however, eg along the Great Glen, parts of Rannochside and Argyll, was both unaesthetic and rather ill-planned, often taking the form of great blocks on the open hillsides, excluding sheep and deer, which normally winter in the glens and straths, from their summer grazings in the moorlands above. The coming of inter-war and postwar hydro-electric schemes in many Highland glens, drowning winter pasture lands, has exacerbated this problem.

The legacy of regimented inter-war planting, which actually lasted until restrained by the outcries of the first leisure invasions of family motorists in the 1950s, is still a very distinctive landscape element, despite the extensive felling and replanting with deciduous species like larch and birch along forest borders which has been tried in the last twenty years. In the inter-war years, Norway and Sitka spruces were planted more extensively than before and the Scots pine was replaced by a North American pine on the poorer upland soils. In special situations, such as the afforestation of the Culbin Sands and Tentsmuir, the Corsican pine was used. All these plantations, however, were only just beginning to mature when the felling demands of World War II intervened. Nevertheless, the suitability of many parts of the Highlands, Southern Uplands, the Central Valley hills and elsewhere, outlier hill masses, mosses, dunes and other intractable areas for timber production was clearly recognizable in the 1920s and 1930s. However, over many upland tracts, land best suited to timber production was frequently also some of the better grazing land and in such areas conflict arose between competing land users, notably the deer/sheep/conifer/hydro-electric reservoir conflict in many Highland glens.

The landscape of 1945 was profoundly different from that at the time of Culloden. In the space of two hundred years, the fastest and most profound changes ever to take place in the Scottish landscape had occurred: not least among these, the new man-made Forests of Caledon had begun to form. Although in the last twenty-five years pressures and technical means have arisen that can change the landscape even faster and more radically, a new type of planning consciousness has arisen to take control of this trend — to varying degrees of success — one which has its roots in the same climate of thought which originally motivated the Improvers. Today, as will be shown in the final chapter, the planner has taken over a process of shaping the landscape which the eighteenth-century landowners began. Suffice to stress, however, that the rural landscape, even that of the remotest Highlands and Islands, is generally far from natural: every part of it, in some measure, has, for good or ill, been affected by human activity. The Scottish countryside has developed, and continues to be, in a delicate state of aesthetic and ecological balance.

7 The evolution of settlement in the Scottish landscape: 18th and 19th centuries

We have already seen that the Improving movement brought about great changes in the pattern of settlements throughout Scotland and this chapter is given over to a more detailed discussion of these alterations and innovations in the landscape. Generally, after *c* 1750, the old nucleated fermtouns began to be replaced by individual farmsteads and crofts and the intaking of waste and extension of arable required farmbuildings and cottages to be built in areas not previously occupied. All these changes made for greater farming efficiency. The size of the new farms depended on the preferences of the landowners: some let out the old townships in two or three large farms: others divided up the ground into small farms and crofts. Usually, the most fertile areas were laid out in large farms and the spaces in between them filled with a more intricate mosaic of small farms and crofts. Many of these new settlements took the name of the old township, adding the prefix Easter, Mid, Upper, Nether or Crofts to indicate the relocated sites.

However, although these new settlements generally formed the basis of modern rural communities, not all of them have survived. Indeed, after 1775, many farms in the North-East, and a number in the central and eastern Lowlands, and the broader straths penetrating the Highlands, proved too small to be economic; even today farms in the North-East remain appreciably smaller than in other lowland areas of Scotland. Also, the North-East has a greater scatter of crofts (smallholdings) than elsewhere, notably around former moss areas (eg Rora Moss in Buchan, where smallholdings were given

¾-1¼ hectares each, with a stone cottage, on the edge of the moss, with a long lease to encourage Improvement). Elsewhere in the North-East and the Central Lowlands, other areas with intractable soils, like moraines and outwash trains, were similarly settled, but not all were successful. From the mid-nineteenth century, such holdings were amalgamated as the leases ran out and settlement generally retreated downhill, below the head dyke. Later, with continued out-migration to the industrial towns and the agricultural depression of the 1880s and 1890s, further amalgamations of holdings occured, as is evident from the ruins of cottages and farmbuildings scattered through the Lowlands and broader Highland straths today.

Settlement changes in the Highlands lagged behind those of the eastern and central Lowlands. As late as 1837, for example, old fermtouns still existed in upper Deeside,[1] but by the mid-nineteenth century changes had occurred almost everywhere in rural Scotland. In contrast to the Lowlands, the townships of the North-West Highlands and Islands were re-sited and/or rearranged to fix each individual homestead on its own parcel of land or croft, replacing run-rig. Today, in these areas, two types of crofting township can be seen: one, possibly the older, with a close grouping of buildings often laid out on the inner margin of a raised beach; the other very loosely strung out with no obvious plan over a distance of 1½-5km. However, houses are occasionally found on the edges of glaciated rocky outcrops and small rocky promontories along the west coast; often isolated, such houses are usually a legacy of the clearances when dispossessed crofters sought land on the coastal margins, either for permanent use or as a temporary home before emigrating to the South or overseas. Today, together with the isolated gamekeepers', shepherds' and coastguards' houses, small fishing jetties and hamlets, lighthouses and often obsolete defence installations, they form the typically dispersed settlement of the western seaboard.

Considerable differences in rural settlement forms exist between the north, east, west and south of Scotland. For example, there are many features — building stones, styles of building, field size, field boundary types, land uses and settlement forms — which distinguish the North-East from the other lowlands of Scotland. In particular (compare north Argyllshire and Renfrewshire)[2] the Aberdeen district has a greater continuity of settlement forms and sites carrying over from the pre-Improvement period than many parts of the Central Lowlands and Strathmore, although everywhere the changes of the last two hundred years have been profound. Place-names like kirktoun, milltoun, cottoun, seatoun, etc indicate something of the former landscape order. In retrospect, we have a picture (Hamilton, 1946)[3] of the Monymusk estate from plans made for Improvements between 1735 and 1750: in the centre stood the kirktoun, with its fine Norman church, school and meal mill driven by the burn – with about a hundred inhabitants. About 400m away stood the mansion, mains and home farm. Beyond were the joint farm touns and cottouns, with farm labourers, a few traders and weavers, together with one or two other hamlets of ecclesiastical or industrial significance. Yet, in comparing Thomson's map of the North-East of 1828 with General Roy's maps of eighty years earlier, we see how much this old landscape order was changed. Most notable, alongside the reorganization and reclamation activities, was the introduction of planned villages. However, beside the rationalizations and Improvements carried out by the eighteenth-century lairds, including the planned villages for estate workers, weavers and fishermen, larger and more diversified villages began to grow around a number of the old kirktouns. With the break-up of the fermtouns in a period of growing specialization, tradesmen and craftsmen, such as blacksmiths and tailors, began to settle in the kirktouns – which often became unofficial markets. During the nineteenth and twentieth centuries some kirktouns remained quite small – despite their becoming local service centres, with a post office and shop – or, more recently, a rural housing scheme added to the original church, manse and smithy, eg Kirktown of Clatt, in western Aberdeenshire.

Planned villages in Scotland

Planned villages, dating from *c* 1730 to 1830, are a striking feature associated with the landscapes of Improvement throughout Scotland, but chiefly in the north-eastern, eastern

and central lowlands. In the North-East, for example, their
regular layouts contrast strongly with the unordered forms of
older small burghs and kirktouns. Quite often, the old
kirktouns provided the site or nucleus for the new planned
villages — but in some cases, eg Rhynie, Aberdeenshire or
Mortlach, Banffshire, such sites were unsuitable. Thus the
Earl of Fife erected Dufftown as part of estate Improvements, in 1817, on the nearest suitable site to the old
kirktoun of Mortlach. Likewise, the planned village of
Bishopton (Renfrewshire) stands near the kirktoun of
Erskine, now reduced to a church among fields and plantations. During the period of village foundation, the coming of
turnpikes and the railways increased the importance of some
of these new settlements, and some remaining from earlier
times, at the expense of others. They also encouraged the
semi-spontaneous growth of hamlets in some remoter districts, and more generally, at road and railway junctions. The
planned settlements were the first real villages to appear in
most parts of Scotland; the nucleated English village, on a
street or round a green, with a church, manor house, inn,
shop and smithy was not found in eighteenth-century
Scotland, except in some places in the south-east that had
been under the occupation or influence of Anglian settlement. There, eg in Dirleton and Stenton in East Lothian and
Ceres in Fife, are to be found some green villages strongly
resembling those of Northumberland. However, even in the
Borders, the medieval pattern of small burghs, fermtouns and
occasionally kirktouns became well established: the contrast
between the well-developed English farm village and the
Scottish fermtoun reflects the very different rural traditions
within the two countries. Even today, the term village tends
to be used in a loose fashion in discussions on Scottish rural
settlement, since the concept is historically an imported one.

Among the pre-Improvement settlement forms in Scotland, fermtouns, kirktouns and castletouns derived from land
and burghal laws and social institutions differing from those
in England. The exclusive marketing monopolies of the
Scottish royal burghs until the sixteenth century were largely
responsible for the lack of village communities until the
second half of the eighteenth century and for the belated
development of rural industries. The baronial markets estab-

lished on estates during the sixteenth and seventeenth centuries were often little more than hamlets performing burghal functions. However, the proliferation of burghs of barony (vassal burghs) between the mid-fifteenth and end of the seventeenth centuries does, to some degree, foreshadow the developments in village planning in the eighteenth century. In 1527, for example, the Earl of Glencairn laid out his burgh of Kilmaurs in Ayrshire. Likewise the Earl of Nithsdale laid out Langholm in Dumfriesshire on the route through the Borders from Edinburgh to Carlisle. In 1677 Walter Stewart, of Kirkcudbrightshire, founded a very successful burgh of barony called Newton Stewart. Stornoway was planted in Lewis by the Earl of Seaforth in the seventeenth century as a fishing burgh; likewise the royal burgh of Campbeltown in Kintyre, under the aegis of the Earl of Argyll. Both settlements had strategic and acculturizing, as well as economic, functions. Inverary village was laid out near the rebuilt mansion of the Campbells (now Dukes of Argyll) in the early eighteenth century.

However, although the planned rural settlement was not a novelty in the eighteenth century, it was expected by Improving landlords to form a focus within a completely new framework for life in the countryside. The building of new villages in Scotland was primarily related to promoting industry and trade. In the spirit of the times, landowners saw the new settlements consuming produce grown on surrounding farms, and providing employment for tenants and subtenants otherwise forced to leave by enclosure. More subtly, the Improving lairds saw the presence of enterprising villagers in a rural society as an example and inspiration to the tenantry without diminishing the landowners' influence over the community. Also, economic changes occurring at the time showed the need of a village society to stimulate industry and trade in areas where an unfavourable environment required types of work supplementary to farming. Some villages were built to promote fishing, whilst some landowners also built villages to beautify their estates. However, some of the older settlements were reconstructed and enlarged, notably in fertile parts of the Lowlands, like Strathmore, adjacent to the improved main roads. New planned villages were very often built along a street, with a small depth of grid layout, creating a pattern which, on 1:25,000 maps and air photographs, contrasts strongly with surviving, much modified forms of the old 'touns' nearby.

Between 1745 and 1770, many 'tradesmen' or 'estate' villages were built, often associated with rural activities and Improvements on private estates. Moreover, like the fashion for timber planting which diffused from the estates of energetic Improvers, that for founding villages spread similarly. Cuminestown, founded by Joseph Cumine of Auchry in Buchan in 1739, like its contemporaries of Crieff in the southern Highlands and Ormiston in East Lothian, produced a crop of imitations, eg New Byth, Aberdeenshire, by James Urquhart in 1764, which was probably the model for the Duke of Gordon's rebuilt village of Huntly nearby. Indeed, the Duke was particularly anxious to attract industry to several other planned villages on his estates in the district, besides Huntly. Village building reached its peak between 1770 and 1795, partly due to the rapid growth of the cotton, flax and woollen industries. Between 1795 and 1845, village building was more closely associated with the erection of settlements in the Highlands, mainly through the later diffusion of the enclosure movement into the Highlands and the clearances for sheep grazing. Altogether, about 150 planned villages appeared in the Scottish landscape between *c* 1750 and 1850.

The idea for making a planned village a place of employment, alongside its function as a market, appealed to many Scottish landowners as a way of absorbing surplus population and avoiding emigration. Eighteenth-century Improvers were well aware of the social disruption the agricultural changes were creating, and the most committed among them were keen to reduce this disruption since they were certain that the changes they were effecting were economically and even morally beneficial. However, reorganization of the farms involved the displacement of many small tenants and subtenants, not all of whom were willing or able to take up work as landless labourers, and the population of both the Highlands and the Lowlands was rising steeply, to complicate the problem of finding rural employment. However, in such a situation, many people vaguely believed that a village community offered the ideal moral surroundings in which to keep a working population virtuous and respectful. This was very much in accord with eighteenth-century thought.

Most villages were founded on either fishing, small rural textile manufacturing, eg linen and hosiery, or a basis of factory employment. When the commissioners of the forfeited estates wanted, after the 1745 uprising, to acculturize the Highlanders into Lowland ways, they conceived of planned villages with linen works, English-style schools, post offices, markets and prisons. Robert Owen, a philosopher-industrialist, familiar with life in the industrial planned village of New Lanark, transformed the settlement under his own management and then proceeded to found Orbiston nearby on similar lines. Most landowners, however, were practical men, seeing the industrial village as a means of increasing their own profits and their hold on the leadership of society. However, for all these designs, industrial employment often failed to arrive, with the result that villages became rural slums like the crofters' settlements in the Highlands. These short-comings were first apparent in the north and south-west. Some times, landowners tried to develop older villages without basic-ally transforming their appearance; for example the Earl of Hopetoun's scheme for rationalizing the scattered isolated mining settlement of Leadhills in the hills on the south Lanarkshire border.

The distribution of planned villages

Planned villages are noticeably absent from Orkney, Shetland and the Outer Hebrides, none of which — except Orkney — was really influenced by the Improvements. Such settlements are also largely absent in the south-east; here the explanation is not isolation, but the fact that there were already large villages that were a legacy of the Anglian settlement, whose buildings did not need reconstruction on a new ground plan. Also, late medieval and seventeenth-century burghs of barony were numerous and well established, especially on both coasts of the Firth of Forth. T. C. Smout (1970)[4] identified eight broad geographical groupings of planned villages. The first group is almost entirely of coastal settlements along the shores of Caithness, Sutherland and Cromarty. Apart from two villages on the Cromarty Firth, they were all built after 1780, stemming largely from the initiative of two men, Sir John Sinclair of Ulbster and the 1st Duke of Sutherland. Most of them were meant to rehouse crofters displaced by the spread of sheep farming inland who were encouraged to settle as fishermen on the coast. Thurso (Sinclair) and Helmsdale (Sutherland) are particularly good examples of such settlements. Lybster, Pulteneytown (Wick) and Halkirk are contemporary developments also, though Halkirk never grew large enough to fulfil its planned market functions.

The concentration of planned villages in Morayshire, Banffshire and north-west Aberdeenshire is greater than anywhere else in Scotland. Some, notably those dating from the early nineteenth century, are primarily coastal fishing villages. More, including the early foundations like Cuminestown, Keith and Huntly, are inland and were initially associated with the linen industry. Part of the reason for this clustering of village foundations in the North-East is undoubtedly individual enthusiasm, eg that of the Dukes of Gordon, but also, since the area had only been pacified a century earlier, there were few old villages, leaving ample room for settlement on open sites and the reconstruction of old fermtouns. The village of Monymusk was rebuilt in the second half of the eighteenth century to house estate workers and craftsmen; Strichen in Buchan was founded by Lord Strichen in the same year as nearby New Byth; his heir laid out New Leeds. New Pitsligo was founded on a derelict Buchan peat moss in 1787 whilst New Deer, a short distance away, founded as a remodelling of a hamlet called Auchreddie in 1805, contrasts sharply with the old-style settlement of Old Deer nearby. The former has two rows of granite houses facing each other across the street, the latter one street branching into two at the kirk-style, with house gables facing sideways on to the road. Huntly and Inverurie form a similar contrast, the former with its gridiron layout intended in the late eighteenth century to be the Paisley of the north, whilst the medieval burgh of Inverurie (and likewise Old Aberdeen) still has the broadening of the main street, originally the site of the market place. Also, other settlements in the North-East, some partially planned, grew up from 1795, several of them on the turnpiked roads out of

Aberdeen, eg those to house granite workers, or workers in the textile and paper industries at Peterculter and in the lower Don valley.

Thirdly, a small group of planned villages exists in the central and southern Highlands, the earliest being Crieff, laid out on a grid plan by the Duke of Perth from 1731. In the straths of Perthshire, where enclosure had been later and more drastic than on the Central Lowlands, many clearance villages were built to house the surplus rural population, several of which were initially dependent on cotton and woollen manufactures. Indeed, in the Highlands, the lack of village life was considered one of the hindrances to economic development in the eighteenth century. Most planned villages in this grouping were inspired or influenced by the commissioners of the forfeited estates after 1745. Others, in the Spey valley, eg Newtonmore, Kingussie, Grantown on Spey and Tomintoul, were founded by private landowners. Of these, Grantown (founded in 1776 by Sir James Grant) and Tomintoul, the highest town in Britain in the hills of south Banffshire (founded by the Duke of Gordon), are among the best-preserved and most interesting of all Scottish planned villages.

The fourth group of planned settlements comprises a small number scattered along the west Highland coast, almost all of them founded after 1780. The British Fisheries Society founded Tobermory and Ullapool in 1788: the former failed as a fishing centre, but took up alternative functions as a local service centre. Ullapool, laid out on a grid pattern on a delta reaching out into Loch Broom, and the Duke of Argyll's Inverary are architecturally very distinctive. On Islay, the three village centres remain as a legacy to the Improving enterprise of the Campbells of Islay, but elsewhere along the coast, plans drawn up rather idealistically for fishing centres, eg at Plockton and Jeantown (Loch Carron) in Wester Ross, failed to materialize. Today these remain picturesque, but undersized, holiday and crofting communities.

The other four groupings identified by Smout all lie to the south of the Highland line. The fifth group in some way resembles the second (ie the North-East; mainly along the Moray plain). These settlements are located in the trough between Callander and Stonehaven, known as Strathallan, Strathmore and the Howe of the Mearns. In east-central Scotland, by the mid-eighteenth century, groups of small burghs had already developed in a close relationship with their local rural hinterlands — eg the old woollen centres in the dens of Fife, using wool from the sheep pastures of the southern Highlands and central uplands and local water for power and washing. Also, a line of market burghs had grown up below the Highland fault-line scarp (eg Dunkeld, Blairgowrie, Alyth, Kirriemuir and Fettercairn) between the fertile vales and the Highland cattle pastures. Moreover, such older burghal centres with their home-based linen and woollen industries, obviated the building of many new villages in Fife, Strathmore and Howe of the Mearns: hence most of the new villages were founded by estates for fostering trade although a few appeared around isolated cotton mills. However, their founders speculatively saw their potential mainly as centres of the linen trade, like their counterparts on the Moray coastlands, and almost all of them were completed before the end of the eighteenth century while the linen trade was still prosperous in rural areas. Nevertheless, many planned or rebuilt villages in the eastern Lowlands derived considerable stimulus from the estates to which they belonged, in an area studded with country seats of the gentry. Dairsie, on the main road through Fifeshire, was laid out after this route was turnpiked in 1790. George Dempster of Dunnichen laid out Letham (Angus) in 1788 and Charles Henderson of Rochelhill (Kincardine) Charleston in 1833; the latter contrasts markedly with the old kirktoun of St Cyrus nearby. In east Perthshire, in the Vale of Strathmore, John Mackenzie founded Spittalfield on his 950 hectare estate of Delvine, and Meikleour on his Meikleour estate close by. However, Callander (founder: Duke of Perth) and Laurencekirk, founded by Lord Gardenstone in 1766 on the turnpike (now A94), are probably the most distinctive amongst these villages.

The sixth group of planned villages lies within the influence of Glasgow and contains the factory villages like Balfron, Deanston, Catrine and New Lanark which often owed their development as much to middle-class industrialists as to the initiative of landowners. Indeed, the rapid and widespread founding of villages from Galloway to lowland

Perthshire in the 1780s and 1790s was associated with the expansion of the Ayrshire and Renfrewshire cotton industry, when it was still regarded as a great advantage, before the widespread use of steampower, to site a cotton-spinning mill on a fast-flowing stream near good communications and a cheap labour supply in the countryside. Such factory villages obtained their raw materials and market outlets in Glasgow under the direction of Paisley manufacturers, and lived a life quite separate from the countryside. Thus the kirktoun of Balfron (Stirlingshire) was rebuilt by Dunmore of Ballindalloch beside the river Endrick, with a print and bleachfield on the opposite bank. The population rose from 50 in 1780 to 1,100 in 1793. Among the villages in the west central Lowlands the spinning and weaving of cotton was readily accepted since the climate made it difficult to obtain a living solely by farming. In Ayrshire, notably in Kyle and Cunninghame districts, the labour and capital for this enterprise came forward from the large baronial estates interspersed with many small but quite prosperous owner-occupiers.

The new villages in the Lothians form only a small group (7) but almost certainly they were much inspired by John Cockburn's early success in his planning of Ormiston (1738). These new or rebuilt settlements were for rural tradespeople and craft workers serving a wealthy rural area in the hinterland of Edinburgh, where previously there had only been a few village-type settlements including old salt and sea-coal settlements on the coast and small rural centres in the Lammermuir Hills. Not all the new settlements were of this type, however: Athelstaneford, for example, was a purely agricultural settlement; Tyninghame was founded by the Earl of Haddington for estate workers pensioned off from his service; and Grangemouth, not strictly a village, was the new port founded by Sir Charles Dundas in 1777 at the eastern terminal of his Forth-Clyde Canal.

Lastly, there was the group of villages along the lowlands north of the Solway Firth. Earlier, a sizeable number of villages had been founded as burghs of barony in the middle and later decades of the seventeenth century and it seems these foundations partly generated the initiative for further planned communities in the eighteenth century. The new villages were varied in function, some being fishing or coast-trade ports like Glencapel and Port William, some with a cotton mill like Kirkpatrick and Durham, and some with linen and woollen weaving like Brydekirk and New Langholm. In some cases, eg Newton Stewart and Castle Douglas, original foundations of the seventeenth century continued to develop, or were re-founded in the eighteenth century. Like north Ayrshire and parts of the North-East, there is rather more continuity of settlement sites and patterns in the Dumfriesshire and Galloway coastlands compared with several other areas of the country.

Types of planned village communities

Smout has identified four types of planned village foundations, although Houston (1949)[5] suggests a further category of inland spas, tourist and residential centres. The last-mentioned developed in the nineteenth century, after the main impetus for village foundation had passed and are considered separately, below, after agricultural villages, villages based on small rural industries, factory villages and fishing villages. (Smout's two categories of industrial villages are discussed below under 'manufacturing villages'.)

AGRICULTURAL VILLAGES
The majority of planned villages began as agricultural settlements, associated with the revolutionary changes in estate management. Later, a good many other planned communities ended up as agricultural settlements, housing farm workers and a few tradesmen, after attempts to bring industrial work to the village had failed. However, some settlements were specially founded to improve the land around them and house the rural population engaged in drainage schemes, lime burning, quarrying, etc. Occasionally, villages such as Racks in Dumfriesshire and Beauly in Inverness-shire were built on lowland peat mosses or near estuarine flats to improve and cultivate wasteland. Some villages in Perthshire, eg Whiteley, Benniebeg, Borland Park, Strelitz and Callander on the Duke of Perth's estate, were small villages, almost hamlets, laid out for Highlanders serving in the Seven Years War; of these, only Callander (through imported trades) had any success. The slate quarries of

Bonawe in Argyll and the Hill of Foundland in Aberdeenshire
gave rise to small hamlets nearby: likewise, those of the
granite workers in the North-East and the lead mining village
of Clifton, founded by Sir Robert Clifton, near Tyndrum
(Argyllshire). In the eastern Highlands, Haugh of Moray and
the North-East, a number of villages were built to accommodate crofters and cottars cleared as a result of estate
Improvements. Examples include Archiestown in Morayshire
(1764) and Longman in Banffshire. The latter, however, lost
its planned character as crofters' individual initiative was
allowed the upper hand.

Usually, the planned layout of the village remained intact
if trade was introduced or if the landowner, for amenity
reasons, was strict about the development of the settlement.
However, where trade was introduced into a nucleated
clearance village it was often difficult to maintain. For
example, in Banffshire, New Mill of Keith, founded by Lord
Findlater in 1750, remained largely agricultural, whilst
nearby Fife Keith (1817) founded, like a number of villages
in the Lowlands, around a linen mill, in an attempt to
complete the local group of new villages, was described soon
afterwards as a complete failure. In Easter Ross and lowland
Caithness, little attempt was made to settle evicted crofters in
such inland farming or trade-based villages; consequently, in
these areas, although farming was improved through means
similar to those used in the North-East and Central Valley,
crofting settlement remains largely scattered, often strung
out along Improvement roads. In the Lowlands, 'tradesmen'
villages were generally more successful, but in these towns,
together with similar settlements in the North-East, any
industrial associations have long since disappeared. Spring-
field, in Dumfriesshire, is an interesting example of a
Lowland tradesmen village, established by Sir William Max-
well in 1791, and advantageously located on the main Carlisle
to Portpatrick and Glasgow road junction, near a coal supply
and a small harbour.

Some landowners designed villages to beautify their
estates, usually to improve the view down the entrance drives
to their mansions. These 'estate villages' were often rebuildings of medieval castletouns: for example, Newcastleton was
built in 1793 by the Duke of Buccleuch to replace the hamlet

near his border keep in Roxburghshire — a gridiron village with two principal streets and a square in the centre. Gavinton in Berwickshire and Gifford in East Lothian were also rebuilt in the second half of the eighteenth century, as were Glamis in Angus by the Earl of Strathmore, and Baledgarno on the marches of Lord Kinnardy's Rossie Priory estate in south Angus. Kenmore village (Perthshire) was rebuilt when the policies (grounds) of Taymouth Castle were radically altered in 1760; it became a part of the new carriage drive between the church and the mansion and was decorated with a village archway. Taymouth Castle was itself rebuilt in the nineteenth century. At Atholl, when Blair Castle was converted to a comfortable residence in 1750, the village was removed over the other side of the road (now the A9). Fochabers, in Morayshire, on the east bank of the Spey at its lowest bridging point, was removed from its original site close to Gordon Castle in the late eighteenth century, to be rebuilt with a new, imposing plan a mile away, including a handsome square and town hall. Smaller estate villages in the Lowlands were often reconstructions of former kirktouns, eg Monymusk.

MANUFACTURING VILLAGES
(villages with small rural industries and factory villages)
Often similar to or hybridized with the 'tradesmen villages' developed from agricultural planned settlements, certain villages were planned with the deliberate intention of introducing small-scale rural manufacturing. They are widely scattered throughout eastern central and southern Scotland and are most numerous and typical of the eighteenth-century Improvers' planned communities. The prototype was John Cockburn's Ormiston in East Lothian (1738) — later came Lord Gardenstone's Laurencekirk in Kincardineshire and George Dempster's Dunnichen in Angus. Sir James Grant's Grantown on Spey had a sawmill and a distillery, and George Ross of Pitkerrie brought brewing, cloth and hardware trades to Cromarty. The Dukes of Argyll replanned Inverary with linen and woollen works, the Dukes of Gordon and Earl of Findlater promoted linen in Moray and Banff and the Duke of Buccleuch set up a woollen weaving trade in his Newcastleton to rival that in the nearby burgh of Hawick.

such villages were built at a time when the countryside still remained an active source of living and when rural surroundings were thought more attractive and healthier for the location of workers than the city. Indeed, English urban workers were actually settled in the village of Gatehouse of Fleet in Kirkcudbrightshire and likewise Irish immigrants at Catrine in Ayrshire. Manufacturing villages were generally isolated settlements with cotton or woollen mills, bleaching yards or iron foundries. When virtually the entire settlement was built or subsequently developed as a source of labour for one factory, the term *factory village* is applicable, for in these the role of the landowner was greatly reduced in favour of that of the enterprising middle-class industrialist. Examples include Spinningdale in Sutherland, Penicuik in Midlothian, Deanston and Stanley in Perthshire, New Lanark in the Clyde valley, Newton Stewart in Galloway and Eaglesham in Renfrewshire. There is a heavy concentration of such settlements, moreover, within 30km of Glasgow. In a number of these, industry and workers' housing later expanded to swamp the original neatly planned layout, eg Eaglesham, New Lanark and Penicuik.

Waterpower or bleachfield sites on the junction of lowland and upland and where trade and marketing opportunities already existed often prove most attractive to manufacturers. Thus Stanley, north of Perth, was founded by George Dempster around his cotton mill, on the banks of the Tay in 1785. Likewise, Luncarty, Stormont and Huntingtower, also near Perth, were sited by the bleachfields of the lower Tay and Almond rivers. Invergowrie (Carse of Gowrie) grew as a bleachfield village in the 1820s; Douglastown, near Glamis, grew up around a flax mill in the early 1790s and Friockheim, founded by John Andson of Arbroath, became an outlier of that town. Pitlochry, Crieff and Aberfeldy acquired small woollen mills in the late eighteenth and early nineteenth centuries, but cotton mill villages like Catrine, New Lanark and Deanston were the most important establishments of this kind. These were sited on a river bank terrace, huddled about the mill and waterpower site. However, with the subsequent decline of the cotton industry, only those villages near a coalfield or early established in the trade were able to survive, whilst manufacturing villages built from the early nineteenth century sometimes never developed. Like the small, picturesque hamlet of Brydekirk in Dumfriesshire, they remained anachronisms of a contemporary ideal.

FISHING VILLAGES

In contrast to the other types of planned village, the fishing villages have a fairly limited distribution around the north, east and west coasts. Favoured in these areas as alternative means of employment, these settlements have nevertheless remained aloof from neighbouring landed interests. Starting in the seventeenth century, with, for example, the founding of Stornoway, the development of fishing communities gained new impetus through the founding of the semi-charitable organization called the British Fisheries Society in 1786, to develop the herring industry. However, the Society built only four villages of its own: Tobermory (Mull), Loch Bay (Stein, Waternish) in Skye, Ullapool in Wester Ross and Pulteneytown also known as Louisburgh) as a suburb of the older royal burgh of Wick. Only Wick succeeded as a fisheries centre, although Tobermory developed an alternative market and port trade. Ullapool, chosen for its central position near the west coast fishing grounds, was originally planned in 1758, but was not laid out until thirty years later. Moreover, poor road communications thwarted ideas for manufacturing in the village and today Ullapool survives on fishing supplemented by a small, but flourishing, summer tourist trade.

A second type of fishing village was that erected by Improving lairds in association with their land clearance schemes. On the west coast, Campbletown and Tarbert in Kintyre and Oban in Lorne were promoted by the Dukes of Argyll, and Brodick by the Dukes of Hamilton in the eighteenth century. Further north, in Wester Ross, private capital in the early nineteenth century tried to develop Plockton and Jeantown (Loch Carron) on similar lines to Ullapool. Likewise, on the north-east coasts, Thurso (c 1810-30) and Lybster (1802) were the work of the Sinclairs (the elegant flagstone layout of the former contrasting strongly with the new estates housing the Dounreay 'atomics'),.Sarclet that of the Dunbars, and Bettyhill and Helmsdale that of the Duke of Sutherland (rehousing the displaced cottars of Straths Naver and Kildonan). Along the Cromarty coast (Easter Ross), a number of fishing villages had earlier been established at the beginning of the eighteenth century, by migrant groups of fishermen from existing fishing settlements further south along the eastern coasts, and on the coasts of Buchan, Banffshire and Moray several fishing communities were promoted by Improving landlords from the early eighteenth century on. For example, East Buckie (1723) was added to Buckie (1650), Findochty was founded in 1716, Down (later Macduff), Gardenstown (by Alexander Garden of Troup) and Crovie in 1720. Buckhaven (Aberdeenshire) was planned in 1780, St Combs in 1771, and Collieston and Burghead in 1800. Fittie (Aberdeen) was moved and rebuilt in 1806 around two squares. Many Improving lairds were quick to see the growing herring industry as an alternative means of employing displaced cottars, and the eighteenth-century settlements of the Banff and Moray coasts, with others founded around the Moray Firth in the early nineteenth century, came into their own with the decline of the rural linen industry.

There is evidence (eg from Pont and Gordon's map of the North-East in 1654, and from Roy's map a century later, together with local excavations like those at Corskellie in 1950) that fishermen had settled along the coast in huddles of earth and thatch houses by the mid-seventeenth century, about a century before the first planned fishing villages appeared. It is known, for instance, that sixteen villages existed along Spey Bay in 1700. Other evidence for the continuity of the fishing industry along the North-East coasts comes, for example, in Cullen (Banffshire), founded 1720; here the original fishing village was enlarged by a crofting community displaced from the land. 'Seatown' with its untidy plan has the gable ends of the houses facing towards the sea, in the direction of the prevailing north-easterly gales, whereas 'New Town', to landward, is built to a regular plan. North and south of Aberdeen, the fishing villages built in the early nineteenth century are now defunct; their very small quays, affording the minimum of shelter, today hold only the occasional fishing boat and a few pleasure craft, and the houses are often occupied by Aberdeen commuters. In Stonehaven there is a clear contrast between the old fishing harbour area, the planned streets behind, the new commuter estates still further back up the hill, inland, and the seaside amenities developed behind the beach further along the bay. Peterhead and Fraserburgh, built respectively in pink and grey granite, with their huge granite harbour moles, owe their present size and distinctive building styles largely to the fisheries boom of the mid-nineteenth century; likewise, Thurso and Wick owe their present size and character to the herring boom in the same century.

Further south, the villages of the Angus and Fife coasts (several of which were founded in the later Middle Ages) also flourished until the eighteenth and nineteenth centuries, eg Inverbervie, Montrose, Arbroath, Crail, Anstruther, Pittenweem and also Eyemouth in Berwickshire. Today Arbroath, like Stonehaven, is a seaside and commuter centre, whilst in Fifeshire many of the former fishing villages are now commuting, retirement or second-home settlements for the well-to-do, many of the oldest houses having been superbly restored by the National Trust for Scotland, as a reminder of the earlier fortunes of these communities in the sixteenth and seventeenth centuries. In the eighteenth and nineteenth centuries, local landlords also improved the fishing harbours and ports of other small coastal towns in the Lowlands such as Girvan, Ardrossan, Largs, Berwick, Portpatrick and Stranraer. The development of fishing villages continued until 1918 when the first Lord Leverhulme developed Leverburgh in an attempt to revive and centralize the flagging fishing industry of the Long Isle but, like many other of his ventures, it failed.

Besides the fishing villages, several small harbours were established in connection with industrial activities, such as the group of slate villages, including Easdale, in Argyllshire. Others include Brora in Sutherland, primarily for the shipment of coal from the local mine (still active) to Helmsdale and other coastal clearance villages. Kingston was erected by a private company at the mouth of the Spey for exporting timber and Ardrishaig (south Argyllshire) engaged in the shipping activities of the Crinan Canal and herring fishing in the nineteenth century. Several small quays were also built along the Galloway estuaries; today these are mostly disused, but make pleasant, off-the-beaten-track attractions for summer tourists.

RESORT CENTRES AND OTHER SMALL SETTLEMENT DEVELOPMENTS.

A group of villages and small towns were developed as inland spas or resorts in various parts of Scotland from the early nineteenth century, in accordance with a fashion of the times. Villages such as Bridge of Earn (Perthshire) and Moffat (Dumfriesshire) were built as select residential resorts, involving the expansion of an older settlement nucleus by the development of large villas on the south-facing slopes of the valley, near the mineral spring. Thus Bridge of Earn consists of a bridgehead village built in 1769 to which an extension was planned in 1832. Some inland spas became more noted as tourist centres. Edzell (Kincardineshire) was a regularly planned nineteenth-century extension in red sandstone built on to an older village; this development did much to boost its reputation as a summer resort. After the mid-nineteenth century, 'Balmoralism' in the Highlands led to the further development of villages already created, such as the military and trading settlements of Fort William and Callander and the tradesmen villages of Pitlochry and Grantown on Spey.

However, the real development of inland and coastal resorts had to await further developments in communications, notably the extension of the railway network. Thus a number of west coast residential resorts grew up in places with easy access from the rapidly growing city of Glasgow, after the coming of the rail and steamship links with Argyll and the Clyde coast, and the popular appreciation of Highland scenery. Dunoon, Oban and Lochgilphead, erected as villages in the early nineteenth century, quickly grew into towns. The burghs of Ayr, Largs, Rothesay and Callander and Crieff in the Trossachs expanded for the same reasons. Peterhead and Ballater were once small spa towns, the latter growing rapidly after Queen Victoria chose Balmoral as her Highland residence. The central square of Ballater surrounding the church is distinctive among such planned Highland settlements. When roads, railways and fashionable tourism moved into the Highlands, the expansion of local centres on the new routes was accompanied by a scattering of shooting lodges in the glens and the creation of some of the finest sporting preserves in Europe. At the same time, during the second half of the nineteenth century, various coastal settlements on the east and south-west coasts developed tourist functions, eg Dornoch, Balintore, Rosehearty, Cruden Bay, Stonehaven, Arbroath, Carnoustie, Girvan and Dunbar. Even Aberdeen has become a prominent seaside resort. A distinctive landscape feature of many such centres (including some inland resorts, like Gleneagles and Pitlochry) is the golfcourse: several famous seaside courses, eg Carnoustie and St Andrews, as well as many lesser municipal ones, are located on the main postglacial raised beach level.

Other rural settlements of the nineteenth century

A number of other settlements grew up at important rail and macadamized road junctions during the nineteenth century: generally, these were not planned, but they are roughly contemporaneous with the development of the resorts. For example, Inverness burgh grew as a rail junction from the 1860s; Newtyle (Angus) at a road junction (1831), Aviemore, Beattock, Riccarton and Carstairs at rail junctions and Ladybank (Fifeshire) as a miniature railway town (like Swindon or Crewe); Crianlarich is also largely a railway creation. Single-line working led to a scatter of small settlements around loops and sidings, eg Dinnet on the former Deeside line, Dava on the former Highland line; Garve on the Inverness-Kyle line; and Dalwhinnie and Tomatin on the Highland line. The same is true for the canals, built several decades earlier, eg Grangemouth on the Forth-Clyde Canal and Port Elphistone on the old Inverurie Canal. Today, with canals and railways often abandoned, it is difficult to see readily the original raison d'etre of many such settlements, which have now completely changed their functions.

On the west coast and Islands, new settlements grew up by quays built during the nineteenth century to serve the expanding steamer traffic, eg Tarbert in Harris, Mid Yell in Shetland, Mallaig and Kyle of Lochalsh. Kyle was founded in 1900. Mallaig and Kyle was associated with competing railheads for the Islands trade. In the south-west, when silting, increased size of ships and new rail links deprived many coastal burghs of their port functions, they often became small service centres and quiet seaside resorts, allowing market and administrative functions to go to newer burghs, eg Dalbeattie, Castle Douglas and Newton Stewart, on the main road (A75) and former rail link between Dumfries and Stranraer. In Hawick, Galashiels, Melrose and Selkirk, on the former Waverley line through the Borders between Edinburgh and Carlisle, the life of the burghs was maintained by the restructuring and relocating of the woollen textile industry within the district in the nineteenth century — an enterprise based initially on local sheep and abundant soft water for power and washing. Today, in each of these towns, and in the textile outlier of Dumfries, the nineteenth century mill architecture is a distinctive feature of the townscapes.

The planned village in the landscape

The planned village built between *c* 1730 and 1830, whatever its intended purpose, was usually a new feature within a new landscape planned by a landowner (eg Kirkowan in Wigtownshire). Some roadside villages (eg Eaglesham, Renfrewshire) were built with sufficient width between the two rows of houses for a village green. Square villages, however, were usually planned to develop easily with the expansion of trade. In contrast to the earlier medieval burghs, trade in the new villages was generated from within the settlement itself, not a hinterland: hence the importance of the central square and regular layout. Where a new settlement was provided with burghal features, yet has remained only a village in size (eg Dufftown in Banffshire), the tollbooth or courthouse is scarcely more than ornamental. Generally, front gardens were discouraged; consequently, small, double-fronted, single-storey houses, with dormer windows added later, and facing right on to the street, are a very typical feature of planned estate villages — a feature as distinctively Scots as the tenements of Glasgow and other large towns and cities in Scotland which expanded rapidly in the nineteenth century. Both these village houses and the tenements conceal some of the highest room occupancy rates in the United Kingdon. Many Scottish villages have long since ceased to be local centres for manufacture and trade. Indeed, in a number of districts it is possible to trace a sequence of change in form and function in such settlements during the last two hundred years. In Strathmore, the clay-built cottages of Leetown in Carse of Gowrie date from the early eighteenth century, and the eighteenth-century houses of Glamis, with gables facing the road, contrast with the double-fronted house styles which came later, eg in Laurencekirk. Late eighteenth-century thatched cottages at Longforgan, near Dundee, still survive, and in many parts, stone, lime mortar and slate did not come into use until the late nineteenth century. All this is evidence of the poverty and late Improvement of life in the Scottish countryside in comparison with that in lowland England. In contrast to the lowly cottars' houses, standing nearby in their magnificent landscaped grounds are the mansions and lodges of the landed gentry, forming with the planned villages, the square farmsteads and the rectangular field boundaries, the focal points of the landscape of Improvement. Whether as the remodelled turretted keeps in the North-East, the baronial-style shooting lodges of the Highland Glens, or the massive, simply proportioned classical mansions of the Lowlands, modelled by the Adam family or their contemporaries (eg Mellerstain, Culzean, Hopetoun and Drumlanrig), these great houses, set against the background of green or purple hills or the great chequerboard of lowland farms, add a final note of dignity to a unique and richly various cultural landscape that is among the finest in Europe.

8 Transport in the Scottish landscape: the legacy up to 1945

Looking at the placid waters of Scotland's largest rivers, it is hard to think of them as important medieval trade routes, when overland communications were very poor. Of the heaviest goods, timber and iron ore were sometimes moved by water, whilst salt and other essentials were carried on rudimentary trackways. Rivers not now considered navigable were often negotiated in medieval times and later by small, shallow-draught vessels and rivers such as the Spey, Dee, Don, Tay, Forth and Clyde were used at various times to float timber. It is also difficult to visualize the former activity of many little ports, notably round the east and south-west coasts, that took part in the timber, fish and small goods trades. Many such small harbours and creeks have become silted up or were abandoned after the coming of deeper-draught vessels in the early nineteenth century, and, later, the railways.* Indeed, parts of the east coast, in particular, have locally changed considerably in profile since historic times. Also, old rotting jetties on the lower courses of Lowland and North-East rivers bear witness to the coastal small boat and lower river barge traffic that existed in the eighteenth and nineteenth centuries before bridges built upstream obstructed navigation. Sometimes, old warehouses — some disused, some adapted to other uses — remain by these jetties, eg at Bonar

*Two factors, in particular, combined to cause the demise of the small harbour trade in Scotland, as elsewhere in Britain in the nineteenth century — the coming of company-owned steampowered coasters, to replace family schooners and boats and, soon afterwards, competition from the fast, bulk-load-carrying freight services on the new railways.

Bridge, Dingwall, Beauly, Newburgh on Ythan, Annan and Dumfries, whilst a number of small river-mouth ports still remain in use, eg Inverness, Montrose, Berwick, Girvan and Ayr.

In the Highlands and Southern Uplands some of the earliest trackways either developed or came to be used as drove roads through the valleys. Until the mid-eighteenth century, sturdy black cattle were ferried in open boats from Skye and the Outer Hebrides to the mainland or were swum across Kyle Rhea to Glenelg. They were then driven southwards along a number of alternative routes across the North-West Highlands and the Grampians, selected according to the prevailing weather and local clan feuds. These trackways crossed the bleak cols and high moorland between glens that could never be negotiated by today's fat cattle, and met in a succession of fairs or trysts on the Highland/ Lowland margins, of which the most notable was the Falkirk Tryst. There, Highland drovers bargained with Lowland dealers, after which the cattle were driven through the Southern Uplands to the meat markets of England. The droveways, where they have not since become parts of modern motor roads, together with old waggonways and old peat-gathering roads in the west Highlands and Islands, form the basis of known rights of way on foot and horseback throughout Scotland. A number, like the Mounth Roads, are now popular with hill-walking enthusiasts. The drove routes had their maximum use in the early eighteenth century, before the 1745 uprising, after which sheep progressively displaced cattle in the Highland economy.

With some local exceptions, the roads linking touns and burghs in the Lowlands until the eighteenth century were little more than narrow, unmetalled foot and bridle tracks with drainage ditches cut along the sides. The alignment, however, is roughly followed by many modern roads. These tracks were rarely causewayed and they quickly became quagmires in wet weather: frequently, there were recognized alternative routes to be used when the tracts of lower ground became impassable. For example, Roy's map (1747-55) shows the road from Aberdeen to Peterhead and Fraserburgh running over sandy beaches to avoid the difficulties of travel inland. After the Act of Union (1707) an Act of 1669, imposing a liability of statute labour for road building and repair, was better enforced. In the Highlands, however, whilst the cattle drovers continued to avoid Improved roads for the sake of their animals' feet, there was little incentive to upgrade and maintain road surfaces. Bridge building in Scotland, which demanded large resources, was generally funded by munificent Improving landowners and/or by voluntary contributions and special levies. Until the early nineteenth century, there were few bridges and these were chiefly situated in the vicinity of large towns like Aberdeen, Dundee, Perth, Stirling, Glasgow, Edinburgh, Dumfries and Berwick. As late as 1803, there were no bridges on the Spey, Conon and Beauly rivers in north-eastern Scotland – only Telford's crossing of the mouth of the Don (below the picturesque medieval Brig o' Balgonie) and one bridge across the Dee from Aberdeen. Similarly, in the Lowlands only the major crossing points on the Tay, Forth, Clyde, Tweed and Nith were bridged. The last two bridges, at Berwick and Dumfries, also remain picturesque anachronisms.

Most of the survivals of eighteenth-century bridge building are located in the Lowlands, although Carrbridge, over the Dulnan in Speyside, was built (by the lairds of Grant) in 1719 and the Doune bridge, over the Ardoch in Perthshire, in 1735. In the Highlands at that time no local enterprise was forthcoming for substantial bridging works and river crossings were made by fords – which were impassable when the water ran in spate – or by ferries, whose former location is frequently recorded today in place-names such as Boat of Garten on the Spey. Similar arrangements existed on the rivers of the Lowlands and North-East, eg Boat of Carputh on the Tay, near Perth. On sea lochs and firths, notably on the west coast, ferries avoided a long journey round. Today, Kylesku, Kyle of Lochalsh and Kyle Rhea ferries still operate, as do those on the Firth of Clyde, and the Corran Narrows and Ballachulish Narrows near Fort William. Strome Ferry in Wester Ross, however, is now bypassed; bridges cross the mouth of Loch Etive, Kyle of Tongue, the lower Clyde, and Firths of Forth and Tay, with plans mooted to bridge the narrows to Skye, Ballachulish and the firths of Easter Ross. Small foot ferries still operate between several points on the western coasts and eastern firths.

Whereas the Lowland routeways often had more choice in alignment, even in the Southern Uplands, those of the Highlands were often canalized in the glens because of the mountainous relief. Consequently, in the past, those — like the cattle drovers — who wanted to follow the most direct route south through the Highlands had to journey over the ridges and high plateaux since most of the valleys ran either east/west or north-east/south-west. There were far more north/south routes in use in the Highlands in the eighteenth century than today, notably the Mounth Roads, between Drumochter Pass (A9) and Aberdeen. On these routes, particularly at valley entrances, castles had earlier been built to control communications and hinder cattle raiding, eg Corgarff (now a youth hostel) on the upper Donside-Speyside route; Kildrummy, an imposing thirteenth-century ruin on upper Donside guarding the route north via Strathbogie to Huntly and the Moray coast; and Kindrochit, near Braemar, controlling the route from the Spey valley via the Larig Ghru where it joined the upper Deeside road before heading south via Glen Clunie (now A93). In the North-West Highlands, the largely east/west valley alignments focused the droving routes into the Moray Firth lowlands and Inverness. The Great Glen, however, was not much used in the early eighteenth century because high passes at Glencoe and Rannoch Moor had to be crossed to reach Glasgow from its south-western end.

Until the time of General George Wade, the only properly-made roads in Scotland had been those built by the Romans in the south, which had long since fallen into decay or disuse. However, after the rising in 1715, in an attempt to pacify the Highlands and curb cattle raiding, the garrison points at Fort William, Fort Augustus, Inverness and Ruthven (in Speyside), together with the original Fort George near Ardensier, were strengthened in 1724. Today, Inverness Castle is the county police headquarters and Ruthven Barracks remain as a prominent ruin on a mound near Kingussie. Roads were built between these strongholds to help prevent any future uprisings of the clans. The Fort Augustus-Fort William road was begun in 1725 (12km), and later extended beside Loch Ness to Inverness (the alignment of the modern A82 road). In seven years, Wade built 242¾ miles (404.5km) of road at £70 a mile (£42 a km) and by 1736, the end of the work, thirty bridges. His roads linked the three forts along the Great Glen with one other and with Dunkeld and Crieff in the south (the latter route forming part of the modern A9).

The terrain was difficult for easy grading, since all the roads were made suitable for hauling artillery, and no less than seventeen hairpins were needed over the Corrieyairrack Pass in the Monadhliaths (pass summit 2,507ft, 770m). Most of the roads built by Wade are now derelict, although their approximate alignment is quite often followed by modern roads. Often, the sharp eye can trace the grassy track of a military road, starting, perhaps, from an old, broken bridge, then rising along the opposite side of a glen from the modern road – then veering away over the moorlands by another abandoned route. The seventeen traverses at Corrieyairrack went out of use for wheeled traffic in the early nineteenth century, but stock was still driven over them until the end of the nineteenth century. Today, like the Mounth droveways, Wade's roads provide miles of good hill-walking tracks.

Road building started again in the Highlands in 1741, and after Culloden (1746) there was a faster growth of mileage until 1767, eg the Stirling-Crieff road 1743, the Dumbarton-Inverary road 1744-9, roads between Stirling, Fort William and Coupar Angus and a new Fort George (the present one, at Ardensier which was built in 1749 to replace the one destroyed by Prince Charles Edward in 1746). Other projects included the Fort Augustus-Bernera and Contin-Poolewe roads, both modern motor routes. Altogether, about a thousand bridges (often no more than culverts) were built on 1,089½ miles (1,816km) of Highland roads. These roads amplified Wade's strategic network by running largely through to key points south of the Highland line, to Dumbarton (A83, A85), to Stirling (A9), Coupar Angus (A93), Fettercairn and Stonehaven, thus opening up the region for commerce and other Lowland and English innovations and ending its isolation.

From 1784, the military roads were gradually turned over to the civil authorities. Mitchell and Telford then built more Highland roads, the most notable being Mitchell's route alongside Loch Laggan between Speyside and Lochaber (A86) and Telford's roads from Fort William to Mallaig (A830), from Invergarry to Kinloch Hourn (a modern motor

road), from Dingwall to Lochcarron (A832/A835), from
Dingwall to Lairg and Tongue (A836) and — best known of
all — Telford's route from Dornoch over the Mound via
Helmsdale to Caithness (1809) over the Ord, now the A9.
The last road was very difficult to build, but ended the long
isolation of Caithness, except for access by sea. Today, over
the Ord, the grass-covered track of Telford's road can still be
seen and also, further north, near the Improvement village of
Lybster, one of the bridges. For the most part, the route
took advantage of raised beaches etc, but the Ord cliff
remains a formidable constraint in driving and road improvement, even today. In the North-East of Scotland, another
group of military roads were built in the second half of the
eighteenth century: between Aberdeen and Banff (A947);
the Slug road, over the Mounth, between Banchory and
Edzell; and the road from Aberdeen to Stonehaven (A92).

In the Lowlands, the turnpiking of the A94 and A92
routes between Perth, Stonehaven and Dundee was carried
out in the late eighteenth century, together with the lower
part of the A9, the A90 (between Broughty Ferry and
Queensferry), the Edinburgh-Glasgow road (A8) and the A1
over the difficult coastal shoulder route between Berwick and
Dunbar and thence to Edinburgh. The Carter Bar route (over
the Cheviots — A68) was similarly improved. Telford constructed the forerunners of the A74 and A73 roads and
another military road was built from Gretna to Ballantrae
(A75). (The Ministry of Transport road numberings were a
creation of the 1920s, on a nationwide sector basis.) The
turnpiking of roads in the Lowlands became extensive after
the first Scottish Turnpike Act in 1750. Thereafter, the
Statute Labour Acts were more rigidly enforced and new
bridges were built in river valleys in various parts of the
country to avoid detours and, especially in the north, ferries.
However, even with improvements like the Stonehaven-
Aberdeen turnpike in 1797, the Deeside road in 1798 and the
Moray coast road in 1799, communications in the North-
East, the Highlands and parts of the Southern Uplands
remained difficult into the first quarter of the nineteenth
century. Generally, progress in road building was slower away
from the main roads: even as late as 1855, turnpikes were
still being constructed in the Lowlands, where statute labour

was still in use. In the western Highlands a number of 'destitution roads' were built after the failure of the potato crop in 1846-7 — as, for example, the road from Braemore Junction to Aultbea (A832), which is still called the Destitution Road. The first road was not built in the Shetland Islands until 1781 and there further impetus was given by the use of local labour in the poor harvest years of the late 1830s. In the central Highlands, however, the road improvements were such that coaches were running by the 1820s between Edinburgh and Inverness (A9).

In the nineteenth and early twentieth centuries, further improvements were made in the Highlands, notably on trunk roads, which involved considerable engineering. Steep gradients, like those on the main road south of Braemar at the Devil's Elbow (A93) and the side road over the Pass of the Cows in Applecross, were negotiated by hairpin bends, whilst roads crossing peat bogs still require much careful maintenance to prevent subsidence. Washouts and rockfalls remain typical maintenance problems on roads in hilly areas throughout Scotland, especially the Highlands. In the Depression of the late 1920s and 1930s more destitution roads were built, eg the new road across Rannoch Moor (1932-5) to replace the one along the line of the old drove road. Most road surfaces in the Lowlands were tar-sealed by 1939, together with many in the Highlands — but many secondary roads, and even trunk roads north and west of the Great Glen, still consisted of single lane roads with passing places before the mid-1960s. Even today, many narrow, picturesque side-roads remain as attractions for tourists in the North-West Highlands. One effect, however, of road improvements in the Highlands and Islands — contrary to the intended result — has been to facilitate further depopulation, producing evidence of fairly recent abandonment (ruined crofts, etc). Similar trends have been evident in parts of the Southern Uplands over the same period of time. In the industrial Central Valley and particularly in the large burghs and four largest cities (Glasgow, Edinburgh, Dundee and Aberdeen), the inter-war period saw the coming of the arterial motor road and bypass, combinations of which now form a meshwork in and between the outer sprawling industrial and residential suburbs of the towns and conurbations of central Scotland. The first big Scottish road bridge, over the Forth estuary at Kincardine, was completed as a Depression project in 1936 and during World War II the Churchill Barrier, topped by a motor road and forming part of the eastern flank defences of Scapa Flow, became a new feature in the Orkney landscape.

Canal development in Scotland was inhibited by the amplitude of relief, but several ventures have still a marked local impact in the landscape. The most famous was Dundas's Forth-Clyde Canal of the late eighteenth century. Two canals were built in the North-East and even two in the Highlands. The Inverurie Canal, between Aberdeen and Port Elphinstone, was engineered by Telford in 1805, with the aim of transporting agricultural produce and stimulating local farming enterprise. Another canal was started farther north in Buchan, in the late eighteenth century, along the bank of the river Ugie. This was aimed at opening up the water transport between Peterhead and the developing industrial village of Pitfour. However, the original plans were dropped and the canal was used to transport shell sand for agricultural improvements in the district. Other canals were planned for the North-East, but the Don valley (Inverurie) canal was the only one that became fully operational. It remained so until its trade was effectively killed by the coming of the railway in the 1840s. The Great North of Scotland Railway Company bought up the canal company, using its drained water-course in places for the bed of its railway to Inverness, via Inverurie. Part of the canal has become a water intake for the paper mill at Port Elphinstone. Elsewhere, local navigation improvements were effected on the lower Tay, Forth and Clyde and several schemes were promoted for canals in the Central Valley, e.g. the Monkland canal. But of the three most remarkable canals built in Scotland, the Caledonian, Crinan and Forth-Clyde, the first two are still in use and the last was closed in 1963.

Stimulus for building a canal through the Great Glen came from several quarters in the late eighteenth century: from the Baltic trade interests, wanting a quick, safe passage between east and west coasts, avoiding the dangers of the Pentland Firth; from those wanting to promote the west coast herring fisheries; and from those seeing its strategic value in the Napoleonic Wars. Some even (falsely) believed that the proposed Caledonian Canal would halt emigration in the western Highlands, since canal building, with agricultural improvements and industrial villages, was a fashionable idea of progress at that time. The physical advantages of the route, a glaciated trough, with its chain of lochs, were obvious. James Watt made a survey of Glen More in 1773 but it was not until 1800 that Telford was engaged to supervise the work, which was one of the major engineering feats of the period. The canal was opened in 1822, but closed again for repairs in the 1840s, reopening in 1847. Small coasters carrying coal, farm produce and building materials and fishing boats used the canal during the remainder of the century. By 1906 it was considered obsolete, since better steampower and navigational aids enabled big ships to get through the Pentland Firth safely; the canal was too narrow and had too many locks (total lift 32m). In this century, rail, then road, drained its traffic, although it was fully used during the two World Wars for strategic reasons. It is still, however, quite often used by fishing boats, although it did little to promote west coast fishing.

The Crinan Canal was built to shorten the distance between the Clyde and the west coast by 90 miles (150km) by cutting through the Kintyre peninsula. It also, like the Caledonian Canal, avoided waters prone to severe storms. It was believed (falsely) that the canal would increase the prosperity of the west coast by making it more accessible to the Glasgow market. Rennie made a survey of the route and the canal opened in 1801. It is now mainly used by Clyde puffers (coasters) and yachtsmen after being rendered obsolete, like the route through the Great Glen, by developing marine technology.

Sir Lawrence Dundas's Forth-Clyde Canal was opened in 1790. The meandering course of the lower Carron, at the eastern end, had earlier been straightened to take barge traffic to Falkirk, but it was the capital and initiative of Dundas, as a wealthy landowner turned industrialist, which made the canal a reality. Work began in 1768 but, because of many setbacks, took twenty-two years to complete. It runs 35 miles (60km) from Dundas's new port of Grangemouth on the Forth to Bowling, on the Clyde near Glasgow, and has thirty-nine locks. Dundas, who owned the land at both ends of the canal, hoped that the project would foster trade and particularly the growth of Grangemouth, since, as he had foreseen, ocean-going ships were too large to go through the canal, necessitating trans-shipment at the ports at each end. Thus, Grangemouth began as a few houses, shops and an inn, to serve the ships in 1777, its hinterland initially restricted to Falkirk. In its heyday, the canal carried three thousand vessels a year. Today it is officially closed, used only by occasional pleasure craft on parts of its length, and angling clubs. It is interesting in passing to note the close alignment of this canal to that of the Antonine wall built for a very different purpose in very different circumstances some sixteen centuries earlier. Local landforms, in that time-span, did not change radically — only man's appraisal of them.

In just seventy years the railways penetrated throughout much of Scotland to become a familiar, occasionally spectacular, feature in the landscape. The earliest railways were local mineral lines in the industrializing Central Valley in the 1830s, but these were soon incorporated into a growing meshwork of lines built by competing railway companies. Edinburgh and Glasgow were linked by rail by 1842, and Glasgow with Carlisle and the south during the 1840s. The coast line northwards, to Edinburgh via Berwick, was completed by 1850, followed later by the Carlisle to Stranraer line (now closed west of Dumfries) and the Waverley route from Edinburgh to Carlisle (also now closed). Between the 1860s and 1890s many branch lines were constructed in the Lowlands and North-East for handling agricultural and industrial goods and passengers. Competition developed between several railway companies resulting in the extension and duplication of routes until the first decade of this century. Even then, however, several unprofitable branch lines were closed, particularly in rural areas. This trend increased somewhat during the inter-war years, only to be succeeded after 1945 by sweeping nationalization and, later, rationalization measures. Indeed, many local branch lines and much of the network which extended into the Highlands never really paid from the outset: the competing lines were merely an attempt to capture trade.

The railways never reached the islands, except for a mineral tramway for working chromite in Unst (Shetland).

There were, however, several schemes for light railways, the last group of which were proposed for Skye and Lewis before World War I. In the Highlands, the greater amplitude of relief, restricted economic development and pattern of line owner-ship resulted in the railway network being largely skeletal, in marked contrast to the dense network of the Central Lowlands. Many interesting stories surround the rivalry of the old railway companies, notably in their extension northwards by competing routes in an attempt to capture what they thought would be a lucrative trade in fish, livestock, minerals, etc with the opening up of the Highlands and Islands. This chapter is not the place to indulge the interest of many railway enthusiasts, but mention should be made of the extension of lines through the central Highlands to Inverness in 1863 and the further extensions north towards Caithness in 1868, 1871 and 1874. The latter were partly stimulated by the Duke of Sutherland who spent £226,300 on building lines through his estates, these becoming, in effect, his own private railway. On them, the building costs were kept so low because he incurred no inflated middle-men's costs and land purchase charges. The last extension of the Highland line was to Wick and then, as a light railway, to Lybster, in 1903. The latter part has long since been closed. There were plans for lines from Inverness, Dingwall and Lairg to the west coast fishing ports which never materialized.

Sometimes private stations were built on lines through prominent estates in both the Highlands and the Lowlands, in return for the landowner's goodwill in speeding the passage of the line — or purely for the personal use of an owner, his retinue and guests. Many of these stations are now closed, but in the central Highlands, Rannoch station, Corrour, Roy Bridge and Tyndrum (originally serving sporting estates and as water and shunting points for steam engines) are still open (1973); likewise Carbisdale on the Caithness line. Moreover, two stations nearby, Culrain and Invershin, lie only a quarter-mile (400m) apart across the Kyle of Sutherland, formerly serving two separate catchments. Occasionally, notably in the Lowlands and North-East, a railway took a long and expensive curve around some influential but obstructive gentleman's estate: today, with the estate reduced or broken up, this reason may no longer be obvious. Elsewhere, technical difficulties forced detours, eg the choice (influenced by the Duke of Sutherland) of the long back-country route to Caithness from the Moray Firth coast to avoid the Ord; and the Rannoch Moor route — a major feat of engineering across peat bogs — to avoid the indented, difficult and circuitous alternative around Lochs Awe, Etive and Leven. However, a line (now closed) was later built from Oban north to Ballachulish slate quarries, via Connel Bridge.

Running west from Dingwall is the Kyle of Lochalsh branch of the Highland line built to carry the fish and mail traffic of the Minch district. Both this line and the North British line extended from Fort William to Mallaig were given government subsidies towards construction costs: they were never intended to pay, but only compete (unprofitably) for an Island trade which never really developed. Many believed that a line to Ullapool from Dingwall would have been a better investment, since Kyle and Mallaig were too close together. Today, as monuments to a laissez-faire age, these railways remain two of the most scenic, well-engineered, but utterly redundant branch lines in Europe. The last 25km of the Kyle route proved particularly difficult to build, a fact endorsed by recent similar experience on the Strome Ferry bypass road above the railway along the shore of Loch Carron. Another railway (the Caledonian) ran from Stirling to Oban, creating the needless anomaly of a crossing at Crianlarich with the North British without a connecting spur linking the two competitive routes. All of the west Highland lines negotiate the glens with some spectacular engineering feats, including stone viaducts and horseshoe curves. The Great Glen was not used as a through rail route, although there was a branch (long closed) from Fort William to Fort Augustus, which connected with a Loch Ness steamer service. Although several schemes were proposed for a link between Fort William and Inverness, traffic would never have justified them. On Deeside, the branch line (now closed) was planned to go up to Braemar, but the move was blocked by landlords in the upper valley — not least at the instigation of Queen Victoria — and it never went further west than Ballater. Plans even existed for a further extension of this line through the Feshie-Geldie valley to Speyside but, like Wade's proposal for a military road over a century earlier, and several road schemes since, nothing has ever materialized.

The railway legacy in the Scottish landscape is extensive. Although modern landscaped motorways can fit harmoniously into the countryside, the railway, with its much smaller width of permanent way, often fits in much better as overgrown cuttings and embankments, tunnels, viaducts and girder bridges. However, it must be admitted that large sidings and grimy railway tracks and buildings, especially in the industrialized Central Valley, are not generally considered pleasant. Some of the best railway scenery, including viaducts, crossings, signals and little Gothic baronial stations and wayside halts, is found in the Highlands and the Southern Uplands, eg the Royal Border Bridge spanning the Tweed (1849), and the Glasgow-Carlisle, west Highland and former Waverley (Borders) routes. Many lines, in their post-Beeching abandonment (since 1963) make attractive walkways, enabling adventurous visitors today to see the countryside at a quiet pace and from an unusual angle. Most spectacular monuments, perhaps, to the Railway Age are the rebuilt Tay Bridge (after the great gale of November 1879) and the cantilever Forth Railway Bridge — now flanked by the new (1963) suspension road bridge — which was opened in 1890. Before then the Firths of Forth and Tay together presented a considerable obstacle to east-coast rail transportation.

9 The legacy of industrial and urban growth in the Scottish landscape up to 1945

The most obvious effects of nineteenth- and early twentieth-century industrialization and urban growth in Scotland are to be seen in the Central Lowlands and further north in Dundee and Aberdeen. Some types of development, like open-cast mining or a power station, although localized, are prominent, intrusive and sometimes even dramatic features in the landscape. It was only the Central Lowlands, together with a few outlying districts, that saw the full impact of the Industrial Revolution: in many rural areas, including some close to coalfield and estuarine industries, settlements escaped the rail sidings, tip heaps, vast spreads of grimy, stone-terraced, slate-roofed houses and tenements, the dock developments, the industrial plant, the smog, the dirt and dereliction that still remain as a poignant reminder of the events of the last century. Those were times of unco-ordinated industrial growth on the coalfields and in large burghs and cities, sometimes the result of greedy enterprise, the landscape consequences of which are still far from being remedied in several areas, despite the efforts of postwar national and local planners.

But if the last 150 years have brought a shadow of visual squalor over parts of central Scotland, these industrial landscapes still retain a distinctly indigenous architectural character in the sooty greyness of the massive stone factories, warehouses, terraces and tenements and the whimsical nuances of 'industrial baronial' on a nineteenth-century textile mill, town hall, school, hospital, or town institute in many of the larger burghs and in the four largest cities.

Particularly evocative is the light of a low winter sun on the rather grimy red or grey stone facades of industrialists' town houses (now often flats or offices), on the pretentious rival neo-Gothic spires of the Episcopal, Presbyterian and Catholic churches in the industrial towns, on the red shale heaps, or bings, of West Lothian, North Lanarkshire and Ayrshire, sharing the skyline with derelict pithead winding gear and other rusting plant, gaunt industrial brick chimneys rising over a weedy, smelly, industrial canal basin, the smoky air mixed with a smell of malt from the breweries, and beyond, street after street of high density, obsolescent, back-to-back working-class housing facing on to granite cobbled roads and alleys – a Scottish paraphrase of the industrial north of England or south Wales. However, whilst the changing weather and seasons, townscapes and social and working life of industrial Scotland combine to give another, special quality of appeal to writers, poets and artists, this chapter will confine itself to the geographer's view of the industrial and urban landscape, noting how certain distinctive constituents and patterns within it have come to take their present form.

Looking first at North-East Scotland, we see that little remains of the textile industry which developed throughout a scatter of towns and villages on the initiative of Improving lairds and entrepreneurs. Here, as elsewhere in rural Scotland, a modest amount of nineteenth- and twentieth-century growth has occurred in practically every small burgh, sometimes, as we have seen, as a planned extension, at other times rather haphazardly. Nearly every settlement of this kind profited to some degree from the general rise in prosperity during the nineteenth century, particularly those well placed on new railways and turnpike roads: the legacy of this is a rather pretentious, distinctively Scots, style of domestic Victorian architecture, often including a small guest house and bed and breakfast trade in centres of some attraction for summer visitors. Frequently, the town may still contain one or more old textile or flour mills, or the distinctive cone roofs and fume vents of a brewery or – sometimes – a distillery. Today, however, such buildings, apart perhaps from the last-mentioned, may be used for purposes very different from their original ones, eg as warehouses, small engineering shops and furniture stores. Locally, away from the industrialized Central Valley, it is still possible to see substantial, rather dignified industrial buildings of the late eighteenth and nineteenth centuries remaining in their original use – as, for example, around Aberdeen, in the eighteenth-century paper mill at Peterculter on Deeside and Gordon's mills and Grandholm mills (paper mill and hosiery factory) in the Don valley to the north of the city. Similarly, the nineteenth-century knitwear, tweed and hosiery mills along the banks of the middle Tweed are distinctive features of the Border towns of Selkirk, Galashiels, Hawick and Melrose.

Throughout the eastern lowlands and southern Scotland, simple red sandstone or weathered grey stone classical or baronial buildings are common to many a rebuilt or planned village and many burghs, with slates used for roofing and flagstones for the pavements. The originally granite-paved streets are now usually covered with tar-seal. In the North-East, characteristic Victorian building styles are often translated into granites which have subtle differences in colour according to the varying proportions of mineral constituents in the local outcrops then quarried for building stone. Whether in sandstone, granite or other types of locally-won stone, these settlements form pleasant focal points in the landscape, the granite, for example, sparkling in sunlight in contrast to the rich red-brown of the sandstone. The coming of the steam coasters and railway transport during the last century also enabled builders to use these same materials in the centres and inner suburbs of Scotland's four largest cities to remarkable effect.

Throughout the Scottish countryside, away from the coalfields, local efforts have also been made to exploit various mineral resources during the past two hundred years – particularly in the Highlands and Southern Uplands. Most of these, however, proved too small and uneconomic to work and only occasionally do old workings form significant landscape features. Local stone quarries enjoyed a period of prosperity with the building boom of the late eighteenth century and the nineteenth, supplying the new villages, expanding burghs and industrial centres, but many of these workings are now abandoned and overgrown, unviable except for road metal, since the introduction of mass building materials and techniques and sophisticated distribution systems in the last fifty years. Locally, the remains of limekilns may still be visible, and also the effects on hillsides of peat cutting, notably in the western Highlands, the Islands and Caithness. The biggest landscape impact comes in the slate quarries of Argyllshire and the granite workings of Aberdeenshire. Before the nineteenth century, many buildings, eg St Machar's Cathedral, Old Aberdeen, were constructed from boulders gathered from the fields, but the boom in granite harbour works all around the coasts of industrialized Britain from the early nineteenth century, together with the growing demands from builders throughout Scotland, enabled the great quarries for various types of granite to be profitably worked, eg the red and pink granites near Peterhead, white and grey granites near Kemnay, and Rubislaw granite (also white and grey) for the public buildings and wealthy inner suburbs of Aberdeen. Also, several of the dams built for the Lochaber Power Company in the central Highlands early in this century used granite aggregate.

Mansion houses, humble workers' cottages, churches, factories and public buildings throughout Scotland were often constructed of local stone until World War II. Only in the inter-war years, and particularly since 1945, have cheaper, sometimes inferior, mass-produced building materials replaced stone. Roofing and paving materials in all but the most recently created Scottish townscapes are also distinctive – indeed, 'Aberdeen Adamant' (aggregate) paving stones are still used throughout Britain, although maintenance costs are often forcing councils to replace them with tarmac. The Foundland slate querries (hill of Foundland) are still a prominent local feature in mid-Aberdeenshire, though, like Ballachulish slate and granite quarries in Argyllshire (in which slate was worked from 1760 onwards), they are now disused. The Bonawe slate quarries on Loch Etive (Argyllshire) were, however, still active in 1973. Evidence of lead working can be seen at Leadhills on the Dumfriesshire/Lanarkshire border, originally promoted by the Dukes of Hamilton, and similarly at Strontian, in northern Argyllshire, worked by the York Buildings Company. Both sites date largely from the early eighteenth century.

Industrial and urban developments in the central and eastern Lowlands are best illustrated by reference to those of the south Fife and Clackmannan coalfièld, the Lanarkshire coalfield, Glasgow and Clydeside, Edinburgh, Dundee and Aberdeen. Aberdeen and Dundee are anomalous in that they do not lie on, or near to, the original coal power base, coal-measure iron ores and other natural assets exploited by nineteenth-century industrialists; nevertheless, their position as harbours on the east coast, the impetus of local trade and industrialists' initiative and the general growth of prosperity, aided by improving land and sea communications throughout the last century, combined to establish their prominence. Between Dundee and Glasgow, the medieval burghs of Perth and Stirling developed rapidly during the nineteenth century as two prominent nodal centres for north/south and east/ west rail and road communications. In the late eighteenth and early nineteenth centuries, through the efforts of the Earl of Perth and others, Perth was replanned on the howe of the Tay on a grid street pattern in mellow grey stone and red sandstone; but subsequently, like Stirling, it spread haphazardly out from the centre during the next hundred years, in common with other, larger, burghs which mushroomed in the Lowland industrial areas in the same period.

The burgh of Hamilton, tributary to Glasgow in north Lanarkshire, illustrates the sequence of events through which many small burghs on or near the coalfields passed during the nineteenth century. The town lies in the heavily industrialized middle Clyde valley which featured substantially in the developments of the past two hundred years. A few kilometres to the south-east, David Dale established his cotton mills at New Lanark in 1783 — which were later used by Robert Owen for his industrial welfare experiment, called Saltaire, in the first quarter of the nineteenth century. In 1759, the famous Carron ironworks was established near Falkirk, a short distance to the north-east, using coke for smelting and marking the start of the Industrial Revolution in Scotland. The iron industry spread into the Clyde valley by 1786. By 1815, dredging and associated engineering works widened and deepened the tidal channel of the river Clyde, allowing sea-going vessels to reach Glasgow; and canal, and later, railway links made Coatbridge, north of Hamilton, a centre for the growing iron industry. In 1850, Coatbridge reached its peak as a producer of pig iron and by that time the Clyde yards were launching 75 per cent of Britain's iron ships. Today Motherwell, across the river Clyde from Hamilton, remains with Coatbridge – a short distance away – the centre of Scotland's steel industry.

Hamilton[1] was created a burgh of barony in 1456 by the first Lord Hamilton; previously it had been a hamlet below a small vassal keep. The settlement became a royal burgh in 1548. Industrial growth was slow, even after the introduction of lace making in the early eighteenth century, but later the town became a leading centre of cambric weaving. Before 1820 the town consisted of a small nucleus dominated by the Duke of Hamilton's palace, together with a barracks and a church – a pattern typical of a post-Reformation burgh. Beyond the core of the settlement a number of mansion houses were built in the second half of the eighteenth century and the early nineteenth century, whilst the Clyde ferry was replaced by a bridge in 1781. The period 1820-60 saw a gradual infilling of housing between the river Clyde and the higher parts of the town. In part this growth reflected the opening of a suburban railway connection with Glasgow which made the town a residential suburb of wealthy Glasgow merchants. The growth of this dormitory function continued during the second half of the nineteenth century. The essential character of mid-nineteenth-century Hamilton, apart from a recently-gained judiciary function, was that of a small country town. However, between 1871 and 1901, the burgh's population doubled from 16,803 to 32,775, this rapid growth being the direct result of industrialization. Coal mining increased in importance, superseding weaving and other trades earlier dominant in the town, and the burgh gradually developed its present unbalanced industrial structure. The typical landscape of mining – pits, flashes, spoil heaps, mineral lines and sidings – came to influence the layout of the town's further outward growth. These pits were worked out by 1939 and Hamilton reverted to its former functions as an administrative and residential centre.

Motherwell acquired its giant steelworks and other heavy industry at the same time as Coatbridge, Airdrie and Wishaw, during the last quarter of the nineteenth century. Tóday, this group of towns still contain many streets of Scottish-style industrial terrace and tenement housing, which in winter can look particularly bleak and depressing. In south Fifeshire and Clackmannanshire coal was easily worked and from medieval times it was used in as many as two dozen places along the north shore of the Firth of Forth, between Kincardine and Leven, to help in the drying of sea salt racked up from shallow evaporating pans, which were periodically flooded by opening sluices to let in the tide. In the nineteenth century, large-scale mining moved in to swell the towns of Cowden-beath, Kirkaldy, Lochgelly, Alloa and Dunfermline, together with the associated growth of coal-fired industries. The resulting industrial landscapes is similar to those around Falkirk and in north Lanarkshire. In West Lothian, the once-active oil-shale industry had left huge tips of red, spent shale, locally called 'bings', which dominate the landscape, but around Linlithgow, thanks largely to the insistence of the local landlord on tidy workings, the area lacks the usual features of a decayed mining district. Generally, in the Forth-Clyde valley, the effects of mining and industry are localized but conspicuous, occurring as whalebacked or conical coal and shale heaps, huge holes and flashes, rusting weed-covered sidings, mineral lines and machinery, ruined buildings, grimy, rotting stations, scruffy patches of farmland or moorland between windswept, grey, treeless, and often ridge-side, towns. The whole forms a distinctive patched blanket of enclosed fields and industrial ribbon development, interspersed with tracts of open hillside.

A great deal of dereliction and visual squalor still remains as a legacy of nineteenth- and early twentieth-century developments, despite reclamation schemes proposed or begun during the past twenty-five years, like the Middle Clyde Valley Regional Park, transected by the M74, between Hamilton and Motherwell. In contrast to the Clydeside conurbation and south Fifeshire, Alloa, West Lothian and Falkirk areas, Edinburgh attracted many more light indus-tries, except for salients of heavy plant developments in the Leigh and Musselburgh areas and the Esk valley (Inveresk, Dalkeith) to the east of the city. West of Glasgow, however, Paisley, founded as a medieval burgh and monastic centre, boomed with the expansion of the textile industry in the late eighteenth and nineteenth centuries, with a legacy today of solid, grimy warehouses, factories and tenements, and the abbey rising above the polluted river. Nearby, Renfrew expanded more as a commuter town for Glasgow, but south-westwards, through the hills, an amorphous semi-contiguous industrial sprawl developed from towns like Kilmarnock, Irvine, Kilburnie and Kilwinning and reached out along the coast between the resorts of Ardrossan-Saltcoats, Troon and Ayr. To the west of Glasgow the shipyards and ancillary developments form distinctive features in the landscape of the lower Clyde; indeed, to the north-west, industry in the last century spread up the Vale of Leven, and was only prevented from further encroachment on to the scenic waters of Loch Lomond through the efforts of Lord Dumbarton, the principal landowner.

The townscape of Glasgow, in contrast to the enclosure, coastal and moorland landscapes around, is considered by many dull or depressing, yet a short way beyond the conurbation lie many small villages and towns which were only modestly expanded by nineteenth-century industrial growth, interspersed with elegant mansions built by wealthy landowners and Glasgow merchants, set in large square fields, with copses and plantations, running up on to the Campsie and Renfrew hills. This is now commuting country, each settlement having its modern estates for Glasgow white-collar workers.

Medieval Glasgow developed on a simple cross-plan in the howe overlooking the (then) lowest bridging point on the Clyde. The street pattern survives, together with several old buildings like the cathedral and the tolbooth (jail). There was little growth until the last two decades of the eighteenth century when gridiron streets of houses grew up around George Square and to the west of Kelvingrove and south of the river in the Gorbals and Hutchesontown. At the same time, the Clyde was deepened and docks developed downstream. Glasgow became a nineteenth-century boom city: the initially very bad housing conditions were relieved during the second half of the century by solid stone tenements, normally four storeys high and with a continuous frontage on to streets that were usually fairly wide. Considered the paragons of working-class housing of their day, they concentrated people at up to 700 to the acre, a density rivalled in the tightly packed terrace and tenement development in other industrial towns in central Scotland which created some of the most crowded districts of any towns in Britain. From the late eighteenth century, Glasgow's centre had begun to shift westwards, but the pleasant gridiron residential area focused on Blythwood Square was invaded during the nineteenth century by massive office buildings, although the street plan was retained. However, Victorian munificence retained or created parks, squares and dignified public buildings in the central area, Kelvingrove, George Square and Glasgow Green, to relieve the closeness of the city fabric, and also to provide space for recreation.

As passenger trains and the Clyde steamers were introduced, by the 1840s and '50s, some fine villa developments occurred, particularly on subdivided private estates south of the river (eg Pollockshields: Pollock estate) and to the north-west of the city. Most of these houses were in the solid, plain, Scottish Victorian style, but some were in more exuberant Gothic or baronial. Moreover, just as the house styles and street patterns of these and other Victorian developments (their shape often controlled by former field boundaries) reflect the activities of the speculators, so topography had considerable influence on railway patterns in Glasgow's townscape. The two railways from the south, into Central and St Enoch's stations (the latter now closed), have to cross the river flats on embankments and viaducts, blocking many cross streets. The other two lines, from the north-east, were confronted with a steep descent into the city centre. The tracks terminating in the rustic, clapboard station of Buchanan Street (now closed) did not make this descent; the other railway drops via a steep tunnelled section, into Queen Street station. North of the river, railways either make wide sweeps around drumlins or tunnel through them. On certain routes, the impossibility or undesirability of avoiding drumlins accounts for the large number of tunnels on suburban lines. Characteristically, each drumlin carried a more or less self-contained community, based on the local railway station for transport to the city centre. Such commuters, especially the pioneers, were well-to-do and consequently demanded good building sites; their type of housing did not spread rapidly out of town but leapfrogged from hilltop to hilltop, often in quite rural surroundings. Thus the little altered kirktoun of New Kilpatrick became the core of the residential suburb of Bearsden during the nineteenth century. Later, less expensive housing often occupied the lower slopes of the drumlins and now looks down into the dismal maze of mineral sidings and other untidy industrial plant in the valleys among the drumlins. Because of this nucleated type of expansion, different classes of housing are often in close juxtaposition, especially in tracts between the drumlins. In contrast, it is mainly in south Glasgow, where the relief is more gentle, that large expanses of one type of housing are to be found.[2]

Fast rail transport connects the built-up Howe of Glasgow with the amenities of the coast and the mountains. In this respect, Helensburgh, overlooking the Firth of Clyde, was laid out on a grid pattern as a commuter and resort town on Lord Dumbarton's estates in the late nineteenth and early twentieth centuries, but has developed to a sufficient size, separated from Glasgow and the lower Clyde, to form a community in itself. To the south-west of Glasgow, the Renfrew hills chiefly confined rail and road developments to through valleys or the coastal margins, eg towards Kilburnie and Port Glasgow, Greenock, Gourock and Wemyss Bay. Greenock and Gourock have distinctive ranks of tenements, grimy and massive, backing the shipyards and steamer terminals. Greenock was created a burgh of barony in 1635, after which the small harbour town grew rapidly. Both Greenock and nearby Gourock saw much dock expansion from the late eighteenth century onwards. In Greenock, the modern pattern of docks and shipyards began with an elegant Georgian custom house of 1818, and by the mid-nineteenth century the town was flourishing, despite competition from Glasgow. The Victoria harbour was built in 1850, the Albert harbour in 1870. The old coaling berths and cranes have now gone, but the ship building, marine engineering and other port industrial plants developed since the mid-nineteenth century form conspicuous features of the scene on the lower Clyde today. Many port buildings, including the docks themselves, are, in a sense, memorials to nineteenth-century enterprise.[3] Across the water, Dunoon has a certain elegance as a high-class commuter and resort centre, with fine houses on the hillsides, and wide views across the Firth. Wealthy Glaswegians built their nineteenth-century baronial-style mansions — usually in isolation — on sites overlooking the estuary, whilst less remote lengths of coastline were occupied by large villas. Further down the Clyde coast, the resorts of Largs and Ardrossan-Saltcoats have a distinctive, though now somewhat dated, resort-style architecture.

At the eastern end of the Forth-Clyde valley, Grange-mouth developed from the late eighteenth century as a port on Sir Lawrence Dundas's canal, a short distance from the medieval burgh of Falkirk, which after 1759 became one of the great industrial centres of Scotland. From humble beginnings as a trans-shipment centre in 1777, Ordnance plans show that Grangemouth by 1860 had gained a floating dock beside the canalized river Carron, with gridiron streets of terraced workers' houses, an iron foundry, saw mills and staiths. Then in 1867, the Caledonian railway, owner of much of the Lanarkshire coalfield, purchased the canal and docks. Throughout this period, the town grew rapidly, having 1,488 inhabitants in 1841 and nearly six times that number (8,386) by 1901. Further expansion continued until World War I, and again after 1919, when the manufacture of dyestuffs came in, followed by petro-chemicals. By 1921, the seaward dock extensions had all been completed and by 1931 considerable expansion had been made on to the fertile carseland nearby. In contrast to the older industrialized burghs, Grangemouth was entirely the creation of the Industrial Revolution and later developments; today, set against the prominent back-drop of the Ochill Hills and the estuary, its oil refineries and ancillary plant constitute a dynamic industrial scene.[4]

After Glasgow, Edinburgh is Scotland's second largest industrial concentration and its administrative and cultural centre. Prominently situated on a ridge running east from a volcanic hill (topped by the famous castle), the old town was well placed to control the narrow lowland route between the Pentland Hills and the sea. For centuries the city was confined within walls on this ridge, although there were some country houses and specialized suburbs outside. Easily defended, the site was nevertheless severely cramped, forcing the citizens to build upwards, adding to the great congestion of the city. Towards the end of the eighteenth century, the city burst beyond its walls and the squares and terraces of the New Town were laid out to the north. New north/south arterial streets were built and a new suburb of grace and dignity emerged. There was less distinguished growth to the south, although the congestion of the old town persisted into the present century. The town houses of the late eighteenth and early nineteenth centuries date from the period of great prosperity which followed the improvements in agriculture and the growth of industry, with the expansion of overseas empire and trade.

Today, the houses in Moray Place, Charlotte Square and adjacent crescents and squares are much too large for modern living and, although their facades are carefully preserved, they are often converted into flats and offices. Together with Calton Hill, the Episcopal cathedral, the North British Hotel, the castle and high street, the Scott Memorial and Princes Street Gardens (laid out on the bed of a drained loch in the early nineteenth century), the houses of the New Town comprise one of the most dignified and well-proportioned townscapes in Europe. As background features, the volcanic crags of Arthur's Seat rise like a miniature mountain behind the Palace of Holyrood, and the Pentland Hills (600m) likewise, immediately south of the city. Victorian expansion, however, outran the designs of the planners, and the Georgian core was surrounded by a ring of tenements of varying standards, industry, shops, etc. At the same time the port of Leith expanded to coalesce with the city proper. Yet, despite the rather chaotic developments, notably in the north-eastern and western sectors of the city, the Victorian and twentieth-century suburbs have further advanced, east-wards, westwards and southwards, to the foot of the Pentland Hills, generally with a dignity not shared by Glasgow. Edinburgh is a much cleaner city, also, despite the incursion of heavy industry, particularly on the eastern flank. The whole city, with its historic buildings, elegant New Town, and abundance of parks and gardens, often giving hilltop views over the city and the Firth of Forth, renders Edinburgh a tourist attraction of a high order.[5]

Dundee grew up below the Dundee Law (hill), topped by

an Iron Age fort or 'dun', overlooking the Narrows ferry point across the Firth of Tay on the east coast routeway. The topography of the oldest part of the town has, however, been much altered. The lower Scouring and Dens burn valleys were infilled, and the castle hill and ridge north of the main street removed, in the late eighteenth century, whilst the high street was itself lowered in 1770 and again in 1830. In contrast, Seagate and Cowgate have been raised over several centuries, through accretion of rubble and debris. The foreshore was reclaimed for railway and port industries in the nineteenth century.

Dundee was an Anglo-Norman foundation of the twelfth century, although the castle was destroyed by the English in the fourteenth century. By the end of the sixteenth century a huddled town of narrow streets had appeared within reconstructed walls: these streets were typical of Scottish medieval towns, with wynds and closes — a few of which remain today, in a modified form. Little development occurred outside the walls — except in the suburb of Hillside, to the north. In the second half of the eighteenth century, the walls and gates confining early growth were removed to ease the increase of traffic and suburbs. Dundee changed rapidly after *c* 1760 with the stimulus of industry, involving both central redevelopment and new suburbs. Murraygate and Wellgate were almost wholly rebuilt and fine new houses shared the view across the Firth from the south-facing slopes of Hawkhill, whilst at Chapelside, Blackscroft and along the old road to Perth the first artisan suburbs developed. The roads out of the town guided growth most easily, as with Glasgow and Edinburgh. The Scouringburn valley attracted a vigorous growth of industry in the nineteenth century, although much of this has since gone. Narrow wynds, however, remain to create modern transport difficulties in a pattern of streets developed for the horse and cart. Housing developed mostly on the south side of the valley, with tenements and terraces extending to link up with the more attractive, cottage-type housing in the centre of Hawkhill. Industry intermingled with housing which developed down the Dens burn valley in the nineteenth century. Hawkhill and Hilltown developed terraced housing and industry in the second half of the nineteenth century, as did the braes (hillsides) below the

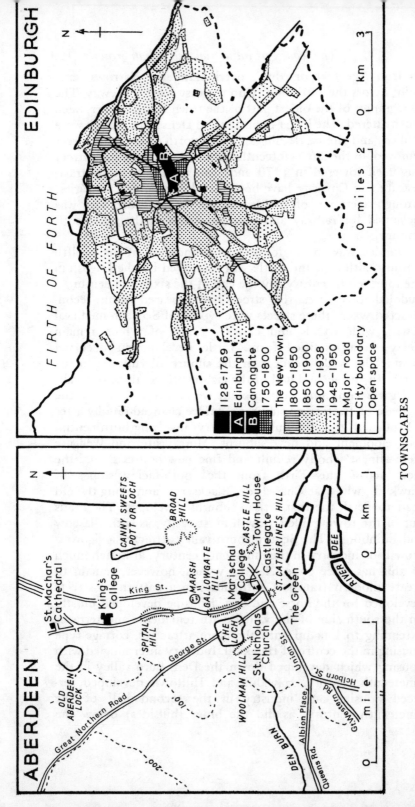

TOWNSCAPES

Fig. 12 Aberdeen: Street plan development

Fig. 13 Edinburgh: growth plan

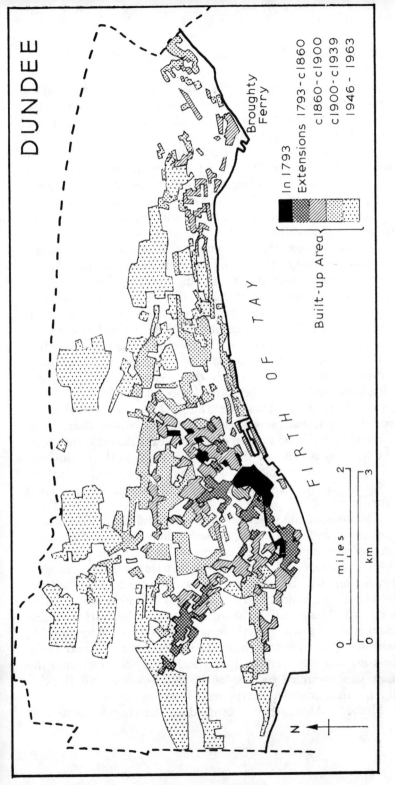

DUNDEE

Broughty Ferry

FIRTH OF TAY

In 1793

Extensions 1793–c1860
           c1860–c1900
           c1900–c1939
           1946–1963

Built-up Area

N

miles 0   1   2
km   0   3

Fig. 14 Dundee: growth pattern

Perth road.

Settlement between Lochee and Dundee coalesced after 1860. Meanwhile, on the braes overlooking the Firth, the expansion of the well-to-do mansion house developments, begun in the late eighteenth century, occurred to the east and west of the town. Later, other attractive parts of Dundee were given over to layouts of quality housing. The peak period of mansion building took place under the patronage of the jute magnates in 1860-90. On the west side of the town, however, some mansions decayed and good-quality terraced housing replaced them.

In the eighteenth and nineteenth centuries, the juxta-position of dissimilar housing patterns expressed sharply the social divisions within the city. In Broughty Ferry, building did not gain momentum until the 1820s, when gridiron patterns, typical of that period, developed below the villas and mansions on the slopes above. Since 1914, however, the amorphous spread of commuter housing had greatly modified this suburb. In the first half of the nineteenth century, considerable middle-class suburbs began to spread towards Monifieth and along the south shore of the Firth after the steam ferry opened in the 1820s. Like their north-shore counterparts, the new residents on the south shore were attracted by the views. Some of the breaks that still survive in the housing pattern of that time derive from the acquisition of amenity feus (plots) to protect such views from the possibilities of overbuilding (*cf* Edinburgh, Glasgow and Aberdeen).

Throughout the nineteenth century and until 1914, linear industrial and residential growth filled out between early arterial developments and coalesced. In the same period, the docks, harbour and associated industries underwent massive expansion. By the inter-war years, Dundee had reached the middle Dight valley, and now spreads from the lower valley west to Menziehill. Within this area, the earlier linear elements of town growth now stand out as older housing within a great tract of new growth. The Craigie and Logie housing schemes were built in the 1920s: ten years later the Law was encircled by residential development and the city temporarily bounded by the wide inter-war bypass.[6]

Medieval Aberdeen was centred on the church, castle and

market, although Old Aberdeen, with the cathedral and university, was then a separate ecclesiastical burgh. Nothing survives of the thirteenth century Anglo-Norman castle. The original town, apparently unwalled, lay between lower Union Street and the upper harbour basin. The town plan first appears in Gordon and Rothiemay's map of 1661. Futtie, or Fittie, was a separate fishing community and, although rebuilt next to the harbour in the early nineteenth century, remains socially very distinct even today. Aberdeen expanded with trade after the Act of Union (1707), and the first docks were built in the late eighteenth and early nineteenth centuries. Nearby, paper mills were established at Peterculter on the Dee in 1751 and at Stoneywood on the Don in 1771. Like Dundee, the town grew around the old core at first, and then as ribbon growth along main roads out of the town, eg Holburn and Gilcomston. The city fathers started to plan the expansion in the early nineteenth century: the new George Street, bringing in the turnpiked road from Inverness, was rapidly followed by the development of Union Street as an entirely new feature, sloping from west to east and bridging the Den burn valley (later occupied by the main line railway and station). King Street, leading to Telford's bridge on the Don, was opened in 1830.

With the building of these main streets, further development occurred to the north-west, where there was the most space available, and the new Union Street became the town focus. In the nineteenth century, port developments proceeded rapidly with the fishing boom and general growth of trade. Later in the century, expansion again involved very considerable planning, although this was not undertaken by a comprehensive city scheme (contrast the New Town of Edinburgh, planned a few years before the building of Union Street, and the other civic improvements mentioned for Glasgow and Dundee). Most of the work in Aberdeen was largely at the hands of influential bodies and individuals in the town encouraging or employing local architects — notably Archibald Simpson, who laid out Golden Square and Albyn Place on much more spacious and elegant lines than the old core. Most of these new streets were straight and planned in geometrical patterns. On the new streets appeared many fine examples of the classical, Gothic and baronial styles of building, notably the music hall and Robert Gordon's academy, in classical style, the old town house and high school for girls (baronial), and many Gothic-style churches, together with baronial-style houses in Albyn Place and Queen's Cross. All these structures, in common with most buildings in Aberdeen, until the inter-war years, were built of grey and white granite, with the result that parts of the city have a townscape approaching the quality of those of Edinburgh or Bath, although employing more massive stone and simpler, more severe styles of building. Even with the postwar influx of new materials, Aberdeen is still very much the 'Granite City'.

Southwards from the centre, the Victoria Bridge across the Dee to Torry was built in 1881, stimulating Torry's distinctive tenement and terrace-type housing developments for the working class. To the north, Rosemount Viaduct (1883) provided another way across the Den burn valley. Town planning in the late nineteenth century cleared the worst slums, and provided public parks as an amenity within the swelling built-up area, eg Union Terrace Gardens and Victoria and Westburn Parks, whilst Duthie Park was donated by a private owner. The Marishall College (University of Aberdeen) in the lower end of the town was rebuilt in 1905, as a fine essay in Gothic, fashioned in granite, although its place in the Aberdeen skyline is now usurped by the solid, starkly functional tower of the new town house across the street. Other foci in the Victorian granite townscape, notably the many church spires, are now being similarly challenged by other high-rise blocks, chiefly of council flats.[7]

In all of Scotland's four largest cities and in a number of large burghs, marked townscape contrasts can be seen between the industrial and housing developments which spread amorphously away from the old town centres during the nineteenth century and the more elegant streets, parks and public buildings which were an attempt by the city fathers to preserve some degree of dignity and rationality. In contrast again are the inter-war developments of housing and industry, often speculative, on fairly cheap land, along arterial routes out of town or as infilling between the main roads. Often, the crescents and avenues of private and council housing built on the debased garden city principle contrast very strongly with the densely-packed housing patterns laid out before 1914 and with the somewhat more tasteful, better-planned housing and industrial estates built beyond them during the last twenty-five years. These and other most recent innovations in the Scottish landscape are considered in the final chapter.

10 The planned landscape of Scotland since 1945

Since World War II the Scottish landscape has become increasingly subject to the direct and indirect effects of comprehensive planning legislation at both the national and local levels. Also, technological processes allow change to occur more widely and more drastically than ever before, a fact which, in turn, emphasizes the vulnerability of both the urban and rural environment to ill-phased developments of various kinds. Indeed, our planning controls are not comprehensive: certain farming practices, including forestry, still do not come under adequate planning control; neither does land used temporarily for mineral working (even if subject to a restitution clause); nor do some uses of land on the fringes of built-up areas (eg the casual dumping of rubbish).

Nevertheless, since 1947, national and local government planners, in an attempt to meet the needs of an increasingly crowded society, with increasing pressures on resources, have effectively taken over the powers for maintaining or changing the appearance and use of the landscape, in town and country, leaving the landowners, industrialists and developers to be more directly concerned with its day to day management. Planners today, in a much more sophisticated way, try to continue the pattern initiated by the eighteenth-century Improvers, who first tried to balance efficiency and amenity in the layout of new fields, farmsteads, villages and woodlands on their estates. To what extent and in what ways the government should control the allocation and use of land is a continuing debate outside the scope of this book: in the past twenty-five years much real progress has been made, but increasing demands for the multiple use of land, especially, for example, in rural areas, have revealed instances of very poor co-ordination between the planners and the public and private interests which manage land, all of which point to the need for a much more positive, consultative planning process.

This chapter will be confined to describing the major innovations in the Scottish landscape during the past twenty-five to thirty years and will conclude by suggesting certain changes likely to occur in the foreseeable future. In this respect, we see the cultural landscape is increasingly being changed by human decision and action, as man becomes emancipated (or rather thinks he does) from the constraints of his environment by improved technology. In fact, *Homo sapiens industrialis* is no less dependent upon his environment than were his palaeolithic ancestors: man's basic ecological relationships in nature do not change, although their implications, not least those arising from man's increasing capacity for landscape changes, are seen to be ever more subtle and complex.

Changes in the Highlands and Islands and Southern Uplands

In the Highlands and Islands, parts of the west coast and the Outer Hebrides were not affected by the actions of consolidating landlords during the last century; there, re-allotment of holdings including, locally, reverses of a landlord's clearances, was carried out by government agencies after the Crofters' Holdings (Scotland) Act of 1886 and continued through into the inter-war years. The 1886 Act gave security of tenure but, together with subsequent legislation, it has tended to fossilize the settlement pattern into holdings which are too small to be worked economically today; moreover, security of tenure makes it difficult to amalgamate vacated croftland into more viable units. Grants are now available to crofters for erecting buildings for ancillary occupations, eg workshops, improving facilities to accommodate tourists (for bed and breakfast), etc, and for refurbishing animal sheds, erecting wire fences and other agricultural improvements. These measures have all tended to preserve the existing pattern of settlement of the west coast and Islands, although abandonment of crofts locally continues as better roads, better jobs and the social attractions in the South and the rising costs of providing services to remote and scattered communities persuade local people to move out of these areas. Remaining settlement and services, partly guided by planning, are concentrated into nucleations where they can be more effectively maintained (eg Portree, Stornoway, Tobermory and Ullapool). Since *c* 1950, little new building has been occurring in the seven crofting counties (and little, for that matter, in the Southern Uplands) — except, for instance, for housing and plant for the Dounreay 'atomics' near Thurso, the Fort William pulp mill, the Invergordon alumina smelter and the ski-ing and summer tourist activities at Aviemore. By contrast, in the Lowlands, industrial decentralization, greater mobility, new and expanded industry and housing schemes, etc are resulting in many new or enlarged settlement foci in the landscape.

At Inverlochy, near Fort William, on the Great Glen cattle ranch, on the Lovat estates in Strathfarrar, and in several other experimental schemes, cattle are once more grazing in the Highland glens, where they have been absent since the second half of the eighteenth century. Pastures that were for long periods closely and selectively grazed and little manured by sheep are now less selectively grazed and better manured by cattle; the grass is more lush and the hillsides are gradually becoming ecologically more stable. In the North-West Highlands and Islands, the improvements in fencing and in the appearance of cottages have come largely since the Crofters (Scotland) Act of 1955. Caravans and tents appear around a number of crofts and upon common (machair) grazings during summer: these, together with some fairly large and conspicuous permanent caravan sites on the east and Clyde coasts constitute a controversial amenity. Moreover, not all the newly whitewashed cottages on the west coast are owned by crofters: in some communities, such as Gairloch and Plockton, between a quarter and half the houses are holiday homes, occupied by their owners or tenants only in the summer months. Some of these second houses are rebuilt on vacated croft sites, taking advantage of certain compromising clauses in the 1955 and 1961 Crofting Acts.

Grants for ploughing, drainage, reseeding and bracken destruction have helped to create lush green, new or reclaimed pastures in many parts of the Highlands and Islands, which stand out in marked contrast to the grey-green and brown colours of acid peat moorlands nearby. Locally, here and there, new creameries dot the landscape. Bracken, the scourge of the Highlands since the mid-eighteenth century, after which it was no longer trampled out by the clansmen's cattle, has been checked, both in the crofting counties and the Southern Uplands, by grazing cattle or by mechanical crushing. The substantial reduction of rabbits by myxomatosis and other agencies has helped the recovery of hill grazings: there are now fewer burrows to start gullies and fewer depredations to young seedlings in plantations and scrubland. In a number of places, the semi-natural birch-oak-pine scrub has begun to creep back a little. However, red deer populations in the Highlands (and red and roe deer in the Southern Uplands), together with sheep and remaining rabbits, continue to be a serious ecological problem.

The culling of red deer is carried out in association with deer stalking in late summer, to maintain the quality of moorland grazings and of deer stocks for sport and venison. Lower stocking densities for sheep and rabbit control measures also help a good deal. High fences (buried also a foot below ground, in some cases) are erected around plantations throughout the hill areas of Scotland to try and keep out deer and rabbits and, in collaboration the Red Deer Commission, Forestry Commission, Department of Agriculture and Nature Conservancy are trying to create a better ecological and aesthetic balance in Scotland's upland landscape. In Orkney and lowland Caithness, however, the windswept Improvers' landscape of small farms (now mostly owner-occupied in Orkney) is now undergoing some changes as fields are enlarged and farmholdings and farmbuildings regrouped for more efficient management, notably in Orkney. These, and similar changes in the Moray Firth district, are akin to those occurring in the eastern and southern lowlands of Scotland during recent years.

Forestry in the Scottish landscape since 1945

Today, about 600,000 hectares in Scotland are owned by the Forestry Commission and Department of Agriculture, two-thirds of this land being north of the Highland line. In addition, there are 2-300,000 hectares of private owned, managed and unmanaged woodland and scrub. Both Forestry Commission and private planting (the latter often done under dedication agreements or by private forestry concerns) is clothing many hillsides in the Highlands and Southern Uplands, even on the moors of Skye, Sutherland and the Moor of Rannoch. Parts of eastern Ross-shire, Speyside, Donside, Deeside, the Perthshire and Angus glens and Argyllshire are now much afforested and both in these areas and in other glens and moorland tracts of the Highlands, long, deep-ploughed furrows up and down slope for drainage, and millions of conifer seedlings planted in rows, are becoming prominent landscape features. Despite continuing controversy, most of the gaps created by premature felling in World War II have now been replaced and new planting is generally much more sympathetic to the contour of the land and better integrated with hill grazing and field sports than pre-1950 afforestation schemes. The Forestry Commission continues to purchase land as it appears on the open market, but has split up glen-side plantations and sometimes planted shelter belts, like some private owners, to help sheep farmers; it has also selectively felled along the edges of its larger forests to blend them more successfully into the landscape, and planted larch stands and deciduous borders along many touring routes through the Highlands and Southern Uplands during the last twenty years. Private estates and commercial forestry undertakings are often working in similar ways. However, large parts of the Forestry Commission's holdings in the Highlands remain unplantable (83 per cent of the Glen Affric estate, 63 per cent of all the North Conservancy's forests, 53 per cent of all the West Conservancy's and 25 per cent of the Eastern Conservancy's holdings) due to altitude and exposure. Such areas continue to be managed for field sports and hill grazing by tenants, in a similar manner to surrounding private estates.

Public forestry is on a much smaller scale in the Central Valley, although several tracts of conifers have been planted in the last thirty years on the upstanding hill masses, eg the Carron Valley Forest on the Campsie Fells. However, *private* forestry has been most active in central and southern

Scotland. Several hundred thousand hectares of moorlands remain grazed by sheep although, in recent years, the financial incentives for afforestation have become much more attractive alongside sheep subsidies; the tradition of sheep farming nevertheless, remains strong.The most recent extensive forestry in the Southern Uplands (11,200 hectares) is that on Eskdalemuir, carried out by a private concern combining timber production with amenities for public recreation and game conservation. Although Argyllshire, Perthshire and Angus have large tracts of public and private forestry, a larger percentage of woodland in relation to other land use is found in the North-East, where Moray and Nairnshire have the highest proportion of land under timber of any counties in the British Isles (25 per cent). By 1963 there were in the North-East 111 dedication schemes covering 32,800 hectares of private woodlands. In the late 1950s there were, within 50km of Glasgow, *c* 14,000 hectares of private woodland, 30 per cent of this being under a dedication agreement or other management plan. Even today, however, despite the forestation incentives, the quality of woodland management still varies considerably between estates.

Many of the larger lowland farms and estates support a woodland management programme that is, to varying degrees, integrated with agriculture; and this combination maintains the dignified, well-proportioned chequerboard landscape originally laid out by the Improvers. Private forestry often occurs on sites of better quality than the Forestry Commission can purchase: this factor, with tradition, accounts for the continued emphasis on deciduous species, often in coverts and shelter belts as well as commercial stands, and with an accent on amenity. The Forestry Commission, facing comment from an increasingly affluent, mobile and leisured public during the last two decades, has most successfully adapted the principles of amenity planting around the edges of its forest parks, such as Argyll, Queen Elizabeth, Glenmore and Glentrool, where the emphasis is increasingly on the provision for public leisure alongside the growing of commercial timber. Birch, beech and oak have been planted along forest rides and motor touring routes, notably in places like the Trossachs, where the scale and intimacy of the landscape have also been conserved, in co-operation with Glasgow Corporation, with the provision or maintenance of vistas and viewpoints through the avoidance of block-planting and clear-felling, and the widening of the grass sward at the side of roads through the forests.

Around Loch Katrine, as at Glentrool and Eskdalemuir, landscape consultants are showing how functional and aesthetic considerations can be integrated successfully in the layout of new forests in the hills and glens, although conflicts, notably between sheep farming, deer management, coniferous forestry and various forms of public recreation, locally continue in upland areas, chiefly in the Highlands. Indeed, sensitive amenity groups are sometimes formed by members of the public who may be inadequately informed about the essential operations and changes occurring in the rural landscape — a factor no less important, albeit in a different way, in their home townscapes. The new Wood of Caledon is as artificial as the moors and regulated lochs of the Highlands or the Improvement landscapes of the Scott country (Tweed valley) and Strathmore which appear so often on illustrated wall calendars in the homes of suburb-anized Scottish and English country-lovers. Moreover, attract-ive areas of deciduous woodland and scrub have to be cleared and replanted, for both ecological and economic reasons, so that rotations of selective, smaller-scale felling and replant-ing — which are much less conspicuous — can be reintro-duced. Trees, like a cornfield, are as much a crop as an object of beauty, only they have a much longer growing cycle. At present, however, forestry, like agricultural operations, is not wholly subject to planning control: this creates a number of problems.

Given the need to inform the average suburban citizen of the realities of rural management, a formidable challenge remains for land managers and planners to ensure much greater continuity and harmony between different activities in the countryside which account for, or sometimes detract from, its intrinsic character and attractiveness. Not least, this affects extensive moorland areas, like the Highlands and Southern Uplands, where tax inroads are resulting in a fragmentation of necessarily large management units that seems to be neither economically nor ecologically desirable. Also, on the lowlands, similar dismemberment of large estates, with the purchase of tenant farms by their occupiers, has resulted in the piecemeal attrition of timber, notably since the mid-1950s, as there is no longer a common woodland management scheme for the locality. Little coverts and belts, which the Improving laird and his successors preserved for game and shelter, are being cleared, mainly for capital gain (sale of timber, removal of hedges for field enlargement, greater mechanization, etc for greater efficiency and profit) — but also to remove cover for foxes and other vermin. A grant-aided tree-planting scheme, operating at county level, would ensure their replacement or continued upkeep. The new Agrarian Revolution of the last fifteen years has also brought tall, shining silos and prefabricated barns on to many lowland farms (both of which — as farm buildings — are exempt from normal planning controls); admittedly a number of people consider silos, if properly sited, to be quite attractive. However, a proliferation of broiler houses, intensive livestock units, etc, notably near the towns and cities of the Central Valley, is also slipping through the same legal loopholes: generally, these are considered to be much less attractive innovations, sometimes suggesting in appearance an agricultural factory or slum.

Hydro-electric schemes in the Scottish countryside

Although the main landscape impacts of hydro-electric generation in Scotland have come during the last thirty years, the Highlands' reserves of power began to be exploited in the late nineteenth century for smelting alumina. The British Aluminium Company started their small hydro-electric station at Falls of Foyers beside Loch Ness in 1896, but this is a very small landscape feature. However, in 1904, to increase output, more conspicuous operations were started at Kinlochleven, near Glencoe, using power from the new Blackwater reservoir dam, above the company village sited at the head of Loch Leven. Further developments, a few years later, involved the construction of underground ducts, the raising of Lochs Treig and Laggan and the formation of the Spey dam reservoir — each involving prominent granite aggregate barrages. The Inverlochy works, near Fort William, was built in 1929. Elsewhere, hydro-electric power stations were installed at Falls of Clyde (Lanarkshire) in 1926, at Loch Rannoch in 1930, at Loch Tummel (below the famous Queen's View, in Perthshire) in 1933 and in Galloway (the Loch Doon and Glenkens scheme) in 1935-6.

In addition, it is convenient to mention here that a number of drinking-water reservoirs were built during the first quarter of the present century; eg the level of Loch Katrine, in the Trossachs, was raised by Glasgow Corporation Water Works. This reservoir was later amplified by Lochs Arklet and Vennacher and, most recently, a scheme for Loch Finglas nearby. The Carron valley reservoir in the Campsie Fells was formed in the inter-war years, and in the last fifty years a number of smaller reservoirs have appeared in central and southern Scotland like the chain of catchments in the Renfrew and north Ayrshire area to serve the Glasgow conurbation, in the Pentland Hills to serve Edinburgh, and the Camps and Daer reservoirs in upland Lanarkshire to supply water to consumers in the middle Clyde valley.

Generally speaking, the dams, water towers, pumping and filter works associated with these schemes are less prominent local landscape features than the service roads, pylons, outbuildings, power stations and conduit terminals of hydro-electric schemes, but in both cases, particularly with drinking-water reservoirs, Forestry Commission and some private planting has helped to blend these new buildings into their surroundings, with a few lochs now being selectively developed as recreation foci. However, although all the trees below the new strand-line on hydro-power and drinking-water reservoirs are cleared, there is quite often a large draw-down, especially in summer, leaving large expanses of loch sand, mud flats, ruined walls, buildings, old bridges and roads, etc with dried up, diverted headwater burns and streams diverted below dams into underground conduits, leaving almost dry beds, depleted of fishing, for the tourists to see in the summer. In particular, the pipes falling down the side of Ben Nevis to an inter-war smelter of dull factory design and the unimaginative council housing nearby on a bare hill above Fort William can hardly be considered attractive landscape features. A short distance away, the Wiggins Teape mill, on

Loch Eil, built in the 1960s, forms a much more positive landscape feature, set against the backdrop of Ben Nevis: the Dounreay establishment and Invergordon smelter have a similar, although controversial, impact on their respective coastal settings. A bad planning error, however, was made in the siting of the alumina works and village in the shaded, hillfoot, pollution-trapping site at Kinlochleven. This, together with the growing amenity lobby, has discouraged any further developments of that type in the Highlands.

Some of the biggest landscape changes in the Highlands during the last three decades have come since the formation of the North of Scotland Hydro-Electric Board in 1943. Although, by statute, considerable efforts have to be made to landscape its schemes, the scale of operations and quality of remedial work on its surroundings have sometimes generated considerable controversy. This began after the construction of projects like the pump storage scheme on the side of Ben Cruachan, in Argyllshire, in 1957, involving a conspicuous dam on the corrie lip and water pipes below it. Indeed, certain informed critics of the board's activities have suggested that several of its amenity restoration and fisheries projects have met with, at best, indifferent success. Beheaded rivers leave an ugly, boulder-strewn gulch, and once-good upstream salmon and trout anglings have been seriously impaired or lost: such streams suffer from powerful, irregular discharges from the dams and from the inadequacy of fish passes. The flooding of certain valleys, as with a number of drinking-water reservoir schemes in the Lowlands, has drowned beauty spots, and the mounting demand for water (although all the major hydro-power potential in Scotland has now been tapped) continues to lead the champions of balancing reservoirs and the growing ecology-amenity movement into open combat on many occasions when a new catchment is proposed.

However, in implementing its Glen Affric scheme, the North of Scotland Hydro-Electric Board — meeting opposition which had prevented its earlier exploitation of this waterpower — did not fill the very scenic Glen Affric with water but, instead, raised and enlarged Loch Mullardoch in neighbouring Glen Cannich, with a long and rather ungainly concrete dam, feeding water into an enlarged, dammed-up

Loch Benevan in Glen Affric via a tunnel 5.6km long. Apart from the mud and sand exposed in this shallow loch in draw-down, some comment has been made concerning the efficiency of the fish passes in the staircase of dams leading north-eastwards, down the Beauly river system. These passes are intended to maintain the quality of angling on this fine salmon water by allowing the fish to move to spawning gravels upstream. Nevertheless, these dams, and others, have become part of the Highland scene, and to its credit, the board has sometimes created new or enlarged lochs which, aided in some cases by sympathetic afforestation, have given certain glens a new water-focus and character that was not there before. On the other hand, innovations like the upper Glen Lyon dam, poorly landscaped and disruptive to fishing, leave a good deal, perhaps, to be desired.

However, the board has, by constructing power stations and maintenance workers' cottages, etc, of local stone, helped to keep alive a good building tradition. Also, the Forestry Commission sometimes builds hamlets for field staff in local wood, which harmonize quite well with their forest surroundings. Some power stations have been built out of sight, underground, eg Clachan on the Glenshirra scheme. Even so, some of the access road scars, buildings and, particularly, the existance and alignment of certain high tension tranmission lines (eg those visible from Queen's View along Rannochside and across the hillsides north of Rannoch Moor and over the Pass of Drumochter) led a number of amenity interests to counter the board's remaining designs in the 1960s. Partly because of this, the small-scale Fionna Fhada scheme in the scenic Letterewe Forest of Wester Ross remains unbuilt, together with several similar schemes elsewhere.[1]

Other power and industrial developments and mineral extraction in the Scottish scene

Elsewhere, other power developments have caused controversial, though striking, landscape impacts; the Hunterston, Chapelcross and Dounreay nuclear power stations each have very different skyline profiles. In particular, Dounreay's spherical reactor standing above the cliffs of Caithness provokes the same kind of mixed reaction as the domes of

Fylingdales distant early-warning station on the North York Moors. In the Central Valley, the largest existing conventional thermal stations, eg at Kincardine on the Forth, Portobello and Cockenzie in Midlothian and the Clyde valley plants, are also distinctive local landscape foci. Between these, and other power stations and consumer cities and industrial sites, are the huge overhead grid-lines, notably the 275 and 400 kilovolt super-grid looping through the Forth-Clyde industrial zone, and the lines striding over the moors beside the A74 and Merse routeways south, to link up with the nation grid.

Pylons — with industry — can make or mar a landscape, depending upon their scale and the skill applied to their design and situation. Sometimes power-lines form prominent, almost majestic, landscape elements, adding focus and proportion to an open moorland or enclosed farm landscape; at other times they threaten to overawe, or be discordant with, a landscape's delicate rhythm and intrinsic character. Likewise, the oil refineries at Grangemouth,[2] viewed from a distance and in different weathers and pollution conditions, produce a mixed reaction among observers: in contrast, the small-scale terminal installations and oil storage tanks at Finart on Loch Long have lent themselves much more readily to landscaping. However, the new oil and iron ore terminals and steelworks complex at Hunterston, on a prominent headland in the scenic Firth of Clyde, will create a very large, dominating and doubtless controversial feature when completed. Already, the huge motor assembly works at Linwood, south-west of Glasgow, and the steelworks of the Clydes Mill, Coatbridge and Motherwell area, form landscape features on a similar scale, notably the complex made up of the continuous strip mill and nearby heavy engineering works at Ravenscraig. There is no doubt, however, that given certain design, light and landscape conditions, modern plant can enhance an industrial landscape: tall chimneys, cooling towers and cracking towers — and even the remaining red shale bings and flashes — have a quality of their own.

The remains of mineral working are still prominent in certain derelict, depressing areas in the Central Valley, despite attempts at reclamation such as the Clyde Valley Regional Park scheme. Although coal and shale are both often worked out, clay, sand, wet gravel and road-metal workings are locally still active near demand centres like the Forth-Clyde industrial zone. Elsewhere in Scotland, small road-metal and building-material workings are well scattered: limestone, diatomite, sandstone, slate and granite are still locally worked on a small scale but with little landscape impact. The landscaping of Associated Portland Cement's workings on the coast near Dunbar (East Lothian) has been remarkably successful. The hummocky, grass-covered remains of old peat workings occur in the North-West Highlands and Islands, whilst a prominent local innovation at Altnabreac, in Caithness, is a pilot peat-briquette works working over 8,400 hectares of moss peat, after the manner of Bord na Mona in the Bog of Allen in Eire. The Brora (Sutherland) and Machrihanish (Argyll, Kintyre) coalfields are still worked privately, as are local diatomite deposits in Skye, all of these having little landscape impact.

However, if successful prospecting for copper, zinc and valuable trace elements proves that working would be economic, this could have very controversial landscape consequences in the Highlands and North-East. The shore terminals for North Sea oil in Shetland, the Moray Firth area and the North-East, and associated industries, could also have considerable impact. Locally, in large and small burghs throughout Scotland, trading estates, with their characteristic light industries using electric power and housed in brick, concrete and asbestos, have sprung up under government encouragement, whilst old and occasionally new-style distilleries continue to mark the local scene in different parts of the country. Fertile arable fields and farms near Invergordon in Easter Ross have disappeared under the new aluminium smelter and dry dock, doubtless to be followed by further industrial growth if the oil boom becomes a reality. At the other end of the Great Glen, however, the pulp mill will probably not be followed by other, conspicuous industrial plant in the foreseeable future, no doubt to the relief of many Highland landscape enthusiasts.

The expansion of towns and cities; new towns; trunk and other road developments

Almost every large and small burgh in Scotland has seen some expansion of its urban area in the last twenty-five years, even places like Lerwick, Portree, Thurso (with its estates for the 'atomics'), Alness and Dingwall (with the Invergordon developments), Fort William (with the paper mill) and Stranraer. Moreover, although mass-produced building materials first came into use during the inter-war years, their greatest impact on the town and village scene has come since *c* 1950. This expansion has responded to a modest net population growth, together with a general increase in affluence and in the number of family units and with a lowering of housing densities, although the latter, notably in the towns and cities of the Central Valley, still remain quite high in some parts.

It is in the Central Valley that the biggest areas and landscape impact of new housing styles and layouts are to be seen. New materials, new methods and the rising costs of materials and construction mean that housing estates, public buildings and blocks of offices and flats now often have tile roofs and are faced with aggregate stone blocks (Fyfe-stone) together with large expanses of 'harling' (pebbledash to English readers) — the rendering being required under the local bylaws for extra protection against the Scottish weather. This practice lends a very distinctive, often pleasing, character to all council and private housing and related developments around the margins of Scottish towns and cities which have been built in twenty-five years. This style contrasts markedly where it has been used in developments surrounding, or infilling older housing and other buildings constructed in local stone and in earlier architectural styles. Slates, however, are sometimes still used on private housing schemes, or special civic housing, refurbishing and conservation schemes, the purple-grey colour remaining a distinctive townscape feature, often forming very pleasing associations with rendered (harling) walls in planned precinct developments, etc. Ridge tiles have been used locally for roofing houses, barns and cottages in parts of the eastern Lowlands since the Improving period, made from local clay, and this style is also continued in certain new housing developments and restorations.

As regards the major towns and cities of Scotland, Aberdeen, firstly, is seen to have extended westwards considerably during the last twenty-five years on to a plateau about 130m above the harbour nucleus, with simultaneous expansion occurring to the north, alongside Donside to Bucksburn and Dyce, to the west-south-west along Deeside towards Peterculter, and towards Nigg in the South[3]. The unimaginative street patterns and functional styles of large corporation housing estates and Scottish Special Housing Association housing in Mastrick, on the bleak, flat hilltop west of the inter-war bypass (now dual carriageway) contrast with the more recent and more attractive council layouts on the hillsides farther down towards the city centre. The latter consist of both two-story closes and tall towers of flats: the flats, with the new town house, rival the granite church spires that form the focal points of the Victorian townscape. South of the Dee, new council estates were built at Kincorth, overlooking the river and the city. Private layouts have been developed at Bucksburn on the Dyce road beyond the Bridge of Don north of the city, to the west along the Deeside road, and into Nigg in the south. Further expansion of private and public housing schemes in the Aberdeen area is likely with the new oil developments. Along the coast, new building and rebuilding of homes for commuters has taken place in the old fishing villages. In between these new developments, industry has come to the Dyce and Nigg Bay area.

Likewise, in Dundee,[4] postwar council estates have spread across the inter-war bypass to the north, and much of the city now looks inland. As in Aberdeen, the new housing layouts are much more extensive and less densely built up than the Victorian and inter-war developments. Among such estates, however, Menziehill is different, being planned as a neighbourhood unit on a hilltop site above Dundee, containing a varity of housing types. Elsewhere in the city, the postwar estate patterns have a characteristic symmetry — usually deriving from the subdivision of shapes initially influenced by a field or farm boundary, stream course and/or the city limits. Building styles are often dull through the dictates of economy and standardization. After the building of Dundee's arterial bypass in the 1920s, light industries developed in estates alongside, especially since 1945. In turn, the road served as a springboard for further inland development, overriding the discipline attempted in postwar planning. Indeed, planning in all Scottish towns since the 1947 Act has had the job of trying to neatly round off, or rationalize, earlier, often unplanned developments — as well as the promotion of orderly new schemes for further expansion. As in all of the four largest cities and many large towns in Scotland, the old buildings in the centre of Dundee are being replaced by shopping precinct redevelopments, parking lots, etc, although, selectively, older elements of the townscapes are being retained. Multi-storey flats and offices are forming new, vertical elements in the city skyline, which are very striking over part of the western end of the town formerly in large mansions and gardens: indeed, many rebuilding schemes in Dundee, as in the other three largest cities, are of a zonal character, replacing sections of the urban fabric developed in earlier stages of growth.

All the large burghs in south Fifeshire, north Ayrshire and the Forth-Clyde valley have undergone considerable postwar growth and infilling. Hamilton,[5] for example, has in the last twenty-five years seen much of the remaining open space, enclosed within the area developed between the wars, taken up for building, together with additional land made available for new housing by burgh boundary extensions. The burgh has come increasingly to function as a dormitory town for nearby industrial and commercial centres, notably Mother-well and Glasgow. Grangemouth has expanded very greatly since 1945 as a result of petro-chemical developments, which now occupy large areas of reclaimed foreshore and former farmland south-east of the town, backed by new housing developments and public open spaces. These form a marked townscape contrast with the timber yards and Victorian, gridiron, terrace-housing patterns.

In the Lothians, Edinburgh now dominates the landscape and pattern of activities very strongly and, since the opening of the Forth Road Bridge in 1963, the city increasingly influences much of south Fifeshire. Large corporation and private housing developments have crept westwards and eastwards from the city over the fertile square fields of the Improvers and southwards up to the foot of the Pentland

Hills. Industrial estates have also appeared in the newly built up areas on the western and eastern sides of the city, whilst heavy industry remains a feature of the Inveresk valley and the dock area. Careful planning, however, has to a noteworthy extent saved the best of Edinburgh's townscape from occlusion by tall office blocks: the New Town, apart from the Princes Street-George Street area, has remained remarkably intact – but innovations like the East End redevelopment behind the handsome, classical Register House and certain inner roadway proposals cause some observers to fear for the future of Scotland's dignified capital.

In contrast to the relatively clean city of Edinburgh, the townscape of Glasgow has suffered neglect perhaps without parallel in Britain. Wide areas of substandard tenements have been cleared, but certain tracts still remain and modern building has spread out to fill every part of the Howe. Until recent years, dereliction came within less than a kilometre of the City hall and subsidence from ill-charted, abandoned coalworkings still renders a number of areas unsuitable for building. Neither are the exposed heights around the city suitable for housing, so the overspill has had to be placed in new townscape areas such as Easterhouse, and the new towns of East Kilbride, Cumbernauld and Irvine. Forty-four hectares of the notorious Gorbals has been demolished and replaced by modern flats, but these only rehoused 10,000 of the original 26,000 inhabitants of that tenement slum area. Today there is very little real countryside left on the lowlands around Glasgow and the challenge remains to rebuild the drab city centre. The latest developments involve a huge ring road scheme, with nearby flats and office block developments, the roadway linking up with the M74 motorway from the south-east, the A8 and M8 to the east, the A80(T) to the North-East, the new Erskine Bridge and M8 link on the south Clyde shore, Paisley in the west, and the A82(T) on the north Clyde shore to the north-west. The new industrial estate on the old corporation airport, the vast Linwood works, the remodelled shipyards and the newest, harled, middle-income, private commuter estates to the north and south of the city contrast dramatically with the grimy, obsolete buildings remaining in the city centre and also, *inter alia,* with the overspill corporation housing scheme at

Easterhouse which has developed new kinds of social problems of its own. But the new office blocks, shopping centre and parking buildings rising in the city centre are rendering the area rather more attractive.[6]

The new towns have had a striking impact on the landscape of the Central Valley, together with a number of town expansions, both largely designed to take overspill population. Of the latter schemes, that in Haddington (East Lothian), involving the grafting of new housing and light industrial estates on to a rehabilitated eighteenth- and nineteenth-century town centre, has proved a particularly successful example. East Kilbride and Cumbernauld, catering largely for Glasgow's overspill, are respectively 13km and 22km from the city centre: the former has about 50,000 inhabitants, the latter 70,000. Glenrothes was developed on worked-over National Coal Board land in south Fifeshire, in an attempt to revive the locality and, similarly, Irvine, near Kilmarnock, in north Ayrshire, taking Glasgow overspill. Livingston in West Lothian, planned for 70,000 people (including 56,000 from Glasgow) and adjoining the industrial developments at Bathgate, has not yet been completed.[7]

Only 1.6km of hilly green-belt land separates the Rutherglen and Clarkston suburbs of Glasgow from East Kilbride. The new town (designated in 1947) is virtually a detached suburb of Glasgow and it incorporates the old kirktoun of East Kilbride, which expanded as a cotton textile settlement in the late eighteenth century. The green belt is enhanced by a further 3.2km gap between the burgh boundary and the developed part of the town (burgh area 4,100 hectares). The altitude is about 150–60m, in attractive, hilly country, with several narrow, winding valleys draining towards the Clyde. These are being preserved as linear parks and walkways to help divide the built-up area into distinctive sections. Between the drainage channels there is a complex pattern of hillocks which have provided sites for housing areas. Slopes of up to 1 in 8 (12 per cent) have been developed for housing. In industrial areas, however, several million cubic metres of rock and earth have had to be removed in order to obtain large enough level sites. In its layout (see map) East Kilbride is typical of the Mark 1 new towns. The town centre is situated at the junction of three radial roads. Looped district

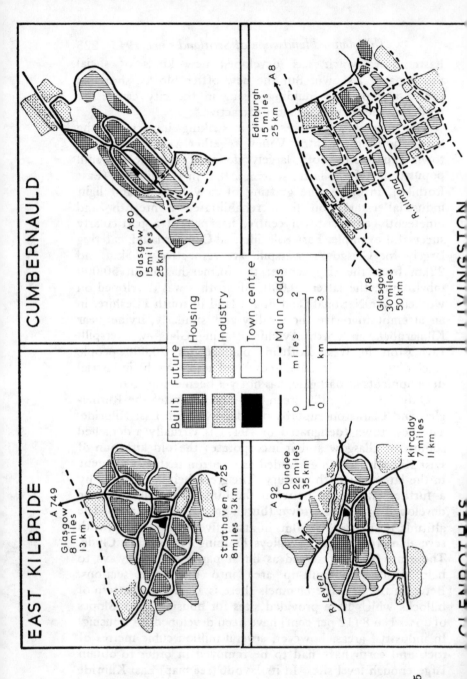

Fig. 15
New towns

EAST KILBRIDE

A 749
Glasgow
8 miles
13 km

Strathaven A 725
8 miles
13 km

CUMBERNAULD

A80

Glasgow
15 miles
25 km

GLENROTHES

A 92

Dundee
22 miles
35 km

Kircaldy
7 miles
11 km

R. Leven

LIVINGSTON

Edinburgh
15 miles
25 km

A8

Glasgow
30 miles
50 km

A8

R. Almond

Built   Future
Housing

Industry

Town centre

Main roads

miles
0   2
km
0   3

roads provide access from these routes to the housing and industrial areas, the former being subdivided by the loops and by the valley parkways into six neighbourhoods, each with its own shopping centre, local shops, schools, churches and recreational areas. The industrial areas are on the outer edges of the town on the three principal roads. The town centre is tightly enclosed by the surrounding housing areas.

Glenrothes, designated in 1948, grew slowly until the sixties and now has a population of c 75,000. The town is on the A92 road from Edinburgh, via Kirkaldy, to Dundee and within an hour's journey of either city via the road bridges over the Firths of Forth and Tay. Ths site comprises 2,292 hectares of gently undulating land at the south-eastern end of the Lomond Hills, altitude around 62-92m. Most of the site slopes gradually towards the Leven valley to the north. In its building styles and layout, Glenrothes is similar to East Kilbride. The original plan contained three residential neighbourhoods south-east, south-west and north of the town centre, each one divided into several precincts focusing on a small group of shops. New housing areas have now been added to the outer edges of these three early neighbourhoods. The road system has been replanned to cater for the greater population and higher car-ownership ratio and the number of local shopping centres reduced — since the mobile population favours the major town shopping centres.

Cumbernauld was, like East Kilbride, designated in 1955, at a convenient distance from Glasgow (22km). The site is on the junction of the A80 from Glasgow to Stirling with the A73 from Airdrie and Lanark which links with the A74 going south to England. The town is in the centre of the Forth-Clyde valley, with easy access to port facilities at either end. Originally, there were two villages on the site (1,660 hectares), Cumbernauld and Condorrat, together having c 3,000 inhabitants. The site is rather smaller than those of the other Scottish new towns, and it has an oblong shape, 8km by 3.2km because of coal-mining areas lying immediately to the north-west and fireclay deposits to the south-east. The layout of the town is very different from those of East Kilbride and Glenrothes, the greater part being on a long, narrow hill rising from 80 to 86m, with fairly steep sides. A flat tract to the south-east is given over to industrial growth.

The notable feature of the rolling site is the wide view from the main hill, especially towards the Kilsyth Hills on the north-west side. It is, however, very exposed: nevertheless, the detailed layout shows due regard for the needs of shelter, compactness and tree planting. The town centre is on the top of the hill, with the whole of the residential area grouped closely around it and extending down the slopes. On the broad scale, the pattern for the town was undoubtedly the hilltop towns of Provence and central Italy, and the view of Cumbernauld from the main approach roads has a dramatic quality not often found in the valley-hugging towns of Scotland (formerly related to river crossings, old waterpower sites, etc). It is easy to dismiss the Cumbernauld concept as out of place in Scottish conditions but, in fact, the housing areas on the hilltop are being built in close-knit groups with some of the enclosure and intimacy of traditional Scottish town architecture. In place of the spires and turrets which are the focal points in existing townscapes, Cumbernauld has several twelve-storey blocks of flats. In addition, three outlying neighbourhoods are being developed, with much the same kinds of local shops, schools and other services as their counterparts in the earlier new towns.

By 1960 it was clear that another town would be needed for Glasgow's overspill population: this is now growing up as Livingston, in West Lothian, with a target of 70,000 people. The site extends over 2,680 hectares, bounded by the Edinburgh-Glasgow road (A8 and M8) to the north and outliers of the Pentland Hills to the south. It is the largest new town scheme planned in Scotland so far, being just 50km from central Glasgow, 25km from central Edinburgh, ten minutes drive from Turnhouse Airport and with excellent road and rail connections with other parts of the Central Valley and with England. The river Almond divides the site of the town, which rises from 92m along the river to 216m along the northern and southern boundaries. The gentle slopes on both sides of the river offer few obstacles to building and road alignments, and the shallow tributary valleys are to be preserved, as in East Kilbride, as linear parkways. The key element in the layout is the decision to build the town centre astride the river Almond in the geographical centre of the site. This will take a linear form, with open parkland at the eastern and western ends left to allow for future growth. The rest of the population will be housed on higher ground 1.6-3.2km from the centre, in three districts, of roughly 10,000 population each, divided by a distinctive pattern of grid roads. This layout (compare Milton Keynes in Buckinghamshire, England) is now being developed to cater for the heavy traffic volume. At the four corners of the site, on suitable flat land accessible to the major road and rail network of central Scotland, are large industrial zones, totalling 400 hectares. In the flexibility of its plan, Livingston clearly benefits from the mistakes made in earlier new town developments in Scotland and England: it also illustrates modern planning priorities, since the site is largely good, grade B, agricultural land.

Irvine, near Kilmarnock (1971 population 23,000), is being developed to a size and plan similar to that of Glenrothes, largely housing overspill population from Glasgow (40km away by road, 50km by electric train). It features prominently in plans to rehabilitate the industrial and urban infrastructure of north-central Ayrshire. The town layout partly involves the expansion of an existing settlement.

Accompanying the new developments in the Central Valley has been the double-tracking of many lengths of trunk road in between the four major cities and the intermediate industrial burghs. The A77(T) to Ayr from Glasgow, the A74(T) to England, the A73(T) and A80(T) and parts of the A92(T) and A94 are dual carriageway: the M74 from Motherwell to Glasgow makes a majestic sweep through the Clyde valley redevelopment area, as do the M90 extending north through the Fifeshire countryside from Edinburgh to Perth, the M8 through the mining landscape of West Lothian and north Lanarkshire, and the M9 being built around Stirling. It will be another decade before these scheduled road improvements are completed, but already, together with the new Tay, Forth and Erskine road bridges, they bring a dynamic innovation into both the industrial and rural landscapes of central Scotland. The opportunities for landscaping, tree planting and even establishing nature reserves along these new routes are being taken up, albeit sometimes rather slowly, and it is clear that the combined landscape impact of the new roads, town developments and industry will rival that of the agrarian landscape created two centuries ago by the Improvers.

Elsewhere in Scotland, significant local landscape changes have come about through road widening, new bridges, car parks, etc, notably on the widened and re-aligned sections of many formerly single-track A-class roads in the Highlands and Islands. However, some of the new roadside construction scars may take some time to recover, owing to slow growth of vegetation and insufficient re-seeding and landscaping, particularly where 'cut-offs' of the old road are left. The rebuilt road from Invergarry to Kyle of Lochalsh A87(T), containing a causewayed section, viewpoints and new and realigned vistas, makes a substantial new contribution to the Highland tourist landscape, as does the widened A850 around Skye. The Uists-Benbecula causeway of the fifties, the new Strome Ferry bypass and Kyle of Tongue causeway and the landscaped link between Glenuig and Loch Ailort built in the sixties and several examples of completely new highway developments in the Highland scene during the last twenty-five years. Other more controversial innovations are the bypass on the A93 around the challenging hairpin section on the Perthshire-Aberdeenshire border, known as the Devil's Elbow, the conspicuous lines of the metalled access roads running up to Coire Cas and Coire na Ciste car parks and ski-slopes at Glenmore on Speyside, the new bridge at Killiecrankie, and some of the hydro-electric board service roads, containing some poorly landscaped sections, running up several scenic Highland glens. Even more conspicuous, to some observers, are the scars of the many new, badly built, private estate vehicle tracks for access on to the bare Highland moorlands for sporting purposes: the scar of the jeep road up to the summit of Ben a' Bhuird on upper Deeside is a prime example.

Also in the Highlands, tourist developments have made prominent, and sometimes very controversial, additions to the landscape in recent years. Some schemes, like the Norwegian-style turf- and heather-roofed log cabins in Glen Derby (Perthshire) and the chalet-style ski-ing facilities at the Cairnwell have some character, albeit not Scottish. The low, tree-skirted facade of the Coylumbridge Hotel, near Aviemore, has received fairly favourable comment, whilst the hillside buildings on the Glenmore and Black Mount chairlift/ ski-ing areas and, notably, the very bold and conspicuous design and siting of the Aviemore Centre, have come under some harsh criticism from sensitive amenity interests. The scarred footpaths, pistes and car park verges on the popular Glenmore ski-slopes have also attracted much adverse comment; their landscape impact in summer is considered particularly detrimental. Reseeding is in progress but grass growth is slow at that altitude (600-800m). Elsewhere, chalets have appeared, as at Leckmelm near Ullapool and Glen Eden near Aberfeldy, and, seasonally, tents and caravans populate the common grazings behind scenic, shell sand bays on the west coast; these also have been the subject of some pointed comment, as has the scattering of a number of essential, but tastelessly designed and sited prefabricated metal climbing huts, bothies and mountain rescue posts in several areas of scenic open moorland in the Highlands popular with hill enthusiasts. Nevertheless, the addition, often insidiously, of such landscape features will undoubtedly increase with the further growth of outdoor leisure demands.

Airports, although another prominent landscape innovation of the last thirty years, have attracted much less adverse comment, mainly because most of them lie outside scenic tourist areas. Down the east coast, a line of abandoned and decaying wartime aerodromes still remains, runways and rusting buildings gathering the weeds and interplanted with grain crops or kept in pasture since the Ministry of Defence restored the land to the farmers. Some sites, however, have been restored to civil use, eg Sumburgh, Kirkwall, Wick, Dalcross and Dyce. Small fields on the Islands, used for the short 'hopping' service linking them with Glasgow and Edinburgh, are merely grass machair fields, or beaches. Other airfields – like those at Kinloss, Lossiemouth, Edzell and Leuchars – continued in use as Ministry of Defence bases, and still others have been taken over by small private flying clubs, particularly in the Lowlands and North-East. The three largest airports, however (Prestwick near Ayr, Abbotsinch near Glasgow and Turnhouse near Edinburgh). have now attracted peripheral industrial growths and are quite extensive. Each covers over 500 hectares of land. Dyce (Aberdeen)

is also attracting some industries around the airport perimeter.

Conclusion

From this account of the making of the Scottish landscape, it can be seen that each formative phase .has involved a combination of additive and subtractive processes, simultaneously or sequentially working for change and contributing, positively and negatively, to the scene which exists today. Millions of years of geological upheaval, erosion, renewed uplift, further sculpturing by wind, water, and, during the last million years, by ice, have produced the form of the ground which we see to be so various in different parts of the country. The centuries of clearing of the primeval forests, resulting in the bleak open moorlands, the building of castles and churches, the founding of burghs, the replacing of medieval run-rig farming in lowland areas by farmsteads set in large square fields with wooded coverts and in the Highlands by sheepwalks and crofting, through the clearances — followed by the spread of the road and rail network, the growth of towns and industry and the building of Highland shooting lodges: together, these events formed the elaborate cultural veneer of the Scottish landscape.

Today, the character of towns and cities is changing as the old fabric, and familiar townscapes, are removed in renewal schemes. New towns, new suburbs, new roads and new industries are laid out in the declining, derelict mining areas and in new sites in the countryside. Over a thousand hectares of rural land are lost to industry, transport and urban expansion annually in Scotland, mainly in areas adjoining the populous and congested parts of the Central Valley through planned location and decentralization schemes. Whilst new conifer plantations, with deciduous borders, are clothing bleak hill pastures in many parts of the Highlands and Southern Uplands, trees and hedgerows are being removed, and new unit-type farm buildings appearing, in lowland areas of the countryside. In turn, with the passage of time, some of these fields and farms near the industrial towns and cities become covered with roads, factories and houses.

The landscape of Scotland, as of any part of the world, is a living entity: a unique, complex and delicate organism, in which not even the remotest parts, like the Highlands and Islands, can escape the consequences of man's increasing capacity to change his environment. In the future, the challenge for planners, and for an increasingly affluent, leisured and educated public, is to ensure that all essential landscape changes are harmonious, through retaining the vital ingredients of amenity and continuity. These are the true constituents of progress in the evolution of a landscape.

Bibliographical Notes

The following notes, relating to indices in the text and to certain additional references, are designed to direct readers who wish to read further to some principal sources. In these, further references to more detailed, local examples, discussions and points of detail may often be found.

SGM = Scottish Geographical Magazine
IBG = Transactions of the British Institute of Geographers.

1 The Form of the Ground

1 Bremner, A., 'The Origin of the Scottish River System', SGM, vol 58, 1942, pp 15-20, 54-9, 99-103.
   Linton, D. L., 'The Origin of the Tweed Drainage System', SGM, vol 49, 1933, pp 162-75
   Linton, D. L., 'Some Aspects of the Evolution of the Rivers Earn and Tay', SGM, vol 56, 1940, pp 1-11, 69-79.
2 Linton, D. L., 'Problems of Scottish Scenery', SGM, vol 67, 1951, pp 65-85.
   Linton, D. L., 'Some Scottish River Captures Re-examined: III the Beheading of the Don', SGM, vol 70, 1954, pp 64-78.
   King, C. A. M., and Wheeler, P. T., 'The Raised Beaches of the North Coast of Sutherland, Scotland', *Geological Magazine*, vol 100, 1963, pp 299-320.
3 Linton, D. L., 'Problems of Scottish Scenery', SGM, vol 67, 1951, pp 65-85.
   Linton, D. L., 'Watershed Breaching by Ice in Scotland', IBG, vol 15, 1951, pp 1-15.

4 Sissons, J. B., 'A Sub-glacial Drainage System by the Tinto Hills, Lanarkshire', *Transactions of the Edinburgh Geological Society*, vol 18, 1961, pp 175-93.

Sissons, J. B., 'The Glacial Drainage System around Carlops, Peebleshire', IBG, vol 32, 1963, pp 95-111.

A full discussion of the work of these and other geomorphologists in Scotland can be found in Sissons, J. B., *The Evolution of Scotland's Scenery*, 1967 (see also O'dell and Walton, *The Highlands and Islands*, Nelson, 1963); and in Sissons, J. B., *Field Studies in the British Isles*, 1964. Further references may be found in the work of C. H. Clapperton and D. E. Sugden relating to the Cairngorms, eg Sugden, D., 'Landforms of Deglaciation in the Cairngorm Mountains', IBG 51, 1970, pp 201-19.

SEE ALSO

Gemmell, A. M. D., 'The Deglaciation of Arran', IBG 59, 1973, pp 25-39.

Small, A. and Smith, J. S., *The Inverness and Strathpeffer Area*, British Landscapes Through Maps series (Geographical Association), O. S. S. Sheets (1″) nos 27 & 28, Study no 13, Sheffield, 1972.

Cruickshank, H. B. and Jowett, A. J., *The Loch Linnhe District*, British Landscapes Through Maps series (Geographical Association), O. S. S. Sheet (1″) no 46, Study no 15, Sheffield, 1972.

2 The Prehistoric, Roman and Dark Age Legacy

GENERAL READING RELATED TO CHAPTER MATERIAL

Childe, V. G., *The Prehistory of Scotland*, 1935.

Newton, R., *Northumberland*, in The Making of the English Landscape series, Hodder & Stoughton, 1972.

Feachem, R., *A Guide to Prehistoric Scotland*, 1963.

Knight, G. A. F., *Archaeological Light on the Early Christianizing of Scotland*, London, 1933.

MacDonald, Sir G., *The Roman Wall in Scotland*, 1934.

Piggott, Stuart (ed), *The Prehistoric Peoples of Scotland*, 1962.

—— *Scotland before History*, 1958.

O'dell, A. C. and Walton, K., *The Highlands and Islands of Scotland*, Nelson, 1963.

Kirk, W., *The Agricultural Colonisation of Scotland*, SGM II, Sept. 1957, p 65.

3 Medieval and Post-Medieval Scotland: c 1100-1707

1 The word *peel* comes from the Anglo-Norman pale, as in paling, meaning stockade. This gives a clue to the original motte and bailey, with stockade. Later, eg in the Borders, characteristic small square stone keeps, intended for lookout, shelter and defence in troubled country, were called peels.

2 Whitehand, J., and Alauddin, K., 'Town Plans of Scotland', SGM vol 85, 1969, p 109.

3 Walton, K., in O'dell, A. C. and Walton, K., *The Highlands and Islands of Scotland*, Nelson, 1963.

ADDITIONAL READING

Steers, J. A., *Field Studies in the British Isles*, Nelson, 1964 (sections of field excursions in Scotland).

The British Association Handbooks, relevant historical chapters: Glasgow meeting 1958; Edinburgh meeting 1953; Dundee meeting 1968; Aberdeen meeting 1963.

Newton, R., *Northumberland*, in The Making of the English Landscape series, 1972.

Fairhurst, H. and Petrie, G., 'Scottish Clachans', SGM vol 80, 1964, p 150.

4 Scotland in the 18th Century

1 Miller, R., 'Major-General Roy', SGM II, Sept. 1956, p 97. Note: in metric units the field plans were at 368m to 1cm approx and final copies at 1472m to 1cm approx.

2 Dodgshon, R. A., 'The Origins and Distribution of Infield-Outfield in Scotland', IBG, 1973.

3 Robertson, Isobel, 'The Head Dyke — a Fundamental Line in Scottish Geography', SGM, 1948.

4 Pears, Nigel, 'Man in the Cairngorms', SGM, 1969, pp 45-55.

5 O'dell, A. C. and Walton, K., *The Highlands and Islands of Scotland*, Nelson, 1963: 'The region before 1800'.

6 Beresford, M. and Hurst, J., *'Deserted Medieval Villages'*, 1961.

GENERAL REFERENCES

The First Statistical Account of Scotland (late eighteenth and early nineteenth century): reports compiled on a parish and county basis, on observations of parish ministers.

The Board of Agriculture Reports, by county, for the various counties of Scotland (late eighteenth and early nineteenth century).

Storrie, Margaret and Third, Betty W., 'The Changing Landscape in the 18th Century Scottish Lowlands', SGM, 1955.

Third, Betty W., 'The Significance of Scottish Estate Plans and Associated Documents', *Scottish Studies*, 1965, pp 39-64.

Third, Betty W., 'Changing Landscape and Social Structure in Scottish Lowlands as Revealed by 18th Century Estate Plans', SGM, 1955, pp 83-94.

The British Association of Handbooks, appropriate chapters on historical aspects of study areas: Glasgow, Dundee, Edinburgh and Aberdeen meetings.

Mather, A. S., 'Pre-1745 Land Use and Conservation in a Highland Glen — an example from Glen Strathfarrar, North Inverness-shire', SGM vol 86, 1970, pp 159-69.

Thomson, W. P. L., 'Funzie-Fetlar — a Shetland Run-Rig Township in the 19th Century', SGM vol 86, 1970, pp 170-85.

5 The Landscape of Improvement

1 Rosalind Mitchison, *'Agricultural Sir John'*, 1962. This is a very readable biography of an important Improver.

2 Adams, I. H., 'The Land Surveyor and His Influence on the Scottish Landscape', SGM, 1968, p 248; also *The Mapping of a Scottish Estate*, pamphlet, University of Edinburgh, Department of Educational Studies, 1971.

3 Lebon, J. H. G., 'Enclosure in the Western Lowlands', SGM, 1946 (article in two parts), pp 7-11 and 100-3.

4 Gailey, R. A., 'Settlement and Population in Kintyre', SGM, 1960, p 89.

5 Storrie, M. C., 'The Census of Scotland as a Source in the Historical Geography of Islay', SGM, 1962, p 152.

6 Coull, J. R., 'The Island of Tiree', SGM vol 78, 1962, p 17.

7 Prebble, J., *The Highland Clearances*, 1963.

8 Gaskell, P., *Morven Transformed*, 1958.

9 Prebble, J., *op cit.*

10Turnock, David, 'Glenelg, Glengarry and Lochiel', SGM vol 83, 1967, p 89; also 'The Improving Movement on a West Highland Estate', SGM vol 85, 1969, p 17.

11Gaskell, P., *op cit.* (*re* 1886 Act).

12Mitchison, Rosalind, *op cit.*; also Coull, J. R., The Economic Development of the Island of Westray, Orkney', SGM vol 82, 1966, p 184.

13Small, A., 'Shetland — Location, the Key to Historical Geography', SGM, 1969, p 155.

14Darling, F. Fraser and Boyd, J. M., *The Highlands and Islands*, New Naturalist series, Fontana, 1972.

15Baker, E. A., *The Highlands with Rope and Rucksack,* 1923.

16Departmental Committee on Deer Forests, 1922, Department of Agriculture and Fisheries for Scotland.

17Darling, F. Fraser, *A West Highland Survey*, 1955.

GENERAL READING

Dodgshon, R. A., 'The Origin and Distribution of Infield-Outfield in Scotland', IBG, 1973.

The First Statistical Accounts and The Board of Trade Agricultural Reports both dating from the late eighteenth century.

Storrie, M., 'Landholders and Settlement — Evolution in West Highland Scotland', *Geografiska Annaler*, Series B, 1965.

Storrie, M. and Third, B. W., 'The Changing Landscape in the 18th Century Scottish Lowlands', SGM 1955.

Davies, G. L., 'The Parish of North Uist', SGM II, Sept. 1956, p 65.

Moisley, H. A., 'North Uist in 1799', SGM vol 77, 1961, p 89.

Kay, G. 'The Landscape of Improvement', SGM, 1962, pp 100-7.

Leeming, F. A., 'Social Accounting and the Old Statistical Accounts', SGM vol 79, 1963, p 34.

Paterson, J. A., 'The Novelist and His Region', SGM vol 81, 1965, p 146.

Whittington, G., 'Land Use in Fife at the Close of the 18th Century', SGM vol 82, 1966, p 184.

Porteus, J., 'The Island Parish of Jura', SGM vol 84, 1968, p 56.

Caird, J. B., 'The Making of the Scottish Rural Landscape',
   SGM, 1964, p 72.
O'dell, A. C. and Walton, K. W., *'The Highlands and Islands
   of Scotland'*, Nelson, 1963.
Turnock, D., 'Scotland's Geography from Valuation Rolls —
   A Highland Example', SGM vol 87, 1971, pp 21-4.

6   Woodlands in the Scottish Landscape

For further reading on the development of forestry in
Scotland since the eighteenth century and until the postwar
years, see the relevant chapters on forestry in the British
Association Handbooks, Dundee, Aberdeen, Glasgow and
Edinburgh. See also O'dell and Walton, *'The Highlands and
Islands of Scotland'*, and Mather A. S., 'Problems of Affores-
tation in Northern Scotland', IBG 54, 1971, pp 19-32.

7   The Evolution of Settlement in the Scottish Landscape: 18th and 19th Centuries.

1 O'dell, A. C. and Walton, K. W., *The Highlands and Islands
   of Scotland*, 1963.
2 Walton, K. W., chapter on rural settlement in Aberdeen
   British Association Handbook, 1963.
3 Hamilton, H., 'Life and Labour on an Aberdeenshire Estate
   1735-1750', *Third Spalding Club, Aberdeen*, 1946. See
   Chapter 8, 'The Region in the Eighteenth Century' in
   O'dell, A. C., and Walton, K. W., *The Highlands and Islands
   of Scotland*, 1963 (for abstract)
4 Smout, T. C., 'The Planned Village in Scotland 1730-1830',
   in Philipson, J. and Mitchison, R. (ed), *Scotland in the Age
   of Improvement,* 1970
5 Houston, J. M., 'Village Planning in Scotland 1745-1845',
   Advancement of Science, 1949, pp 129-32.

8   Transport in the Scottish Landscape: The Legacy up to 1945

GENERAL REFERENCES AND FURTHER READING
Vallance, D., *The Highland Railway*, 1965.
Moir, D. G., 'The Roads of Scotland', SGM, 1957, pp 101
   and 167.

Farr, A. D., *The Royal Deeside Line*, 1969.

O'dell, A. C. and Walton, K. W., *The Highlands and Islands of Scotland*, Nelson, 1963.

The British Association Handbooks (appropriate chapters): Edinburgh, Glasgow, Dundee and Aberdeen meetings.

9 The Legacy of Industrial and Urban Growth in the Scottish Landscape up to 1945

1 Green, P., 'The Burgh of Hamilton', SGM vol 83, 1967, pp 174-92.
2 The British Association Glasgow Handbook, chapter on growth of city, 1958.
3 Kinniburgh, I. G., 'Greenock: Growth and Change', SGM 1960, p 89.
4 Semple, D., 'The Growth of Grangemouth', SGM, 1958, p 65.
5 The British Association Handbook for Edinburgh, chapter on growth of Edinburgh; see also chapter on central Scotland in Steers, *Field Studies in the British Isles*, 1964.
6 Turner, W. H. K., 'The Growth of Dundee', SGM vol 84, 1968, p 76.
7 Walton, K., Mellor, R. and Hamilton, P., 'Aberdeen', special issue of SGM vol 79, 1963, p 69.

ADDITIONAL READING

Warren, K., 'Locational Problems of Scottish Iron and Steel Industry since 1760', SGM vol 81, 1965, pp 18 and 87.

10 The Planned Landscape of Scotland since 1945

1 Lea, K. J., 'Hydroelectric Developments in Scotland', SGM 1969.
2 Semple, D., 'The Growth of Grangemouth', SGM 1958, p 65.
3 Walton, K., Mellor, R. and Hamilton, P., 'Aberdeen', special issue of SGM vol 79, 1963, p 69.
4 Turner, W. H. K., 'The Growth of Dundee', SGM vol 84, 1968, p 76.
5 Green, P., 'The Burgh of Hamilton', SGM vol 83, 1967, pp 174-82.
6 The British Association Handbook for Glasgow, relevant

chapter.

7 McGovern, P. D., 'The New Towns of Scotland', SGM vol 84, 1968, pp 29-44.

ADDITIONAL READING

King, R. Bruce, 'Vegetation Destruction in the Subalpine and Alpine zones of the Cairngorm Mountains', SGM vol 87, 1971, pp 103-15.

Glen, A. and Williams, M., 'Scotland from the Air', Heinemann, 1972.

Selected Bibliography

SGM = Scottish Geographical Magazine
IBG = Transactions of the Institute of British Geographers

Adams, I. H. 'The Land Surveyor and his Influence on the Scottish Landscape', SGM Dec. 1968, p 248

Bailey P. *Orkney* (Islands series), David & Charles, 1971

Batsford, H. and Fry, C. *The Face of Scotland*, London, 1933

British Association for the Advancement of Science. *Dundee and District*, published for the Dundee meeting, 1968

British Association for the Advancement of Science. *The North-East of Scotland*, published for the Aberdeen meeting, 1963

Caird, J. B. 'The Isle of Harris', SGM vol 67, 1951, pp 85-100

Childe, V. G. *The Archaeology of Scotland*, 1935

Collier, Adam. *The Crofting Problem*, Cambridge, 1953

Cooke, G. A. *A Topographical Description of the Southern Division of Scotland*, London, 1805.

Coppock, J. T. (ed). 'Symposium on the Scottish Countryside', SGM vol 84, 1968, pp 201-68. This special section contains articles by Kenneth Walton, David Linton, Kerrin J. Lea, Ian H. Adams and D. Turnock

Coull, R. J. 'The Economic Development of the Island of Westray, Orkney', SGM vol 82, 1966, p 184

Coull, J. R. 'The Island of Tiree', SGM vol 78, 1962, p 17

Crawford, O. G. S. *Topography of Roman Scotland — North of the Antonine Wall*, Cambridge, 1949

Cruickshank, H. B. and Jowett, A. J. *The Loch Linnhe District*, British Landscape Through Maps series, O. S. Sheet (1″) no.46, Study no.15, 1972

Darling, F. Fraser. *West Highland Survey – an Essay in Human Ecology*, Oxford, 1955

Davies, G. L. The Parish of North Uist', SGM vol 72, 1956, pp 65-80

Department of Agriculture and Fisheries for Scotland Advisory Panel on the Highlands. *Land Use in the Highlands and Islands*, Edinburgh, 1964

Emery, F. V. 'The Geography of Robert Gordon 1580-1661 and Sir Robert Sabbald 1641-1722', SGM vol 74, 1958, pp 3-12

Emery, F. V. 'A Geographical Description of Scotland prior to the Statistical Accounts', *Scottish Studies* 3, 1959, pp 1-16

Fairhurst, H. 'The Rural Settlement Pattern of Scotland with Special References to the West and North', in Steel, R. W. and Lawton, R., *Liverpool Essays in Geography*, 1967, pp 193-209

Fairhurst, H. 'The Geography of Scotland in Prehistoric Times' *Transactions of the Glasgow Archaeological Society*, New Series, vol 13, 1954

Feachem, R. *The Guide to Prehistoric Scotland*, 1963

Finlay, I. *The Lothians*, Collins, 1960

Fleming, B. J. 'Some Relations between Town and Country in Scotland', SGM vol 68, 1952, pp 1-12

Gaskell, Philip. *Morven Transformed*, Cambridge, 1968

Geddes, Arthur. 'Statistical Accounts of Parish, County and Nation *c* 1790-1825 and 1835-45,' *Scottish Studies*, 3, 1959, pp 17-29

Green, Peter. 'Some Planning Problems of a Large Burgh – Hamilton, Clydeside', SGM vol 83, 1967, pp 174-82

Haldane, A. R. B. *The Drove Roads of Scotland*, Nelson, 1953

Hance, W. A. 'Crofting in the Outer Hebrides', *Economic Geography*, 28, 1952, pp 13-21

Houston, J. M. 'Village Planning in Scotland 1745-1845', *Advancement of Science*, 1949, pp 129-132

Kay, George. 'The Landscape of Improvement', SGM, 1962, pp 100-8

Kermack, W. R. '*Historical Geography of Scotland*', Edinburgh and London, 1927

Kinniburgh, I. G. 'Greenock; Growth and Change', SGM, 1960, p 89

Kinniburgh, I. G. 'New Developments in Clydeport', SGM vol 82, 1966, pp 144-53

Kirk, W. 'The Primary Agricultural Colonisation of Scotland', SGM vol 73, 1957, pp 65-90

Kirk, W. 'The Agricultural Colonisation of Scotland', SGM II, 1957, p 65

Lea, K. J. 'Hydro-Electric Power Generation in the Highlands of Scotland', IBG 46, 1969, pp 155-65

Lebon, J. H. G. 'Enclosure in the Western Lowlands', SGM, 1946, pp 7-11 and 100-3

Leeming, F. A. 'Social Accounting and the Old Statistical Account', SGM vol 79, 1963, pp 34-45

Lindsay, Jean. *The Canals of Scotland*, David & Charles, 1968

Linklater, Eric. *Orkney and Shetland: An Historical, Geographical, Social and Scenic Survey*, Robert Hale, 1965

Linton, D. L. 'Problems of Scottish Scenery', SGM vol 67, 1951, pp 65-85

McCann, S. B. 'The Main Post Glacial Shoreline of Western Scotland from the Firth of Lorne to Loch Broom', IBG 39, 1966, pp 87-99

McGovern, P. D. 'The New Towns of Scotland', SGM vol 84, 1968, pp 29-44

McLaren, M. *The Shell Guide to Scotland*, London, 1965

McLellan, Robert. *The Isle of Arran*, David & Charles, 1970

McMillan, Helen. 'Raised Beaches in Scotland – a Problematic Study', *Drumlin* (Glasgow) 2, 1966, pp 25-30

Macnab, P. A. *The Isle of Mull*, David & Charles, 1970

McVean, D. N. and Lockie, Jas D. *Ecology and Land Use in Upland Scotland*, Edinburgh, 1969

Mather, A. S. 'Pre-1745 Land Use and Conservation in a Highland Glen – an Example from Glen Strathfarrar, North Inverness-shire', SGM vol 86, 1970, pp 159-69

Matthew, Sir R. H. and Johnson-Marshall, P. E. A. The Lothians Regional Survey, vol 2: *Physical Planning Aspects*, Scottish Development Department and West and Mid Lothian Joint Planning Advisory Committee, HMSO, 1966

Meikle, John. *The Settlements and Roads of Scotland – a Study in Human Geography*, Edinburgh, 1927

Miller, Ronald. 'Orkney – a Land of Increment', in Miller, R. and Watson, J. W. (eds), *Geographical Essays in Memory of Alan G. Ogilvie*, 1959, pp 7-15

Miller, Ronald. 'Orkney Quincentenary' (editorial), SGM vol 84, 1968, pp 143-8

Miller, Ronald. 'The Road North' (re General Wade), SGM, 1967, p 78

Miller, Ronald. 'Land Use by Summer Shielings', *Scottish Studies*, 2, 1967, pp 193-221

Miller, R. and Tivey, J. *The Glasgow Region — a General Survey*, for the British Association for the Advancement of Science, Glasgow meeting, 1958

Miller, Ronald. 'Major General Roy', SGM II, 1956, p 97

Miller, Ronald. 'The New Face of Glasgow', SGM vol 86, 1970 pp 5-15

Moir, D. G. 'The Roads of Scotland', SGM, 1957, p 101

Moir, D. G. 'The Roads of Scotland — Part II', SGM, 1957, p 167

Moisley, H. A. 'North Uist in 1799', SGM vol 77, 1961, p 89

Murray, W. H. *The Hebrides*, Heinemann, 1966

Newbigin, N. I. *The Kingussie District — a Geographical Study*, London, 1906

Nicolson, T. R. *Shetland* (Islands Series) David & Charles, 1972

O'dell, A. C. and Walton, K. *The Highlands and Islands of Scotland*, Nelson, 1963

O'dell, A. C. 'A View of Scotland in the Middle of the 18th Century', SGM vol 69, pp 58-63

O'dell, A. C. *The Historical Geography of the Shetland Islands*, 1939

O'dell, A. C. Highlands and Islands Developments, SGM vol 82, 1966, pp 8-16

O'Sullivan, P. E. 'Land Use Changes in the Forest of Abernethy, Inverness-shire 1750-1900 A.D.', SGM vol 82, 1973, pp 95-106

Paterson, J. H. 'The Novelist and his Region — Scotland through the Eyes of Sir Walter Scott', SGM vol 81, 1965 pp 154-52

Pears, Nigel. 'Man in the Cairngorms — a Population-Resource-Balance Problem', SGM vol 84, 1968, pp 45-55

Piggott, S. *Scotland before History*, 1958

Porteous, J. D. 'The Island Parish of Jura', SGM vol 84, 1968, p 56

Prebble, John. *The Highland Clearances*, 1963

Robertson, I. 'The Changing Form and Function of Settlement in SW Argyll, 1841-1961', SGM vol 83, 1967, p 29

Semple, David. 'The Growth of Grangemouth', SGM vol 74, 1958, pp 76-85

Sissons, J. B. *The Evolution of Scotland's Scenery*, Oliver & Boyd, 1967

Skelton, R. A. 'The Military Survey of Scotland 1747-55', SGM vol 83, pp 5-16

Small, Alan. 'Shetland — Location the Key to Historical Geography', SGM vol 85, 1969, pp 155-61

Small, A. and Smith, J. S. *The Inverness and Strathpeffer Area*, British Landscape Through Maps series, (Geographical Association), O.S. Sheets (1") nos 27 & 28, Study no 13, Sheffield, 1972

Small, Alan. 'The Historical Geography of the Norse viking Colonisation of the Scottish Highlands', *Norsk Geografiska Tidschrift* (Oslo), 22, 1968, pp 1-16

Smith, P. J. 'Glenrothes: Some Geographical Aspects of New Town Development', SGM vol 83, 1967, pp 17-25

Soons, Jane M. 'Landscape Evolution in the Ochill Hills', SGM vol 74, 1958, pp 86-97

Steers, J. A. 'The Coastline of Scotland', *Geographical Journal*, 118, 1952, pp 180-90

Steven, H. M. 'The Forests and Forestry of Scotland', SGM vol 67, 1951, pp 110-23

Storrie, M. C. 'An Evaluation of the Nidisdale Map', SGM 1968, p 160

Storrie, M. C. 'Landholdings and Settlement Evolution in West Highland Scotland', *Geografiska Annaler*, 47B, 1965, pp 138-61

Storrie, M. C. and Third, B. W. 'The Changing Landscape in the 18th Century Scottish Lowlands', SGM, 1955

Storrie, M. C. 'The Census of Scotland as a Source in the Historical Geography of Islay', SGM, 1962, p 152

Strawburn, J.(ed.) *Ayrshire at the Time of Burns*, Ayrshire Archaeological and Natural History Society, 1959

Sugden, D. 'Landforms of Deglaciation in the Cairngorm Mountains', IBG vol 51, 1970, pp 201-19

Thompson, F. *Harris and Lewis*, David & Charles, 1968

Thomson, W. P. L. 'Funzie-Fetlar — a Shetland Run-Rig

Township in the 19th Century, *Scottish Geographical Magazine*, 86, 1970, pp 170-85

Tivy, Joy. *The Geography of the Garth Area — the Central Highlands in Miniature*, Glasgow: Scottish Field Studies Association, 1960

Tivy, Joy. *Some Physical and Social Factors in the Evolution of a Mining Landscape*, Scottish Field Studies Association 1960

Turner, W. H. K. 'The Growth of Dundee', SGM vol 84, 1968, p 76

Turnock, David. 'Regional Development in the Crofting Counties', IBG 46, 1969, pp 189-204

Turnock, David. 'North Morar — The Improving Movement on a West Highland Estate', SGM vol 85, 1969, pp 17-30

Turnock, David. *Patterns of Highland Development*, Macmillan 1970

Turnock, David. 'Glenelg, Glengarry and Lochiel — an Evolutionary Study of Land Use', SGM vol 83, 1967, pp 89-104

Walton, K. 'The Ythan Estuary, Aberdeenshire', in Eyre, S. R. and Jones, G. R. (eds), *Geography as Human Ecology*, 1966

Walton, K., Mellor, R., Hamilton, P. *et al* 'Aberdeen', special issue of SGM vol 79, 1963, p 69

Warner, K. 'Locational Problems of Scottish Iron and Steel Industry since 1760', pts I and II, SGM vol 81, 1965, pp 18 and 87

Whitehand, J. W. R. and Alauddin, K. 'The Town Plans of Scotland: some Preliminary Considerations', SGM vol 85, 1969, pp 109-21

Whittington, G. 'Land Utilisation in Fife at the Close of the 18th Century', SGM vol 82, 1966, pp 184-93

Whittington, G. 'Landscape Changes in the Vale of Menteith' in Whittow, J. B. and Wood, P. D. (eds), *Essays in Geography for A. A. Miller*, Reading University, 1965, pp 188-206

Whittington, G. and Soulsby, J. A. 'A Preliminary Report on an Investigation into Pit Place Names', SGM vol 84, 1968, pp 117-25

Williamson, K. and Boyd, J. M. *A Mosaic of Islands*, Edinburgh, 1963

Index